Genesis 1 as Ancient Cosmology

Genesis 1
as
Ancient Cosmology

John H. Walton

Winona Lake, Indiana
EISENBRAUNS
2011

Library of Congress Cataloging-in-Publication Data

Walton, John H., 1952–
   Genesis 1 as ancient cosmology / John H. Walton.
      p.   cm.
   Includes bibliographical references and indexes.
   ISBN 978-1-57506-216-7 (hardback : alk. paper)
   1. Biblical cosmology.   2. Bible. O.T. Genesis I—Criticism, interpretation,
etc.   3. Cosmogony.   I. Title.
   BS651.W274   2011
   231.7′65—dc23
                                                                    2011034236

Contents

Preface

During my first 20 years of teaching Genesis 1 to classes of all sorts, I experienced the nagging feeling that I was missing something very important that was just out of my grasp. Since my wife was trained as a scientist, conversations between us about the interface of Genesis 1 and science were common. All of my own training and research in Hebrew language and exegesis as well as in ancient Near Eastern languages and literature brought regular insights and progress, but there were still too many pieces that weren't fitting together.

All of this changed rather dramatically in the fall of 1998. I was teaching a Hebrew Exegesis class, and we were working through Genesis 1. We got to v. 5, and I posed a question to the class: "Why didn't God call the light "light?" The device of metonymy was one that I had included in my lectures for years (thus "light" was understood as "period of light"), but putting the question in this way began to make a few new connections for me. Explaining that the naming procedure indicated that it was day and night that were being created, more than light, and that light was not an object but should be understood metonymically, I concluded with the blunt statement, "So on Day 1, God created time." As an observation, it was more mundane than brilliant, but the world suddenly tilted on its axis as I made the next, logical observation: "We ought then to think of creation in terms of functions rather than material objects." The remainder of the class period was spent "working the problem": What were the ramifications? Did this concept prevail throughout the rest of the chapter? Rather suddenly, all of the exegetical insights that I had been gathering through the years, and all that I had learned about the ancient Near East began to fit into place, and in a very short time I had devised the position that I have now presented in detail in this book. No longer did it seem true what Heidel had suggested and so many scholars (including me) had repeated throughout the decades, that one of the key differences between ancient Near Eastern cosmological texts and Genesis 1 was that in the ancient Near Eastern texts the gods were merely organizing and ordering creation, while in Genesis 1 God was really making something—true creation, as it were. This no longer appeared to be a valid distinction.

Research led me to understand that many of the "pieces" of my hypothesis had indeed been found previously, but they had not been compiled into a single perspective on the text. As I continued to think through all the aspects, converse with students and colleagues, interact with my wife, and began writing down my findings in various contexts, I was able to refine, support, and communicate my position more effectively. As I lecture widely both at my institution and around the country on the topic, I am constantly amazed at how difficult it is for us moderns to set aside our cultural preconceptions in order to begin to think in new ways. The ancient Near Eastern mode of thought is not at all intuitive to us, but our understanding of ancient perspectives can only approach accuracy when we begin to penetrate ancient texts on their own terms rather than impose our world view. In this task, we are aided by the ever-growing corpus of literature that is being recovered and analyzed.

After an introduction to present some of the history of comparative studies and the ways that comparative methods have been applied to the study of ancient texts in general and cosmology in particular, I focus in the first half of the book on the ancient Near Eastern texts that inform our understanding about ancient ways of thinking about cosmology. Of primary interest are the texts that can help us discern the parameters of ancient perspectives on cosmic ontology—that is, how the writers perceived origins. Texts from across the ancient Near East are presented, including primarily Egyptian, Sumerian, and Akkadian texts, but occasionally also Ugaritic and Hittite, as appropriate. My intention, first of all, is to understand the texts but also to demonstrate that a functional ontology pervaded the cognitive environment of the ancient Near East. This functional ontology involves more than just the idea that ordering the cosmos was the focus of the cosmological texts. I posit that, in the ancient world, bringing about order and functionality was the very essence of creative activity. I also pay close attention to the ancient ideology of temples to show the close connection between temples and the functioning cosmos.

The second half of the book is devoted to a fresh analysis of Gen 1:1–2:4. I offer studies of significant Hebrew terms and seek to show that the Israelite texts also evidence a functional ontology and a cosmology that is constructed with temple ideology in mind, as in the rest of the ancient Near East. I contend that Genesis 1 never was an account of material origins but that, as in the rest of the ancient world, the focus of the creation accounts was to order the cosmos by initiating functions. I further contend that the cosmology of Genesis 1 is founded on the premise that the cosmos should be understood in temple terms. All of this is intended to demonstrate that, when we read Genesis 1 as the ancient document it is, rather than trying to read it in light of our own world view, the text comes to life in ways that help recover the energy it had in its original context. At the same time, it provides a new perspective on Genesis 1 in relation to what have long been controversial issues. Far from being a borrowed text, Genesis 1 offers a unique theology, even while it speaks from the platform of its contemporary cognitive environment.

I am grateful to the individuals who have been conversation partners along the way and have helped me to shape and define my thinking. These include colleagues, students, family, and listeners in audiences around the country who ask perceptive questions and interact in productive ways so that I can continue to refine my thinking and my communication. I am also grateful to Jim Eisenbraun and his staff for being willing to sponsor my efforts to offer some fresh thinking. What I have presented here is a work in progress. I hope that many who read this book will be stimulated to deeper thoughts and more connections that can strengthen the perspective that I have launched, even as the theory may eventually take on different forms or elements.

Abbreviations

General Abbreviations, Versions of the Bible, and Ancient Works

ASOR	American Schools of Oriental Research
BD	Book of the Dead
CT	Coffin Texts
Ee	*Enuma Elish*
EWO	*Enki and World Order*
JPS	Jewish Publication Society Version
LXX	Septuagint
NIV	New International Version
NJPSV	New Jewish Publication Society Version
NRSV	New Revised Standard Version
NBC	Nies Babylonian Collection of the Yale University Library
PT	Pyramid Texts
REB	Revised English Bible

Reference Works

AEL	Lichtheim, M. *Ancient Egyptian Literature*. 3 vols. Berkeley: University of California Press, 1973–80
AnBib	Analecta Biblica
ANET	J. B. Pritchard, editor. *Ancient Near Eastern Texts Relating to the Old Testament*. 3rd ed. Princeton: Princeton University Press, 1969
AOAT	Alter Orient und Altes Testament
AoF	*Altorientalische Forschungen*
BAR	*Biblical Archaeology Review*
Bib	*Biblica*
BJRL	*Bulletin of the John Rylands Library*
BMS	King, L. W. *Babylonian Magic and Sorcery*. London: Luzac, 1896
BR	*Bible Review*
BZAW	Beihefte zur Zeitschrift für die alttestamentliche Wissenschaft
CAD	Oppenheim, A. L., et al., editors. *Chicago Assyrian Dictionary of the Oriental Institute of the University of Chicago*. Chicago: University of Chicago Press, 1956–2011
CANE	Sasson, J., editor. *Civilizations of the Ancient Near East*. New York: Scribners, 1995
CAT	Dietrich, M.; Loretz, O.; and Sanmartín, J. *The Cuneiform Alphabetic Texts from Ugarit, Ras Ibn Hani, and Other Places*. 2nd ed. Münster: Ugarit-Verlag, 1995

CBQMS   Catholic Biblical Quarterly Monograph Series
CHANE   Culture and History of the Ancient Near East
COS   Hallo, W. W., and Younger, K. L., editors. *Context of Scripture.* 3 vols.
           Leiden: Brill, 1997–2002
CTJ   *Calvin Theological Journal*
DCH   Clines, D. J. A., editor. *Dictionary of Classical Hebrew.* Sheffield:
           Sheffield Academic Press, 1993
DDD²   Van der Toorn, K.; Becking, B.; and van der Horst, P. W., editors.
           Dictionary of Deities and Demons in the Bible. 2nd ed. Grand Rapids,
           MI: Eerdmans, 1999
FAT   Forschungen zum alten Testament
HALOT   Koehler, L.; Baumgartner, W.; and Stamm, J. J. *The Hebrew and
           Aramaic Lexicon of the Old Testament.* Translated and edited under
           supervision of M. E. J. Richardson. 5 vols. Leiden: Brill, 1994–2000
HAR   *Hebrew Annual Review*
HBT   *Horizons in Biblical Theology*
HSM   Harvard Semitic Monographs
HTR   *Harvard Theological Review*
HUCA   *Hebrew Union College Annual*
IBHS   Waltke, B., and O'Connor, M. *Introduction to Biblical Hebrew Syntax.*
           Winona Lake, IN: Eisenbrauns, 1990
JANES   *Journal of Ancient Near Eastern Studies*
JAOS   *Journal of the American Oriental Society*
JBL   *Journal of Biblical Literature*
JCS   *Journal of Cuneiform Studies*
JNES   *Journal of Near Eastern Studies*
JNSL   *Journal of Northwest Semitic Languages*
JR   *Journal of Religion*
JSOT   *Journal for the Study of the Old Testament*
JSJSup   Journal for the Study of Judaism Supplements
JTS   *Journal of Theological Studies*
KAR   Ebeling, E., editor. *Keilschrittexte aus Assur religiösen Inhalts.*
           2 vols. Wissenschaftliche Veröffentlichungen der deutschen
           Orientgesellschaft 28, 34. Leipzig: Hinrichs, 1919–23
KTU   Keilalphabetischen Texte aus Ugarit
LCL   Loeb Classical Library
LHBOT   Library of Hebrew Bible / Old Testament
NAC   New American Commentary
NICOT   New International Commentary on the Old Testament
NIDOTTE   VanGemeren, W. A., editor. *New International Dictionary of
           Old Testament Theology and Exegesis.* 5 vols. Grand Rapids, MI:
           Zondervan, 1997
NIVAC   New International Version Application Commentary
OBO   Orbis Biblicus Orientalis
OEAE   Redford, Donald B., editor. *Oxford Encyclopedia of Ancient Egypt.*
           3 vols. Oxford: Oxford University Press, 2001

OEANE	Meyers, E. M., editor. *Oxford Encyclopedia of the Ancient Near East.* 5 vols. New York: Oxford University Press, 1997
Or	*Orientalia*
OtSt	Oudtestamentische Studiën
RIME	Royal Inscriptions of Mesopotamia, Early Periods
RlA	Ebeling, E., et al., editors. *Reallexikon der Assyriologie.* Berlin: de Gruyter, 1928–
SAA	State Archives of Assyria
SBLDS	Society of Biblical Literature Dissertation Series
SBLMS	Society of Biblical Literature Monograph Series
SBLWAW	Society of Biblical Literature Writings from the Ancient World
ScrHier	Scripta Hierosolymitana
SJOT	*Scandinavian Journal of the Old Testament*
TCBAI	Transactions of the Casco Bay Assyriological Institute
TDOT	Botterweck, G. J., and Ringgren, H., editors. *Theological Dictionary of the Old Testament.* Grand Rapids, MI: Eerdmans, 1974–2006
TLOT	Jenni, E., editor, and Biddle, M. E., translator. *Theological Lexicon of the Old Testament.* 3 vols. Peabody, MA: Hendrickson, 1997
TynBul	*Tyndale Bulletin*
UBL	Ugaritisch-Biblische Literatur
VAT	Vorderasiatische Abteilung Thontafeln
VT	*Vetus Testamentum*
VTSup	Vetus Testamentum Supplements
WBC	Word Biblical Commentary
WO	*Die Welt des Orients*
WTJ	*Westminster Theological Journal*
ZAW	*Zeitschrift für die alttestamentliche Wissenschaft*

Chapter 1

Cosmology and Comparative Studies: Methodology

Cosmology has always been a matter of interest to humanity. From the earliest speculations found in Sumerian and Egyptian mythologies to the modern debate about the relationship between science and faith and the controversies surrounding Evolution and Intelligent Design, people have proposed a wide variety of theories of origins and at times have argued heatedly about the superiority of one view over another.

For millennia, the account in Genesis 1 served as the foundation of cosmology for those who embraced a biblical faith, and through them, for the Western world.[1] This foundation was first challenged philosophically in the aftermath of the Enlightenment, when the idea of the supernatural—that there were forces beyond nature—was called into question. Consequently, a dichotomy between "natural" and "supernatural" became entrenched and people began to see cosmology in more naturalistic terms. The foundation built on Genesis 1 was challenged scientifically when evolutionary biology blossomed out of the research of Charles Darwin. And finally, it was challenged theologically when archaeologists recovered ancient mythological accounts that provided a literary context for Genesis 1.

Because of these developments, the confidence of the Western world in Genesis 1 as a foundation for cosmology has eroded, even among individuals who embrace a biblical faith. One response has been to attempt to transform Genesis 1 into a veiled cosmology, accessible only to the trained modern eye that is able to detect an uncanny correspondence with contemporary scientific knowledge. This concordist approach wants to read Genesis 1 as modern cosmology. Others have claimed that Genesis 1 has only a literary or theological role, which virtually removes it from discussion of cosmologies even while it retains a sometimes vague theological point. Finally, many have positioned Genesis 1 in the context of literature

---

1. Of course, there has always been variety in the interpretation of Genesis 1.

1

emerging from the ancient world, where it becomes just one more mythological cosmology, borrowed from the common stock of ancient tradition and of interest only to those with antiquarian curiosities. This book explores Genesis 1 as an exemplar of ancient cosmology and attempts to understand it as such.[2]

Reading Genesis 1 as ancient cosmology requires that the cognitive environment (how people thought about themselves and their world[3]), as it can be understood within the broad spectrum of ancient Near Eastern cosmological texts be taken into account. This claim, however, leaves open the question whether Genesis 1 used any ancient texts as sources—whether as patterns or templates or as foils. The premise of this book is that many attempts to trace literary trails from ancient Near Eastern texts to Genesis have been too facile and the results too simplistic. Though we should not abandon consideration of the potential literary relationship between specific texts, we also need to recognize that the transmission of traditions is a complex process. We should not be optimistic that we will find demonstrable literary connections in the varied remnants of ancient literature.

Reconstructing literary relationships often becomes an elaborate connect-the-dots game in which the results resemble more the apparent randomness of a Rorschach inkblot test than the clear literary links that are claimed. Our efforts should focus on using all the literature at our disposal to reconstruct the ancient cognitive environment, which can then serve as the backdrop for understanding each literary work. Rather than employing comparative methodology as an apologetic serving our own ideologies, promoting theological or antitheological agendas, we must as careful scholars allow the text, as a product of its cognitive environment, to be interpreted within the context of this cognitive environment.

For decades, comparative study of ancient Near Eastern texts and the Bible has been trying to climb out of the morass that resulted from the aftermath of Franz Delitzsch's Babel-Bibel lectures. As methodology has been

---

2. Significant contributions have already been made in defining how ancient cosmologies differ from modern views of cosmology. See R. J. Clifford and J. J. Collins, "The Theology of Creation Traditions," in *Creation in the Biblical Traditions* (ed. R. J. Clifford and J. J. Collins; Washington, DC: Catholic Biblical Association, 1992), 1–15. Clifford and Collins (pp. 9–10) define the key distinctions as involving process (personal), product (organized human society), manner of reporting (drama), and criterion of truth (plausibility). I agree but will try to move beyond these categories to consider additional issues.

3. Other terms could be used: conceptual world view, philosophical *Sitz im Leben*, *Zeitgeist*, and undoubtedly others.

refined through the study of many throughout the decades since then, a clearer focus has emerged to take literary context into account and show more sensitivity to both comparisons and contrasts. The discussion also began to be expanded beyond basic literary comparisons into the conceptual realm through studies by Speiser, Finkelstein, Jacobsen, Lambert, and many others.

When comparative study is carried out at this conceptual or cognitive level, some adjustments in methodology need to be made. When literary pieces are being compared to consider the question of dependency among them, the burden of proof has been on the researcher to consider the issues of propinquity and transmission. After all, if Israelite literature were to be suspected of borrowing an Akkadian text, the claim of borrowing would need to be substantiated by evidence that the Israelite writers were aware of the Akkadian text and could plausibly have had access to it. Questions of literary genre, structure, and context would all need to be investigated, as well as the geographical, chronological, and national or ethnic context from which the literature had arisen.[4] When one considers the cognitive environment, however, the purview is broader and the demands of literary context are not as stringent, although they cannot be ignored altogether. There is a great difference between explicit borrowing from a specific piece of literature and creating a literary work that resonates with the larger culture that has itself been influenced by its literatures. As a modern example, when Westerners speak of the philosophy lying behind the common saying "Eat, drink and be merry, for tomorrow we die," they resonate with an idea that has penetrated society; many who use the phrase would not recognize it as borrowed from the writings of the Greek philosopher Epicurus. Over time, the philosophy of Epicurus has seeped into the culture, and modern statements reflect this penetration and reflect his philosophy without quoting it directly.

A second example, more pervasive in our world today, comes from Newtonian physics. Few moderns read Newton. Many have no idea that many of the ways they think about the world (that is, their cognitive environment) are linked to Newtonian physics. The premises of Newtonian physics have permeated the culture so deeply that they have become part of the common understanding of the culture. In cases like this, the demands of propinquity

---

4. For example, see Tigay's criteria in "On Evaluating Claims of Literary Borrowing," in *The Tablet and the Scroll* (ed. M. Cohen et al.; Bethesda, MD: CDL, 1993), 250–55.

can be relaxed considerably. A cultural trail is not as well defined as a literary trail, nor will tracking it require the same criteria.

As a result of half a century of the persistent scholarship of Assyriologists, Hittitologists, Egyptologists, Ugaritologists, and Sumerologists, we are now in a position to add significant nuance to the ways we think about the effects of the ancient Near Eastern cognitive environment on the authors and editors of the Hebrew Bible.

We are now able to create a spectrum of categories that help to define the varieties of differences and similarities between various bodies of literature, both inside the Bible and in the ancient Near East. We will begin on the negative side, that is, the side of the spectrum in which the Hebrew Bible totally ignores ideologies that are found in ancient Near Eastern literature and presents a quite different view (e.g., certain notions of theogony are discarded). At a small gradation toward the other side of the spectrum are topics in which the Hebrew Bible evidences at least a hazy familiarity with the ancient Near Eastern ideas: for instance, the caricature or ridicule of other nations' deities (e.g., comments that reflect contact with the idea that a god could take a nap). In a third category, the Hebrew Bible demonstrates more-detailed awareness of viewpoints current in the ancient world but rejects them in favor of a carefully articulated alternative (e.g., it is aware of polytheism but clearly rejects it). Further over on the spectrum are the issues in which the Hebrew Bible does not reject outright the views current in the ancient Near East but expresses disagreement, either through polemical statements or even by providing an alternative perspective (e.g., the role for which humans were created). A fifth category features a clear awareness of an idea that has been adapted and transformed by Israelite authors (e.g., the idea that humans were made from the dust of the earth). A sixth kind of relationship is found in areas in which the Hebrew Bible consciously imitates concepts current in the ancient world (e.g., descriptions of temple architecture and ideology). Finally, in regard to a large number of issues, evidence supports the idea that the Hebrew Bible subconsciously reflects a shared heritage from the cognitive environment of the ancient Near East (e.g., the notion that the deity rests in a temple).

In this book, I will address some of the ways that Genesis 1 has been and can be reassessed in light of this conceptual spectrum. Early study comparing the Hebrew Bible with the ancient Near East focused primarily on individual features (e.g., creation by the spoken word; people created in the image of deity) but this soon developed into speculation concerning outright literary borrowing. As the discipline matured and the complexity of literary relationships became more apparent, most scholars recognized that much more information would be necessary in order to achieve sufficient confidence to be able to reconstruct a literary trail. By now, the individual features had been treated extensively in the secondary literature, and as a result of growing reticence to make broad claims regarding the literary connections, attention appropriately turned to the study of the cognitive environment. This shift is specifically documented with regard to the cosmology texts in the work of R. Simkins, who calls for precisely this realignment of emphasis.

> This common creation model suggests that the Israelites shared a similar conception of reality, rooted in basic experiences of the human body and the earth, as their ancient Near Eastern neighbors. Indeed, the Israelites were part of the larger ancient Near Eastern cultural milieu in that they shared similar understandings of the world with their neighbors. The differences between the Bible and other Near Eastern literature can only be understood from within the context of their similarities. These differences reflect the cultural particularities of each people, not extensively different and unrelated cultures.[5]

Early studies identified the obvious differences, such as the Bible's monotheism in contrast to ancient Near Eastern literatures' polytheism, the absence of theogony in the biblical text, and the absence of theomachy in Genesis despite vestiges of it in the poetic and wisdom literatures. Recently, aspects of the ancient Near Eastern cognitive environment that appear to be reflected in Genesis 1 have been identified in studies focusing on the relationship between cosmos and temple and a related concept, the importance of deity entering rest.[6]

---

5. R. Simkins, *Creator and Creation* (Peabody, MA: Hendrickson, 1994), 89.

6. J. Levenson, "The Temple and the World," *Journal of Religion* 64 (1984): 275–298; J. M. Lundquist, "What Is a Temple? A Preliminary Typology," in *The Quest for the Kingdom of God* (ed. H. B. Huffmon, F. A. Spina, and A. R. W. Green; Winona Lake, IN: Eisenbrauns: 1983), 205–20; G. J. Wenham, "Sanctuary Symbolism in the Garden of Eden Story," in *I Studied Inscriptions from before the Flood* (ed. R. S. Hess and D. T. Tsumura; Sources for Biblical and Theological Study 4; Winona Lake, IN: Eisenbrauns, 1994), 399–404; M. Weinfeld, "Sabbath, Temple and the Enthronement of the Lord: The Problem of the Sitz im Leben of Genesis 1:1–2:3," in *Mélanges bibliques et orientaux en l'honneur de M. Henri Cazelles* (ed. A. Caquot and M. Delcor; AOAT 212; Kevelaer: Butzon & Bercker / Neukirchen-Vluyn: Neukirchener Verlag, 1981), 501–12. See discussion of this and other accounts of temple building and its relationship with rest in Victor Hurowitz, *I Have Built You an Exalted House* (JSOTSup 115; Sheffield: JSOT Press, 1992), Appendix 5, pp. 330–31.

Identifying Cognitive Environment

Cognitive environment can be inferred and reconstructed from non-contemporary cultures only through three resources: the texts that are left to us, artifacts that archaeology exhumes, and the iconography found on objects and architecture from the ancient world. As with any other attempt to place ideas in context, comparing *and* contrasting the cognitive environment are both important. One of the most obvious dangers in this process is that we impose our modern cognitive environment on the ancients simply because we have failed to recognize that our own categories are not relevant to the ancients' way of thinking. For instance, it was long claimed that *Enuma Elish* should not be considered a creation text because nothing was actually "made" by Marduk. This claim arises out of a basic assumption that the ancient understanding of the creative act should correspond to our own—or even more so, that creative activity can only be construed in one way (our modern way!). Consequently, the first important guideline to bear in mind is that we cannot seek to construe *their* world in *our* terms.

An example of the way this guideline functions can be found in the study of cosmic geography. Specifically, we cannot begin with our modern conception of cosmic geography when we try to understand the ancients' cognitive environment or the texts that derive from it. When we use ancient texts and iconography as witnesses to the ancients' cosmic geography, a cognitive environment can emerge featuring both diversity and broad commonality. For example, we find ample evidence that the ancients believed that a material (often conceived as solid) sky was suspended above the earth. This is common ground that can be confirmed across a variety of cultural, chronological, and geographical boundaries. At the same time, variations concerning the material that is involved (cloth? stone?) and what holds it up (ropes or chains from above? mountains below? gods?) are observable. As information of this sort is gathered, we can consult the biblical text to determine whether it displays evidence that reflects the common ground, along with whatever variations from the common ground are also discernible. This specific detail is only one of many characteristics that need to be investigated to understand the basic shape of the cosmic geography common to the ancient world as a whole, as well as the points at which differences emerge. We will discover that the ancient materials at our disposal sometimes reflect cosmic geography in political terms (see, e.g., some of the Egyptian diagrams), in theological terms (e.g., again, Egyptian diagrams, and Mesopotamian astrolabes), in topographical terms (e.g., the Babylonian map of the world), in mythological terms (e.g., the treatment of Tiamat in *Enuma Elish*) but never in terms even remotely related to modern understandings of cosmic geography (a spherical, rotating earth with several major continents, surrounded by an atmosphere and revolving around a star, the sun, in an orbit that is spaced among the other eight planets of our solar system in a galaxy of billions of stars that itself is one of billions of galaxies in an expanding universe). Furthermore, cosmic geography is only one element of a cosmological cognitive environment.

Even as we engage in this process, we must recognize that some dangers exist. First, we must be wary of a tendency toward overextrapolation from unclear, ambiguous, or isolated texts. An example of this is the overzealous generalization that, in the ancient world, mountains were believed to hold up the sky. This view is certainly present in the ancient Near East, but it cannot be claimed to be the common view. Sometimes, overextrapolation is reflected in a failure to engage the ancient view fully (e.g., projecting the Greek notion of chaos onto the ancient Near East). A second danger is overinterpretation, which can happen easily when we deal with iconography, as can be seen in some of the more imaginative treatments of the cosmic role of the sacred tree.[7] A third danger is the inclination to link too closely elements that are only remotely related, thereby creating a pattern of commonality where none exists. There is good reason to see overinterpretation as being the culprit when connections are drawn between the Mesopotamian primordial goddess Tiamat and the Hebrew word *tehom* (Gen 1:2). A fourth danger is the failure to explore a cultural feature in its own context (textual or cultural) before assigning it a larger role in the cognitive environment. An example of this can be found in the discussion of the translation of the Hebrew word *ruah* 'wind' versus 'spirit' in Gen 1:2. Finally, scholars sometimes are too quick to assume that a shared cultural idea exists even when the text is silent, or at least not explicit, on the very topic being considered. An example of this is the assumption that theomachy forms the backdrop of Genesis 1 even though no evidence of it is found in the text of Genesis. The fact that various scholars have differing criteria and differing presuppositions concerning comparative studies means that one scholar may feel that he or she is applying a rigorous methodology to a particular study, while another scholar may conclude that the first scholar

---

7. Cf. S. Parpola, "The Assyrian Tree of Life," *JNES* 52 (1993): 161–208.

has succumbed to an excess of enthusiasm and offers a marquee example of the dangers discussed above. Inevitably, some readers will conclude that this book falls prey to the very dangers that it warns others about. But this is precisely why we must continue to engage in the corporate exercise of comparative study—so that many minds and hands may work together to produce useful studies and reach conclusions that can be supported by many if not all scholars.

Comparing Cognitive Environment

In preparation for exploring the way that Genesis 1 presents its version of ancient cosmology, we need first to identify the basic elements of the cognitive environment that are present throughout the ancient Near East with regard to cosmology. The basic components of the shared ANE cosmology will be introduced and explored in depth in the following chapters based on the evidence found in ancient Near Eastern literature; then, we will explore these components in relation to Genesis 1.

Ontology

To create is to bring something into existence that did not exist prior to the act of creation. Consequently, if we are to understand ancient ideas about creation we need to gain an understanding of *ancient ideas regarding existence*. This puts understanding the cosmic ontology of ancient peoples center stage. Modern cosmic ontology—*our* cosmic ontology—is primarily material, and the result is that when we think of the act of creation, we think mostly about the origins of matter in its various forms throughout the universe. This way of thinking is not the only ontological option, and I will propose that it is not the option that was current in the ancient cognitive environment.

Centrality of Order/Disorder

It is clear from the cosmological literature of the ancient Near East that order in the cosmos and the control of the functions of the cosmos were more prominent in the ancient thought world than any consideration of the material origins of the cosmos. In what follows, I will show that ancient Near Eastern literature is concerned primarily with order and control of functions of the world that exists rather than with speculations about how the material world that exists came into being.

Metadivine Functions

The attributes, or factors, that were thought to define the shape and operation of the cosmos (Sumerian ME, imperfectly translated by Akkadian *parṣu*) and the tablet of destinies (containing decrees concerning the job descriptions of all members of the cosmos) both offer valuable evidence for understanding ancient perspectives on the cosmos, revealing what ancient peoples thought was most important about the world in which they lived. Though Egyptian literature does not have terminology to describe control features, the same concepts nevertheless are central there, as in Mesopotamia. A study of these concepts reveals how pervasive the issues of rule and authority were for ancient thinking. The model of the cosmos as a kingdom was more relevant in the ancient world than our modern model of the cosmos, which typically portrays it as a machine.

Position of Deity in the Cosmos

Throughout most of the literature of the ancient Near East, it is clear that deities are viewed to a large degree as being inside the cosmic system, as being a part of it. Order in the divine world was considered to be an essential part of the same order that humans experienced in their world. Concurrently, the literature suggests that there are aspects of the cosmic system that are beyond the divine realm. Thus, while divine control extends far beyond human control, it is not all-encompassing and there are parts of the cosmos that it does not reach.

Theogony/Cosmogony

A long-recognized aspect of ancient Near Eastern cosmology is the interrelationship of theogony and cosmogony. It could be noted that this interrelationship is itself a reflection of the ontological concepts identified above: that is, if existence was understood primarily in terms of the *functions* of the constituent parts of the cosmos, then both the gods and these parts exist only by virtue of their *functions*. So, for instance, neither the sun nor the sun-god has functions independent of the other; they are identified with each other.[8] When the functions that they jointly represent came into being, they both came into being and began to function in tandem. Thus, theogony is inseparable from cosmogony. It is the fact that the function of

---

8. See especially F. Rochberg, "'The Stars Their Likenesses': Perspectives on the Relation between Celestial Bodies and Gods in Ancient Mesopotamia," in *What Is a God?* (ed. B. N. Porter; TCBAI 2; Winona Lake, IN: Eisenbrauns, 2009), 41–91.

the material object—the sun—overlaps with the function of the deity—the sun-god—that creates a cognitive environment in which theogony and cosmogony are deeply intertwined.[9]

Theomachy

The idea that creation came about through conflict among the gods—that is, *theomachy*—is most evident in Akkadian sources. Theomachy is nearly absent in Sumerian sources and has much less significance in Egypt. Furthermore, not all theomachy in Akkadian sources is related to cosmology, so it cannot be assumed that creation is the focus in a given literary text merely on the basis that theomachy is evident. In the investigation below, I attempt to ascertain the extent to which theomachy is a part of the general ANE cognitive environment.

Cosmic Geography

Cosmic geography offers a description of the shape of the cosmos. As already mentioned, however, the "shape" is rarely understood in purely material terms. Where texts describe the processes by which the cosmos was given its shape, we can gain information about how the ancients thought about origins.

Temple/Rest

One of the major constituent elements of the cognitive environment with regard to ancient cosmology that has been identified in recent years is the relationship between the cosmos and the temple. Because of this relationship, and because how the ancients thought about each illuminates the other, we find that texts concerned with temple building and temple dedications provide information about issues related to the cosmos. One of the most important of these issues is the concept of divine rest—the idea that deities in the ANE find rest in temples and that temples are built for the deity to rest in. As we investigate the notion of divine rest in both temple and cosmology texts, its place in the cognitive environment becomes increasingly important for our subject.

---

9. This blending of theogony and cosmogony in Egypt is termed "cosmotheism" by J. Assmann, *The Mind of Egypt* (New York: Metropolitan Museum of Art, 1996), 204.

Role of Humanity

A final major component of the cosmological cognitive environment is the role attributed to people in the cosmos. Investigating how ancient peoples thought about the centrality of humans, the function/role of humans, the component parts of humans (dust, clay, blood of gods, etc.), and the image of deity are all significant to our understanding of their belief systems.

In all of these areas, naturally, we must apply careful methodology to guard against adopting premature generalizations into our inventory of components of the broader cognitive environment. The cognitive landscape is replete with variety, and the variety must be recognized and allowed to stand in its uniqueness.[10] At the same time, there is much common ground to be identified. Note, for instance, the assessment of J. Allen, who, after studying the rich variety of Egyptian cosmological texts, comments:

> Like later philosophers and scientists, the Egyptian thinkers must have speculated, discussed, and passed on their concepts to subsequent generations. This continuity of tradition is reflected in the creation accounts we have examined. Despite differences in age and origin, imagery and subject matter, these sources all reflect an understanding of creation that was remarkably consistent throughout the 2300 years of history they span.[11]

We would find that the same is true at the most basic level for Mesopotamian sources and in more general terms, when Egyptian and Mesopotamian traditions are compared. This is not to ignore the important differences but simply to note that it is important to recognize common ground when it exists. And we will explore the extent to which ancient Israel shared this common ground.

Even before we look at the evidence, we may wish to ask: should we expect to find any uniqueness in the Hebrew Bible? Levenson has suggested that cultural purity is a chimera:

> First, the quest for the distinctive in Israel is a wild-goose chase. The number of unparalleled elements shrinks yearly, and one can suspect that if we come into any substantial body of texts from Israel's most immediate neighbors—Edom, Moab, and Ammon—it might approach zero.

---

10. See the call for careful synchronic analysis by L. Lesko, "Ancient Egyptian Cosmogonies and Cosmology," in *Religion in Ancient Egypt* (ed. B. Shafer; Ithaca, NY: Cornell University Press, 1991), 122.

11. J. Allen, *Genesis in Egypt* (New Haven, CT: Yale University Press, 1988), 56.

This is not to say that institutions come into Israel unchanged. On the contrary, nothing changes cultures without changing. . . . The crucial fact is that Israel emerged in history. Unlike Sumerian kingship, it was not lowered from heaven, nor was it an immediate product of the "big bang." Thus, the critical historian must assume that every element in Israel has ancestors or at least relatives among the "pagan" cultures. [12]

Though we may not share Levenson's willingness to include all matters Israelite in his sweeping statement, his general point is well taken. In ancient Israel's literature, we will find far more similarity with other ANE literatures than distinctiveness from them, and the distinctions that we discover may often turn out to be ripple effects that resulted from the modifications brought about through interaction with one or two important, distinctive theological tenets.

The Hermeneutics of Comparative Studies and the Cognitive Environment

All literature is dependent on the culture from which it emerges and on the literature of the cultures with which it is in contact. This is no less true if the literature being discussed is mundane business texts, government reports, "high" literature, or texts considered to be holy or canonical because they were thought to be divinely revealed. That all literature is dependent, however, does not rule out the possibility that new ideas or perspectives may emerge; it only recognizes that no literature or idea is without a precursor of some sort, even if there is something in the "new" literature that departs from the "old." For interpretation to be legitimate, it must acknowledge the debt that the "new" owes to the "old" and explore the intertextual linkage between the two. It would be foolish to study Midrash in isolation from an understanding of the world view represented in and promulgated by the Mishnah. Study of the Christian Church Fathers would be flawed without understanding the pervasive influence of the New Testament on the world in which they lived and wrote. Calvin or Aquinas, later in Christian history, need not quote Augustine or Aristotle directly, but their writings spring from the world that was shaped by these earlier philosophers. Though the New Testament often alludes to the literature of the Old Testament and thus assumes familiarity with the earlier literature on the part of its hearers/ readers, at the same time, the Old Testament has shaped the world and

---

12. Levenson, "Temple and the World," 281.

world view of Second Temple Judaism and the New Testament interacts
with that cognitive environment in many different ways (sometimes being influenced by the Hellenistic world at the same time). We should not
be surprised, then, that understanding the Hebrew Bible requires its interpreters to recognize the pervasive connection that ancient Israel had with
the legacy of ancient Near Eastern literature and thought. This relationship,
however, is not merely a matter of literary adoption at some point in time;
that is, we cannot simply consider what we may think Israel has derived
from contemporary literature. The relationship is more complex, because
Israelite literature reflects the broad ancient stream of culture from which
it was watered in the course of centuries or even millennia. As a result, the
issue is not whether Israel borrowed or adopted another culture's ideas. The
stream was so pervasive and persistent that some of the ideas we are consid-
ering had become a "native" way of thinking; they had long been a part of
the conceptual framework of the ancient world and had much earlier taken
root in whatever context(s) the Israelite cognitive environment took shape.
H. H. Schmid expressed these same ideas several decades ago in contrast to
the model offered by G. von Rad.

> Wherever we looked we saw, to be sure in manifold variations but still
> with great clarity, that the controlling background of OT thought and
> faith is the view of a comprehensive world order and, hence, a creation
> faith in the broad sense of the word—a creation faith that Israel in many
> respects shared with her environment. . . . Israel participated fully in the
> thought world and in the creation faith of the world of the ancient Near
> East and understood—and indeed could only understand—her particular
> experiences of history and experiences of God in this horizon. As would
> be expected, Israel's historical experiences necessitated some modifica-
> tions, but that was the case also with other cultures of the ancient Near
> East which likewise gave their own relatively independent expression to
> the common way of thinking. In short, it has been shown that, contrary
> to what von Rad's position would logically lead us to believe, Israel did
> not create from her own faith a peculiar realm of life and experience.
> Rather, from the outset Israel's experiences occurred in the context of
> and in vigorous engagement with the already given sphere of common
> ancient Near Eastern way of thinking, particularly creation thought.[13]

---

13. H. H. Schmid, "Creation, Righteousness, and Salvation: 'Creation Theology' as the
Broad Horizon of Biblical Theology," in *Creation in the Old Testament* (ed. B. W. Anderson;
Philadelphia: Fortress, 1984), 102–17; quotation from p. 111.

That one culture shares a world of ideas with another culture suggests neither priority (in time) or superiority (in value or quality) of the ideas, nor that one system is "primitive" because it is older or "secondary" because it is more recent. Neither Shakespeare's debt to the Bible nor the innumerable ways that his literary works reflect (his own) Elizabethan times leads to characterizations of this sort.

The author and audience meet in communication. Communication is based in the context of language, culture, and world view as it engages the world of ideas and perspectives that affect branches of learning that in modern times we have come to call economics, sociology, philosophy, psychology, and so on. No aspect of human existence escapes context: from unrecognized subtleties to the most blatant idiosyncrasies, people live in context, learn in context, and can only communicate in context. Interpretation must therefore take stock of context. When we come to the Hebrew Bible, this is a mandate whether we are inclined to think of the text as the very words of God or as human, northwest Semitic texts.

Let us consider for a moment each of these extremes. Individuals who consider the biblical text to be the very words of God in the narrowest sense are most inclined to isolate it from its cognitive environment and cultural context, believing that the pure character of the text would be sullied and its authority compromised by any dependency on extrabiblical literature or cultural influence. In this perspective, any hint of human origins of the literature of the Bible is considered to be a dilution of its value at best or, more likely, a direct attack on the divine nature of sacred writ. It is understandable that the occasional uneducated or uninformed layperson might cling to this perspective out of fear, but we expect more from academically trained persons than obscurantism of this sort.

Those who are more inclined to think of the text of the Hebrew Bible as nothing more than northwest Semitic texts, presented in a thinly veiled repackaging, must also consider more carefully the subtleties of cultural sharing and exchange. Each culture has distinctive perspectives, even if it also shows various kinds of dependencies. Today, we are well aware of this as we observe the influence of Western culture throughout the world, sometimes good, sometimes bad. Even cultures that are intentionally engaged in overhauling their cultural traditions in favor of Western ideals do not adapt every idea or practice that they encounter.

Certainly the Israelites were no different. Even scholars who are not willing to grant credence to the divine activity that the Israelites claimed, the

Israelite belief that there *was* divine activity in various ways and contexts itself defines a set of distinctives.[14] It is true that the more we discover from the ancient world through excavation of artifacts and study of its excavated literature, the more the distinctives of ancient Israel diminish—or, perhaps better, the more the distinctives change categories. For example, the laws found in the Pentateuch can no longer be considered distinctive when compared with the legal texts of the ancient Near East, but they still must be recognized as representing a distinctive theory of law.

We should expect that, as discoveries are made and our understanding is advanced, the distinctiveness of cultures will be understood in new ways (and this is true of all cultures; it is hardly unique to ancient Israel). But some distinctives will always be retained; they will never be reduced to zero. All interpreters would agree that cultures modify and adapt in unique ways the elements of culture that they have in common with the peoples around them. Israel's adaptation of ideas or materials from surrounding cultures was guided by what the people of Israel believed about their interaction with Israel's god, Yahweh, and modern interpreters can choose to agree with the Hebrew Bible's perspective or not. Whatever the modern interpreter's assessment of the divine role, the Israelites' self-identity was based (eventually—we need not quibble about the time-frame here) on the belief that there was only one God, and God chose their forefathers to be in a unique relationship with them (a relationship defined by the covenant).[15] Other cultures in other times may have had some form of monotheism, but it was never identical to the Israelite form. Perhaps we will someday find evidence that another ancient culture believed that their god chose them and made a covenant with them, entering into a special sponsorship relationship with them. But if this proves to be the case, to be fair both to Israel and to any other yet-to-be-discovered covenant people, each group's distinctives will nonetheless need to be evaluated fairly.

I have been discussing the extreme ends of the spectrum but do not intend to imply that a choice must be made between two extremes: (1) the view that the Hebrew Bible is entirely distinctive at every point in contrast with (2) the view that it has nothing distinctive to offer. These extremes are

---

14. This is similar to P. Machinist's question, "How did Israel, in its biblical canon, pose and answer the distinctiveness question for itself?" See "The Question of Distinctiveness in Ancient Israel: An Essay," in *Ah, Assyria!* (ed. M. Cogan and I. Eph'al; ScrHier 33; Jerusalem: Magnes, 1991), 196–212 (quotation from p. 202).

15. Machinist, "Question of Distinctiveness," 205.

clearly artificial but have been chosen to make the hermeneutical points clear. Most individuals find themselves somewhere in between the extremes, and any number of variations on positions between the extremes of the spectrum are possible. Once we acknowledge that there *was* an ancient cognitive environment and that it is reflected even some of the time in the Hebrew Bible, then it becomes our responsibility as interpreters to acknowledge this reality and come to terms with understanding it. On the other hand, once we recognize that there *are* distinctives, however slight they may be, it also is our responsibility to recognize the distinctives and to evaluate their effect on our understanding of the Hebrew Bible.

At this point, we are far beyond the usual whipping boys of borrowing or accommodation. All of us need to move beyond the "fundamentalist" and "liberal" labels; whether we consider the Bible to be God's holy Word revealed through the apostles and prophets or one people's adaptation of common ANE themes and tropes (to cite again the two extremes), or anything in between, we need to sharpen our hermeneutics. We can no longer ignore the vast literature of the ancient Near East and the possibilities of insight into the Israelite literature preserved in the Hebrew Bible that they offer. Nor can we retain a position that is so disrespectful of ancient Israelite culture that we rule out the possibility that it was a unique culture with its own claim to a self-identity based on distinctive cultural perspectives. The goal of this book is to follow a path that seeks the commonalities that resulted from a shared cultural environment but also attempts to understand the nature of the Israelite "stamp" that shaped its own cosmology.

Chapter 2

Creation in
Ancient Near Eastern Literature

In this chapter, I present two tables that summarize the segments of creation that appear in various strands of ancient Near Eastern literature. The notes that follow provide information about the analysis presented in the tables.

Notes to the Tables

A few important observations may be made about the columns and rows that are empty as well as those that show a concentration of shared elements.

In the "Features" chart (table 2.1), the columns for the Sumerian composition *Bird and Fish* is empty, as are the columns for the Akkadian works *Worm and Toothache, Two Insects, Tamarisk and Palm,* and *Great Astrological Treatise.* All of these are included in the chart, however, because they contain information used in the second table (table 2.2: "Elements"). The absence of information for these works in the features chart is the result of the literary genre to which the works belong: all but the last belong to the wisdom dispute category. The cosmogonic introductions of these pieces tend to focus specifically on the parties that will be involved in the dispute.

Empty columns in the features chart are noticeable for three items. Theomachy is absent from all of the Sumerian sources surveyed and is represented only once in passing in the Egyptian material, and apart from *Enuma Elish* is represented only in late sources in Akkadian. "Separating as an act of creation" is absent in both Sumerian and Akkadian sources but is well represented in Egyptian sources. I am distinguishing "separating as an act of creation" from the original separation of heaven and earth, which is much more prevalent (see below). Outside Egypt, separation as a creative act at various levels of creation is lacking. Also absent from the Sumerian

[[Text continues on p. 22]]

Table 2.1. Summary of Features Appearing

Primary Sources	Egyptian						Sumerian										
	Hermopolitan: pBremner-Rhind BM 10188	Hermopolitan: CT spell 76–80	Heliopolitan: CT 335/Book of the Dead, 17	Theban: Papyrus Leiden I 350	Memphite Theology	Instruction of Merikare	Huluppu Tree	Ewe and Wheat	Bird and Fish	E-engura Hymn	Song of the Hoe	Enki and World Order	Enki and Ninhursag	Enki and Ninmah	Eridu Genesis	NBC 11108	KAR 4
Precreation Condition	•	•	•	•			•				•				•		
Separating Heaven and Earth		•	[•]				•				•			(•)		[•]	•
Theogony Mixed with Cosmogony	•	•	•	•	•				•						•		
Theomachy						•											
Naming as Act of Creation					•		•	[•]							•		
Separating as Act of Creation	•		•														
Creation of People		•	•			•	•						•	•	•	•	•
Temple Connection					•	•						•	•	•	•		
Rest					•												

(•) = implied; [•] = stated as not yet having occurred

in Ancient Cosmological Accounts

Primary Sources	Akkadian								
	Atrahasis	*Enuma Elish*	*Dunnu Theogony*	*Worm and Toothache*	*Two Insects*	*Tamarisk and Palm*	*Great Astrological Treatise*	*VAT 17019*	Seleucid Foundation prayers
Precreation Condition		•							•
Separating Heaven and Earth		(•)							•
Theogony Mixed with Cosmogony		•	•						•
Theomachy	•	•	•						
Naming as Act of Creation		•							•
Separating as Act of Creation									
Creation of People	•	•						•	•
Temple Connection		•							•
Rest		•							

Table 2.2. Summary of Elements Appearing

Primary Sources	Egyptian						Sumerian										
	Hermopolitan: pBremner-Rhind BM 10188	Hermopolitan: CT spell 76–80	Heliopolitan: CT 335/Book of the Dead, 17	Theban: Papyrus Leiden I 350	Memphite Theology	Instruction of Merikare	Huluppu Tree	Ewe and Wheat	Bird and Fish	E-engura Hymn	Song of the Hoe	Enki and World Order	Enki and Ninhursag	Enki and Ninmah	Eridu Genesis	NBC 1108	KAR 4
Gods		•	•	•	•									•		[•]	
Heaven and Earth	[•]	•		•	•	•	•		•	•	•			•		[•]	•
Sky		•														[•]	
Waters									•	•		•					•
Dry Land	[•]	•															
Plants and Fedundity						•	•		•	•	•	•					•
Birds and Fish		•				•			•	•		•					
Animals		•				•			•	•	•		•	[•]	•		
Society or Civilization					•	•	•	[•]	•	•	•	•	•	•	•	[•]	•
Celestial Bodies				•	•												

(•) = implied; [•] = stated as not yet having occurred

in Ancient Cosmological Accounts

Primary Sources	Akkadian								
	Atrahasis	*Enuma Elish*	*Dunnu Theogony*	*Worm and Toothache*	*Two Insects*	*Tamarisk and Palm*	*Great Astrological Treatise*	*VAT 17019*	Seleucid Foundation prayers
Gods		•	•						•
Heaven and Earth		•		•	•		•		•
Sky		•	•						
Waters	•	•		•		•			•
Dry Land	•					•			•
Plants and Fedundity			•						•
Birds and Fish									
Animals			•			•			•
Society or Civilization							•		•
Celestial Bodies							•	•	

material and only represented once in Egyptian and once in Akkadian is the element of divine rest associated with creation.

The most frequent features in the Egyptian sources are the references to the precosmic condition and the attention to theogony. In the Sumerian documents, the separation of heaven and earth is prominent, and the creation of human beings is most common in both Sumerian and Akkadian sources. It is worthy of note that the Egyptians focus more on divine origins while in Mesopotamia the greater focus is on human origins.

In the "Elements" table (Table 2.2), there are no empty rows. A glance at the columns shows there is no reference in Egyptian sources to the origins of the waters—and this category does not include the primordial waters that are present at the beginning (instead of being created). There is only one reference to the creation of (??) the sky (although the god Shu is important and ubiquitous in the sources) and only one reference to plants. Note that, generally, in the Egyptian portion of the tables, comment in the sources is sparse once the origins of the gods and of heaven and earth are addressed.

In Sumerian sources, the empty columns pertain to the emergence of the dry land and the creation of the celestial bodies and the sky. The imbalance in the columns is probably due to the fact that so many of the sources are either cosmogonic introductions to wisdom stories (and therefore more narrowly focused) or myths connected to Enki, the deity who naturally is active in the terrestrial or chthonic realms. In Akkadian, the only blank column pertains to the creation of birds and fish, but this absence may simply be due to lacunae in *Enuma Elish*.

The heaviest concentration of references to specific elements in the Egyptian sources is found in the first two columns, which deal with the origins of the gods and the origins of heaven and earth. In the Sumerian material, the three major categories are heaven and earth, fecundity (Enki's influence again), and aspects of society or civilization, demonstrating that these elements are just as much the object of creation as the "natural" world. In Akkadian sources, the distribution is fairly even.

One item that is not reported in the tables should be mentioned: among all of these cosmogony works, only *The Instruction of Merikare* mentions that people are made in the image of deity. This will be discussed in more detail in chap. 3.

Chapter 3

The Ancient Cosmological Cognitive Environment

In the following chapters, I present data from the ancient Near East that articulate the ancient cosmological cognitive environment, organized according to the categories presented in chap. 1. It is my intention to highlight both the commonality and the diversity evident in the data. This analysis will then serve as a template for my investigation of Genesis 1 in the second part of the book.

Ontology

The philosophical concept of *ontology* can be applied to many different ideas (such as, e.g., evil, belief, the cosmos), but here we are dealing specifically with *cosmic ontology*. Understanding ancient peoples' cosmic ontology must precede discussion of their understanding of cosmic origins because ontology determines what aspect of origins will be of interest and ultimate significance.

In the post-Enlightenment Western world, the framework of cosmic ontology has become strictly material—that is, the cosmos is perceived to exist because it has material properties that can be detected by the senses. The functioning of the cosmos is consequently understood as resulting from its material properties, and its origins are described in material terms. In a material ontology, something is created when it is given or otherwise gains its material properties. In material ontology, there is great interest in investigating and understanding the physical nature of reality, especially in terms of its building blocks, from the smallest constituents, including molecules, atoms, cells, quarks, and so on (the constituent parts), to the largest agglomerations of constituents, including planets, solar systems, and galaxies. In a material ontology, material origins are of ultimate importance and of central concern.[1]

---

1. It should be noted that the situation may gradually be changing in postmodern thinking. F. B. Burnham ("Maker of Heaven and Earth: A Perspective of Contemporary Science," *HBT* 12 [1990]: 3–16) identified a transition to what he termed "relational ontology."

However, we have no reason to think that cosmic ontology in the ancient world was conceived as having a material basis. Though an ancient material cosmic ontology cannot be ruled out, it certainly should not be assumed as the starting point for our consideration. Good methodology demands that we take our lead from the texts themselves when thinking about how the ancients framed their own ontological perspectives.[2] If their ontology was not material, then they likely would have had little interest in material origins. The focus of their ontology would also naturally be reflected in their accounts of origins.

By asking three questions, I will establish what the ancients believed was required for something to exist: (1) What did they consider to constitute nonexistence? (2) What activities do they describe as bringing something into existence, and what is the situation "before" and "after" these acts? and (3) How did the ancients describe the existing cosmos that they perceived with their senses—that is, the elements that they considered to be foundational building blocks of the cosmos? Based on these three questions and other studies, I will suggest that cosmic ontology in the ancient world was a *functional ontology*—that is, everything exists by virtue of its having been assigned a function and given a role in the ordered cosmos.

Nonexistence

Egyptian literature addresses most directly the categories of what can be considered to exist in contrast to what does not exist, using very clear terminology.[3] E. Hornung at first appears to affirm the material nature of

---

Classical Newtonian science was atomistic and reductionistic. It reduced the basic stuff of reality to distinct, elementary particles which could be isolated, measured and predicted. In the postmodern scientific picture, reality cannot be broken down into separate particles or discreet material entities. Nothing can be isolated from its environment. Instead, reality is constituted by events and relationships. Relationships, not things, are fundamental. (p. 5)

This is much closer to the ancient ontology that I believe emerges from the texts, but we must always remember that we should not impose any modern or postmodern ontology (our own ontology) on ancient texts. Burnham's comment does demonstrate the point, however, that a material ontology is not the only option.

2. Ontology per se has received little direct attention in the discussions of ancient Near Eastern thought. For one example from Mesopotamia, see the brief comments by T. Jacobsen, "The Graven Image," in *Ancient Israelite Religion* (ed. P. Miller, P. Hanson, and S. D. McBride; Philadelphia: Fortress, 1987), 18–20; Jacobsen suggests that the ontology of the ancient inhabitants of Mesopotamia included both what was tangible and what was intangible. For Egypt, see E. Hornung, *Conceptions of God in Ancient Egypt* (Ithaca, NY: Cornell Univ. Press, 1982), 172–85.

3. Particularly the negations of the verb 'to be', *tm wnn, nn wn*, as well as *jwtj/jwtt*; see Hornung, *Conceptions*, 173–74.

existence in Egyptian thinking when he notes that the absence of matter is included in what Egyptian texts classify as the nonexistent. Nevertheless he follows this comment immediately with the observation "that which is nameless does not exist," implying that material properties are not criteria for the distinction.[4] In fact, he later admits that "everywhere in the landscape we would come across the non-existent, especially in the desert, which contains fabulous animals that do not exist."[5] He maintains that the existent and the nonexistent together compose the totality of all that is conceivable.[6] With this distinction between existent and nonexistent in mind, we see that, for the Egyptians, creation did not involve transformation of the nonexistent into the existent (which is what most moderns would most easily consider to be the definition of "creation").[7] Instead, space is created for the existent as the nonexistent is pushed behind boundaries or beyond limits while yet remaining alongside that which is existent.[8]

> For the world of creation, the elements from which the state before creation is constituted—primeval flood, primeval darkness, weariness, and negation—are present in two ways. They are the final limit, or the realm beyond all boundaries, which is encountered when one reaches outside the limited world of being; and they are also present in our midst within the ordered world of creation.[9]

Thus, living beings may encounter the nonexistent in a variety of ways.[10] When a pharaoh such as Ramesses II is said to "make rebellious foreign lands non-existent," it does not mean that he annihilates them or sends them into oblivion but that he drives them out of the realm of the existent beyond the boundaries into the realm of the nonexistent.[11] Hornung offers his summary conclusion: "For [Egyptians] the nonexistent is the inexhaustible, unrealized primal matter."[12]

---

4. Hornung, *Conceptions*, 175. In fact, what he appears to mean is not the total absence of matter (i.e., anything material) but the absence of differentiated forms of matter, since every statement that he makes shows that the primeval oneness had a material aspect (though its material aspect was irrelevant).

5. Hornung, *Conceptions*, 180.

6. Hornung, *Conceptions*, 176; it would be an intriguing exercise to think about this in comparison with modern discussions about matter and anti-matter.

7. Hornung, *Conceptions*, 177; S. Morenz, *Egyptian Religion*, (Ithaca, NY: Cornell University Press 1973), 171–72

8. Morenz, *Egyptian Religion*, 168.

9. Hornung, *Conceptions*, 177.

10. Hornung, *Conceptions*, 179; Assmann, *Mind of Egypt*, 205–6.

11. Hornung, *Conceptions*, 180. In Egypt, death and the netherworld are part of the existent.

12. Hornung, *Conceptions*, 182.

While Hornung considers the precosmic status to be characterized by the nonexistent,[13] Assmann, in contrast, observes that "the Egyptian concept of 'nothingness' is not a part of the extracosmic or precosmic sphere but of the 'inner cosmic.'"[14] Hornung's evaluation is supported by a statement in Papyrus Leiden 1 350: "You began evolution with nothing, without the world being empty of you on the first occasion."[15] Hornung's conclusions about the nonexistent bring out the salient features that are significant for our study:

> One could say that in Egypt "the nonexistent" signified quite generally that which is inchoate, undifferentiated, unarticulated, and unlimited; or in affirmative form, the entirety of what is possible, the absolute, the definitive. In comparison with the nonexistent, the existent is clearly defined, and articulated by boundaries and discriminations.[16]

Allen, though choosing different terminology, follows the same line of thought when he describes the antithetical nature of the two realms.

> What lies outside the biosphere of earth, sky, and Duat is not "nothingness" but a universe that is the antithesis of all that defines the world. It is infinite, where the world is bounded; formless and chaotic, where the world is shaped and ordered; inert, where the world is active; and wholly uniform in substance (water), where the world is materially diverse.[17]

This Egyptian view of nonexistence is not found throughout the ancient world and thus constitutes a unique element of the Egyptian cognitive landscape. But the inchoate nature of this nonproductive, nondiversified, nonfunctional precosmic state is evidenced more widely and in a variety of forms, as can be discerned by evaluation of the literature left by other ancient cultures. Whether one accepts Hornung's or Assmann's interpretation of the continuity or discontinuity between precosmic and inner cosmic nothingness, both conclude that the Egyptian view of nothingness/nonexistence points to the fact that the Egyptian ontology was nonmaterial. It is this belief that we will show was common throughout the ancient Near East.

---

13. Hornung, *Conceptions*, 176.

14. Assmann, *Mind of Egypt*, 206. He identifies two kinds of chaos: the precosmic/extracosmic chaos, primarily the primal waters, which is characterized by oneness, and an inner cosmic chaos characterized by "nothingness, destruction, entropy." It is the latter that would be what Hornung calls the nonexistent.

15. J. Allen's translation in *COS* 1.16 from the 80th chapter. Allen comments in a footnote that the text indicates that Amun began evolving "without what exists."

16. Hornung, *Conceptions*, 183.

17. Allen, *Genesis in Egypt*, 57.

In reference to Mesopotamia, Clifford observes, "The cosmogonies do not express nonexistence abstractly as nothingness, but as a period when essential institutions did not yet exist."[18] In the past, the precosmic condition was often labeled "Chaos," and this terminology often included a personification or characterization of this condition as evil.[19] In the Classical world, Chaos in Hesiod's *Theogony* and in Virgil's *Aeneid* is personified as the primal state in which earth, sky, and seas were all merged.[20] More generally, *chaos* is the opposite of *cosmos*, which refers to the *ordered whole*.[21] It is this latter juxtaposition that is particularly evident in the ancient Near East. Egyptian philosophers conceived of the precreation state as the opposite of the created state. In Mesopotamian views of the precosmic condition, chaos was personified only secondarily in the conflict myths in which the created order was considered to be at risk. In this cosmological literature, the creatures posing the threat must be overthrown and order reestablished.[22] "The conflict myth is a secondary development, a personification, of these primary creation metaphors of separation and differentiation."[23]

Whether the term *Chaos* is appropriate as a label for the precreation state depends, naturally, on how it is defined and used. One option is to define it as the opposite of order and functionality; it is that which is unproductive. In this definition, chaos is neither a gaping void nor a personified enemy of order.[24] In the ancient Near East, creation involves bringing order and organization to the cosmos. In modern discussions of this topic, this (sometimes) threatening disorder is often labeled *chaos*, and we can retain the terminology as long as this careful definition is maintained. It is better,

---

18. Richard J. Clifford, *Creation Accounts in the Ancient Near East and the Bible* (CBQMS 26; Washington DC: Catholic Biblical Association), 64.

19. Examples abound from H. Gunkel's, *Creation and Chaos in the Primeval Era and the Eschaton: Religio-Historical Study of Genesis 1 and Revelation 12* (Grand Rapids, MI: Eerdmans, 2006) to B. W. Anderson, *Creation versus Chaos* (New York: Association Press, 1967) and S. Niditch, *Chaos to Cosmos: Studies in Biblical Patterns of Creation* (Scholars Press Studies in the Humanities 6; Chico, CA: Scholars Press, 1985)—just to name a few that contain *chaos* in the title.

20. *Aeneid* 4.707; *Theogony* 2.116–53. This was adopted and further refined by the Gnostics; see E. Hornung, *Conceptions*, 177 n. 127.

21. G. E. R. Lloyd, "Greek Cosmologies," in *Ancient Cosmologies* (ed. C. Blacker and M. Loewe; London: Allen and Unwin, 1975), 200.

22. Here we refer to creatures such as Tiamat and her cohorts in *Enuma Elish* and Anzu in the *Tale of Anzu*.

23. Simkins, *Creator and Creation*, 78.

24. All of this is thoroughly sorted out and discussed in a monograph by R. S. Watson, *Chaos Uncreated: A Reassessment of the Theme of "Chaos" in the Hebrew Bible* (Berlin: de Gruyter, 2005).

however, to avoid the multivalent senses that *chaos* has and instead to use *precosmic condition* (Greek *kosmos* implies order) as our term in order to avoid misunderstanding the various uses of *chaos*.[25] In the ancient Near East, the precosmic condition is therefore neither an abstraction nor a personified adversary. The primordial Sea, which is the principal element of the precreation condition, is personified as Nammu in Sumer[26] and as Nun in Egypt.

Before-and-After Pictures, and Activities Involved with Bringing into Existence

As noted above, Hornung's description of the creation cosmology of ancient Egypt entails ordering the realm of the existent.[27] This ordering takes place through a number of different processes, some directed by deity (procreation, fashioning, or use of bodily fluids), and others that are expressed in a sort of middle voice: they 'evolved' or 'developed'.[28] In all of these cases, origination in Egypt is a process of transitioning from one to many, from unity to diversity.[29] The god Atum is conceptualized as the primordial monad—the singularity embodying all the potential of the cosmos, from whom all things were separated and thereby were created.[30] Egyptians were not concerned with abstractions such as the eternality of matter, nor were they interested in the origin of matter per se; but the *continuity* of matter from the original precosmic condition to the current state of differentiated elements was of utmost importance.[31] Creation involved the transition from primordial unity to the diversity of the world that they experienced.

---

25. I prefer *precosmic condition* or *precreation* over *chaos*, and in this book, unless I capitalize *Chaos*, I will use the word only in a nontechnical, nonpersonified sense.

26. This is a general statement and as such is reductionistic. For further discussion of the variety of primal materials in Sumerian thinking and a thorough analysis of them, see J. Westenholz, "Heaven and Earth: Asexual Monad and Bisexual Dyad," in *Gazing on the Deep: Ancient Near Eastern and Other Studies in Honor of Tzvi Abusch* (ed. J. Stackert et al; Bethesda, MD: CDL, 2010), 293–326.

27. Hornung, *Conceptions*, 184.

28. The Egyptian term is *hpr*; see translations in *COS* 1.2; 1.5; 1.9; 1.10; 1.14; 1.15; 1.16; and frequent textual notes in Allen, *Genesis in Egypt*, 74–95 and commentary on p. 29.

29. Assmann, *Mind of Egypt*, 206.

30. Allen, *Genesis in Egypt*, 57–58: "Creation is the process through which the One became the Many."

31. Allen, *Genesis in Egypt*, 14.

The world is the creator's own self-realization, his development into the elements of nature. All things that exist are developments (*hprw*) of the creator himself: "he created the identities of his parts."[32]

In all of this, however, it should be recognized that these creative activities focused on the gods first and foremost and only indirectly on the cosmic parties that they represented. In other words, the Egyptian texts are much more interested in the theogony side of the spectrum than on the cosmogony side, although the two are inevitably connected. The very fact that they *are* inseparable says much about ontology in ancient Egypt. CT 261 expresses this teleology as well as the underlying functional ontology by the claim of the creator:

> I am the one who gave life to the Ennead.
> I am Acts-As-He-Likes, father of the gods,
> High of stand,
> Who made the god functional in accordance with that which he who
>   bore all commanded.[33]

Though creation in Egyptian texts is more developmental than causal,[34] transitive verbs do occur in the texts. Egyptian terms that relate to creation include *írí* 'to make', *msí* 'to beget', and *km* 'to form, fashion'.[35] A survey of the literature shows that, in cosmic contexts where a deity is the subject, the objects of these verbs are primarily functions rather than anything strictly material. The texts are more interested in the unfolding process than the means or mechanisms by which the unfolding was accomplished.[36] First and foremost, creation was considered to be not an account of the manufacturing of material things but a teleological account that reflected divine purpose.[37] "In the Egyptian understanding of reality, all the elements and forces that a human being might encounter in this world are not impersonal matter and energy but the forms and wills of living beings."[38]

---

32. Allen, *Genesis in Egypt*, 33, quoting from CT 335 = BD 17.

33. Allen, *Genesis in Egypt*, 37. This is actually a speech by Magic, that is, the magic that was wielded by the creator-god to bring about the development of all of creation by the spoken word. Thus, it is an intriguing parallel to Dame Wisdom in Proverbs 8.

34. Allen, *Genesis in Egypt*, 36.

35. For discussion of the terminology, see J. Bergman, "*Bara*': Egypt," *TDOT* 2:242–44.

36. Allen, *Genesis in Egypt*, 36.

37. Allen, *Genesis in Egypt*, 36; notice CT 714: "It was as I wished, according to my heart, that I built myself."

38. Allen, *Genesis in Egypt*, 62.

This is further illustrated by the "before" and "after" portrayals of creation found in Egyptian literature. The precosmic condition, whether or not it can be labeled *nonexistent,* can be defined both by components that are cited as lacking and by components that are present. Absent components include the spatial world (not yet separated), inhabitable places, life and death, procreation, time, conflict, and diversity.[39] The positive description features limitless waters and total darkness.[40] There are many examples of this, in which components are counted among the "existent," even though these elements had not yet come into being at the beginning—despite the fact that the precosmic state is not labeled "the nonexistent." The existent entities had not yet come into being because they had not been separated out from the initial oneness or given a name.[41] As noted above, Atum was conceptualized as the primordial monad—the singularity embodying all the potential of the cosmos, from whom all things were separated and thereby were created. Everything else was brought into existence by being differentiated. The "after" picture is consequently one of immense diversity.[42]

In addition to there being no names and no diversification, the "before" picture has no space for life to exist. The Heliopolitan text CT 80 portrays the primordial condition before creation described by Shu as having no "Place."[43]

> Not finding a place in which I could stand or sit,
> Before Heliopolis had been founded, in which I could exist;
> Before the lotus had been tied together, on which I could sit;
> Before I had made Nut so she could be over my head and Geb could
>   marry her[44]

As with all of this literature, this text does not deal with material origins but reflects a continuum between origins and life in the everyday world.[45]

---

39. Hornung, *Conceptions,* 174–76.

40. Hornung, *Conceptions,* 177; CT 80; *COS* 1.8; also anticipated as the condition the earth will return to at the end of time; see the Book of the Dead chap. 175: "I shall destroy all that I have made, and this land will come back into Nun, into the floodwaters, as in its beginning."

41. See Papyrus Berlin 3055, 16:3–4 and its quotation in Morenz, *Egyptian Religion,* 165.

42. Hornung, *Conceptions,* 171; Morenz, *Egyptian Religion,* 173. Texts include Pyramid Text 1208c (Morenz, 173); CT 4 36 (spell 286) (Morenz, 173); Heliopolis (Morenz, 173); Stele Leyden 5.12 (Morenz, 173); "Ptah, Lord of maat . . . who lifted up the sky and created things that be" (Morenz, 174); *Memphite Theology,* line 14: Ptah, creating through the Ennead, is identified as the one who "pronounced the identity of everything."

43. Allen, *Genesis in Egypt,* 25

44. CT 80 48–51.

45. Allen, *Genesis in Egypt,* 25.

In Akkadian, the main verbs meaning 'create' are *banû* and *bašāmu*.[46] The former is used generally, with an extensive range of meanings, including "build, construct, form, make, manufacture" and is sometimes translated 'create'. When a deity is the subject in a cosmic context, objects include:

- mankind or individual humans
- heavens [see "When Anu had created the heaven, the heaven had created the earth, the earth had created the rivers," etc.]
- offices (high-priestess, kingship)
- mountains
- various abstract features (e.g., womb [not the female organ] that produces features, warfare, conjuration, justice)
- cosmic features (e.g., evil wind) and physical things that are given cosmic qualities (e.g., barley, flax)
- items created to perform functions (stars created to destroy evil ones)
- a plan or a situation

The second verb, *bašāmu,* is used more narrowly. Its objects include:

- buildings or plans for them (usually sanctuaries)
- pictures (e.g., reliefs on steles)
- arable land (e.g., by building dikes)
- people in the womb
- strategies
- weapons (magical ones for the gods)
- divine images
- cosmic components (constellations, firmament [*burumu*])

When creation activities are documented in Sumerian and Akkadian sources, we are able to observe the situation both before and after the activity, as well as what sorts of verbs are used. This helps to determine the focus of the creative activity. We will begin with Sumerian texts.

NBC 11108

Earth was in darkness, the lower world was [invi]sible;
The waters did not flow through the opening (in the earth),
Nothing was produced, on the vast earth the furrow had not been made.
The high priest of Enlil did not exist,

---

46. See some discussion of additional verbs in Clifford, *Creation Accounts,* 71–72; H. Ringgren, "*Bara*': Mesopotamia," *TDOT* 2:244; *CAD* B 88–89 for *banû*; *CAD* B 137–38 for *bašāmu*. Sumerian verbs for the creation of humanity are discussed in G. Pettinato, *Das altorientalische Menschenbild und die sumerischen und akkadischen Schöpfungsmythen* (Heidelberg: Carl Winter, 1971), 48–57, and Akkadian verbs cited there, pp. 57–60.

The rites of purification were not carried out,
The h[ierodul]e (?) of heaven was not adorned, she did not proclaim
　　[the praises?]
Heaven and earth were joined to each other (forming) a unit, they were
　　not [married].
Heaven showed its shining face in Dagan [= heavenly dwelling],
As it coursed, it could not reach the fields.
The rule of Enlil over the land had not yet come about,
The p[ure lad]y? of E'anna had not yet [receiv]ed [offerings]?
The gr[eat gods], the Anunna, were not yet active,
The gods of heaven, the gods of ea[rth] were not yet there.[47]

The "before" picture here comprises darkness, water, and the nondiscrete
heaven and earth (on the positive side) and the absence of productivity, of
the gods, and of the operation of the cult (on the negative side). Creative
activities then alter this landscape. An alternative perspective can be seen
in *Enki and Ninhursag*, where it is not the cultic system that is absent but
the social system.[48]

Gilgamesh, Enkidu, and the Underworld (or The Huluppu Tree)

in days of yore, when the necessary things had been brought into
　　manifest existence,
in days of yore, when the necessary things had been for the first time
　　properly cared for,
when bread had been tasted for the first time in the shrines of the Land,
when the ovens of the Land had been made to work,
when the heavens had been separated from the earth,
when the earth had been delimited from the heavens,
when the fame of mankind had been established,
when An had taken the heavens for himself,
when Enlil had taken the earth for himself,
when the nether world had been given to Ereškigala as a gift;[49]

Clifford points out the focus on organization evident in this account.[50] Origins are introduced in the first two lines, and then the specifics of what this
refers to are detailed in the following lines. Areas that are addressed include

---

47. Clifford, *Creation Accounts*, 28, translated into English from J. van Dijk's French trans-
lation in "Existe-t-il un 'Poème de la Création' Sumérien?" in *Kramer Anniversary Volume:
Cuneiform Studies in Honor of Samuel Noah Kramer* (ed. B. Eichler et al.; AOAT 25; Kevelaer:
Butzon & Bercker, 1976), 125–33.

48. Clifford, *Creation Accounts*, 36.

49. Electronic corpus of Sumerian Texts translation, http://etcsl.orinst.ox.ac.uk lines 4–13.
"Necessary things" = Sumerian niĝ$_2$-du$_7$ 'that which is proper or appropriate'.

50. Clifford, *Creation Accounts*, 24–25.

the operation of the cult, cosmic separation, naming of mankind, and juris-
dictions of the major gods.

Similar observations can be made concerning major pieces of literature
such as *Enuma Elish*. The initial primordial context is addressed very briefly
in theogonic terms. The situation before creation is described in terms of
the absence of names, gods, and destinies.

> I 1–2: When on high no name was given in heaven, nor below was the
> netherworld called by name . . .
> I 7–9: When no gods at all had been brought forth, none called by
> names, none destinies ordained, then were the gods formed.
> I 10: Laḫmu and Laḫamu were brought forth, were called by name
> I 16: Then Anu begot in his own image Nudimmud[51]

Later in the piece, after Marduk has defeated Tiamat's forces, a more extensive account of creation provides details of his work. Note the following
excerpts, which have been chosen to highlight the terminology.

IV 138–44

Half of her he set up and made as a cover, heaven.
He stretched out the hide and assigned watchmen,
And ordered them not to let her waters escape.
He crossed heaven and inspected its firmament,
He made a counterpart to Apsu, the dwelling of Nudimmud.
The Lord measured the construction of Apsu,
He founded the Great Sanctuary, the likeness of Esharra.

V

1: made the position(s) for the great gods
2: established (in) constellations the stars. Their likenesses
3: marked the year
4: set up twelve months of three stars each
5: patterned the days of the year
12: made the moon appear, entrusted (to him) the night
54: he opened underground springs, a flood was let flow
55: From her eyes he undimmed the Euphrates and Tigris
61: He set her crotch as the brace of heaven,
62: Spreading half of her as a cover, he established the netherworld[52]

Marduk then proceeds to assume his prerogatives (V 65) and takes the throne
(V 78–104). The other gods then proclaim: "Over all things which your hands

---

51. *COS* 1.111.
52. *COS* 1.111.

have created, who has authority, save for you?" (V 133–34). In this way, it is clear that all of the previous description was part of the act of creation.

The principal acts of creation are naming, separating, and temple building. While separating holds a prominent position in Egyptian and Sumerian texts, the significance of naming can be seen in its role in *Enuma Elish*, as observed by B. Foster.

> The poem [*Enuma Elish*] begins and ends with concepts of naming. The poet evidently considers naming both an act of creation and an explanation of something already brought into being. For the poet, the name, properly understood, discloses the significance of the created thing. Semantic and phonological analysis of names could lead to understanding of the things named. Names, for this poet, are a text to be read by the informed, and bear the same intimate and revealing relationship to what they signify as this text does to the events it narrates.[53]

All of this indicates that cosmic creation in the ancient world was not viewed primarily as a process by which matter was brought into being but as a process by which functions, roles, order, jurisdiction, organization, and stability were established. This makes it clear that creation in the ancient world was defined by the determination of functions and, in turn, demonstrates that the ontology of ancient peoples was focused on a thing's functional, rather than its material, status.[54]

A final example from Mesopotamia, from the Seleucid period (ca. 3rd–2nd century B.C.E.), is a work entitled:

Cosmogony and the Foundation of Eridu

All lands were sea
The spring in the midst of the sea was only a channel
Then Eridu was made, Esagil was built,
Esagil that Lugaldukuga erected in the heart of the apsu
Babylon was made, Esagil was completed.[55]

---

53. B. Foster, *Before the Muses* (3rd ed.; Bethesda, MD: CDL, 2005) 437–38. The relationship between naming and creation is also affirmed in J.-J. Glassner, "The Use of Knowledge in Ancient Mesopotamia," in *CANE*, 3.1818.

54. An uncritical reading of Allen, *Genesis in Egypt*, 45–46 and 59–63, could potentially lead to the conclusion that he thinks otherwise, because he repeatedly refers to "substance" and "material reality" throughout the discussion as he writes about what Ptah created according to the *Memphite Theology*. A more careful reading, however, makes it evident that what he means by the "material" is not what we mean by "matter" but the "forces and elements of the world" (p. 45). The distinction Allen is trying to make is the contrast between the perception of Ptah—i.e., his concept of the world—and the resulting reality (p. 47), which is what he refers to by the word "material."

55. Clifford, *Creation Accounts*, 63.

In this text, the primordial state is once again the familiar unbounded waters. The creative act referred to, however, is the founding of city and temple. This feature was already present in some of the earlier works, particularly *Enuma Elish*, where it was one part of the activity (and the climax of the creative activity), but here it is the first of a number of other activities (creating humans, animals, Tigris and Euphrates, etc.).

Separating Heaven and Earth

Often, the transition from the precosmic condition to the activities involved in creation is the separation of heaven and earth. In Egypt, the separating of heaven and earth is not frequently mentioned as a major event but as one of many stages involved in the one becoming many. In Mesopotamian accounts, the separation is simply mentioned, without any statement about the mechanism involved.[56] On the other hand, Egyptian accounts focus more on what separates heaven earth—namely, the sky god Shu—than on the separation itself. The Coffin Texts describe this process:

> For I [Shu] am weary at the Uplifting of Shu,
> Since I lifted my daughter Nut atop me,
> That I might give her to my father Atum in his utmost extent.
> I have put Geb under my feet.[57]

Allen identifies the separating of heaven and earth as the first act of creation and a necessary precondition for the rest of creation:

> Shu's role, however, is the pivotal one, both in the created world and in the process of its creation. Before the creation, all things were undifferentiated in the primordial Monad, Atum. The creation of a void (Shu) within that unity inevitably produced, at the same time, a distinction between top and bottom—between sky-vault above the void and the earth beneath it, with the void separating the two.[58]

To the Egyptians, the universe consisted of a limitless ocean (Nun) above the sky, paralleled by waters under the earth.[59] The waters above the sky and under the earth were separated by Shu, the god of the air.

This notion is referred to again in the Book of the Dead chap. 17:

---

56. For extensive discussion see J. Westenholz, "Heaven and Earth: Asexual Monad and Bisexual Dyad," in *Gazing on the Deep: Ancient Near Eastern and Other Studies in Honor of Tzvi Abusch* (ed. J. Stackert et al; Bethesda, MD: CDL, 2010), 293–326, especially pp. 304–7.

57. CT 76 10–13, translation by Allen, *Genesis in Egypt*, 18.

58. Allen, *Genesis in Egypt*, 20–21.

59. Allen, *Genesis in Egypt*, 4

I am Atum when I was alone in Nun. I am Re in his appearances in glory, when he began to rule that which he had made. Who is he? "Re when he began to rule that which he had made" means: when Re began to appear in the kingship which he exercised as who existed before the liftings of Shu had occurred, while he was on the hill which is in Hermopolis.[60]

In Hittite literature, heaven and earth were understood to have been cut apart with a copper cutting tool.

When they built heaven and earth upon me, I was aware of nothing. And when they cut heaven and earth apart with a copper cutting tool, I was even unaware of that.[61]

It is in Sumerian accounts that the most frequent references to the separation of heaven and earth are found but often only in passing.

Song of the Hoe
Not only did he [Enlil] hasten to separate heaven from earth, and hasten to separate earth from heaven, but, in order to make it possible for humans to grow in "Where Flesh Came Forth" (the name of a cosmic location), he first suspended the axis of the world at Dur-an-ki.[62]

Huluppu Tree
In "The *Huluppu* Tree," a section in *Gilgamesh, Enkidu, and the Netherworld* (see translation above, p. 32) the separation is accomplished by An carrying off heaven and Enlil carrying off earth. Also translated above, in NBC 11108, the future separation of heaven and earth is noted as not yet having taken place. Two other sources mention the separation briefly in passing.

Lugalbanda in the Mountain Cave
When in ancient days heaven was separated from earth, when in ancient days that which was fitting . . . , when after the ancient harvests . . . barley was eaten (?), when boundaries were laid out and borders were fixed, when boundary-stones were placed and inscribed with names[63]

---

60. Lesko, "Ancient Egyptian Cosmogonies and Cosmology," 113.
61. H. Hoffner, "Song of Ullikummi," in *Hittite Myths* (SBLWAW 2; Atlanta: Society of Biblical Literature, 1990), 59, §61. The speaker is Ubelluri, a god whose place is similar to Atlas in Greek mythology, who holds up the cosmos from his place in the netherworld.
62. http://etcsl.orinst.ox.ac.uk 5.5.4.
63. http://etcsl.orinst.ox.ac.uk 1.8.2.1.

Silver and Copper

(Copper speaks:) ". . . the heavens were separated from the earth, there was no drinking water."[64]

The theme of separation of heaven and earth is less common in Akkadian sources.[65] It is not explicitly mentioned in *Enuma Elish* but is perhaps alluded to in the first two lines, which indicate that the heaven and the earth had not yet been named. This may imply they had not yet been separated. In line 12, Anshar and Kishar are formed and named, representing the now-identified totality of heaven and earth.[66]

Finally, in *KAR* 4, the Sumerian version begins, "When Heaven had been separated from Earth—hitherto they were joined firmly together. . . ."[67] Because this text is preserved in both the Sumerian and Akkadian versions, it might have provided the only Akkadian text that referred explicitly to the separation of heaven and earth. Unfortunately, the Akkadian version of line 1 is not preserved.

This survey shows, then, that a precosmic condition is followed by the first step in creation, which often is the separation of heaven and earth. From this step forward, a variety of creation verbs are used in the description of the subsequent stages of creation, and these verbs find their correlates in the basic building blocks of creation.

Building Blocks, Causation, and Teleology

In this section, based on what the texts reveal, I will demonstrate that, when the ancients thought about the component parts of the cosmos—even as it is expressed in statements about cosmic geography, they focused on function rather than material. When they ponder causation, their thinking reflects a world in which divine activity moves objects rather than a world of material objects acting in accordance with natural laws.[68] The perspective of the ancients on the nature of the material world and causation firmly

---

64. http://etcsl.orinst.ox.ac.uk 5.3.6.

65. In fact, reading the entries in the *CAD* on *nesû, zâzu, šamû, burūmû, qaqqaru,* and *erṣetu* turned up no references to the separation of heaven and earth (as distinguished from the separating of the waters in the splitting of Tiamat's body).

66. See Foster's note in *Before the Muses,* 439 n.4.

67. Clifford, *Creation Accounts,* 49. For details of the controversy surrounding this poorly preserved line, see G. Pettinato, *Das altorientalische Menschenbild und die sumerischen und akkadischen Schöpfungsmythen* (Heidelberg: Carl Winter, 1971), 79 n. 1. The separation of heaven from earth in this text, however, is not controversial.

68. Note W. G. Lambert, *RlA* 6:218–19: "In ancient Mesopotamia there was comparatively little interest in cosmogony as such. Few texts deal in any detail with the processes whereby

support what is patently obvious to anyone reading the texts—that they viewed cosmic origins and operations in teleological terms.[69] Purpose and intentionality characterized the work of the gods. Though their purposes were not always transparent, and no overarching plan was evident to human beings, the gods had their reasons and were acting in accordance with those reasons. Even when no specific goals could be discerned by mortals, the cosmos was driven from beginning to end by the purposes of the gods.

> [Ptah's] heart and tongue have control over all limbs showing that he is preeminent in every body and in every mouth—of all gods, all people, all animals, and all crawling things that live—planning and governing everything he wishes.[70]

That all of the world was governed by the gods' activities is an integral element of the cognitive environment of the ancient world, and it is diametrically opposed to the reigning modern paradigm, which is thoroughly dysteleological: origins and causation are seen in impersonal terms, the simple result of random reactions within the bounds of natural laws, discernible only within an empirical framework.

In the *Memphite Theology*, important components of creation are listed in terms of functions, such as male life-principles, female life-principles, what is loved, what is hated, life to the calm, death to the wrongdoer, construction and craft, working hands, walking feet, and movement of limbs. The *Memphite Theology*'s description of the created world singles out the most important aspects of creation, as it was understood by the Egyptians.

The late demotic Papyrus Insinger, which M. Lichtheim dates to the Ptolemaic period, contains a series of instructions made up of individual proverbs. The 24th instruction concerns the wisdom of recognizing the role of deity and how foolish it is to discount the gods. Toward the end of column 31, a couple of rhetorical questions introduce a list of what god has created.

> How do the sun and moon go and come in the sky?
> Whence go and come water, fire, and wind?
> Through whom do the amulet and spell become remedies?
> The hidden work of the god, he makes it known on the earth daily.

---

the physical universe originated and attained its present form. A much greater interest was taken in the ancestries of the gods, and these frequently have cosmogonic associations."

69. I am using *teleology* to refer to the branch of cosmology that deals with final causes; specifically, teleological affirmation reflects a belief that origins are driven by intention and purpose. This intention or purpose does not necessarily include a final goal for the end of time, though it may do so.

70. *Memphite Theology*, column 54; see *COS* 1.15.

He created light and darkness in which is every creature.

He created the earth, begetting millions, swallowing (them) up and
begetting again.

He created day, month, and year through the commands of the lord of
command.

He created summer and winter through the rising and setting of Sothis.

He created food before those who are alive, the wonder of the fields.

He created the constellation of those that are in the sky, so that those on
earth should learn them.

He created sweet water in it which all the lands desire.

He created the breath in the egg though there is no access to it.

He created birth in every womb from the semen which they receive.

He created sinews and bones out of the same semen.

He created coming and going in the whole earth through the trembling
of the ground.

He created sleep to end weariness, waking for looking after food.

He created remedies to end illness, wine to end affliction.

He created the dream to show the way to the dreamer in his blindness.

He created life and death before him for the torment of the impious
man.

He created wealth for truthfulness, poverty for falsehood.

He created work for the stupid man, food for the common man.

He created the succession of generations so as to make them live.[71]

Examples such as this demonstrate that, across all periods, in Egypt the
components of the real world convey a functional view of reality, not a material view, and that causation emanates from the divine, not from within
the material world itself.

In Mesopotamia, the situation is no different. A full discussion of the
archetypal functions (Sumerian ME) will be undertaken below (pp. 46–62),
but for now it should be observed that these are the building blocks of the
cosmos.

Enki and World Order

Counting the days and putting the months in their houses, so as to complete the years and to submit the completed years to the assembly for
a decision, taking decisions to regularise the days: father Enki, you are
the king of the assembled people. You have only to open your mouth for
everything to multiply and for plenty to be established. Your branches . . .
green with their fruit, . . . do honour to the gods. . . . in its forests is like a
fleecy garment. Good sheep and good lambs do honour to. . . . When . . .

---

71. M. Lichtheim, *AEL*, 3:210–11.

the prepared fields, . . . will accumulate stockpiles and stacks. . . . there is oil, there is milk, produced by the sheepfold and cow-pen. The shepherd sweetly sings his rustic song, the cowherd spends the day rocking his churns. Their products would do honour to the late lunches in the gods' great dining hall.

At my command, sheepfolds have been built, cow-pens have been fenced off. When I approach heaven, a rain of abundance rains from heaven. When I approach earth, there is a high carp-flood. When I approach the green meadows, at my word stockpiles and stacks are accumulated. I have built my house, a shrine, in a pure place, and named it with a good name. I have built my Abzu, a shrine, in . . . , and decreed a good fate for it.[72]

The text goes on to describe Enki's role in assigning functions to the gods, the temples, and the cosmos. The functions fall mainly into the categories of time, weather, and fertility, though aspects of culture and society are also mentioned. In this document, we can see both the essential building blocks of the cosmos (the functions represented by the Sumerian ME) and the location of causation, which is fully in the realm of deity.

Inanna and Enki

Aspects of human society and culture are even more evident in *Inanna and Enki*, which preserves a list of nearly 80 ME. This list should not be considered comprehensive (perhaps it lists only those that become associated specifically with Inanna and her town of Uruk), but it is sufficiently representative to provide an understanding of the kinds of items that the composers of this story considered to be the building blocks of the cosmos.

heroism, power, wickedness, righteousness, the plundering of cities, making lamentations, rejoicing, deceit, the rebel lands, kindness, being on the move, being sedentary, craft of the carpenter, the craft of the coppersmith, the craft of the scribe, the craft of the smith, the craft of the leather-worker, the craft of the fuller, the craft of the builder, the craft of the reed-worker, wisdom, attentiveness, holy purification rites, the shepherd's hut, piling up glowing charcoals, the sheepfold, respect, awe, reverent silence, the bitter-toothed (?), the kindling of fire, the extinguishing of fire, hard work, the assembled family, descendants, strife, triumph, counselling, comforting, judging, decision-making, the office of *en* priest, the office of *lagar* priest, divinity, the great and good crown, the royal throne, the noble sceptre, the staff and crook, the noble dress, shepherdship, kingship, the office of *egir-zid* priestess, the office of *nin-diĝir* priestess, the office of *išib* priest, the office of *lu-mah* priest, the office

---

72. http://etcsl.orinst.ox.ac.uk 17–31 and 89–95.

of *gudug* priest, constancy, going down to the underworld, coming up from the underworld, the *kur-ĝara* priest, the sword and club, the cultic functionary *saĝ-ursaĝ*, the black garment, the colourful garment, the standard, the quiver, sexual intercourse, kissing, prostitution, forthright speech, deceitful speech, grandiloquent speech, the cultic prostitute, the holy tavern, the holy *niĝin-ĝar* shrine, the hierodule of heaven, loud musical instruments, the art of song, venerable old age.[73]

From the list of these items, it is evident that the ME include both cosmic and cultural operations and that both kinds of activities equally define the way the created world functions. The context likewise makes it clear that the administration of these functions belongs in the divine realm.

Enuma Elish

One more example should suffice to illustrate what the ancients thought constituted the main building blocks of the cosmos and what were the most important elements to include in any description of origins in a cosmogonic account. In tablet V of *Enuma Elish*, Marduk is "creating the cosmos," though his activity could just as easily be described as "reorganizing" the cosmos. It is difficult, however, to distinguish between these two labels, for when functions are involved, creation and reorganization overlap considerably.

The tablet begins with Marduk's organizing the celestial sphere with regard to the stars, constellations, and the phases of the moon (lines 1–24). Lines 25–45 are not represented in many of the translations included in major modern anthologies of ancient texts. Even in their broken form, however, these lines' basic content can be discerned.[74] In lines 38–40, Marduk makes the night and day and sets it up so that there is an equal number of hours of light and hours of darkness throughout the course of the year.[75] In line 46, he fixes the watches of night and day. All of these creative activities clearly have to do with organizing time.

Lines 47–52 are more readable, though a few breaks still hamper our understanding.[76] These lines deal with the creation of the clouds, wind, rain,

---

73. Taken from http://etcsl.orinst.ox.ac.uk Segment D lines 1–24; Segment F 16–34.

74. See Foster, *Before the Muses*, 464; W. Horowitz, *Mesopotamian Cosmic Geography* (MC 8; Winona Lake, IN: Eisenbrauns, 1998), 117–18.

75. For this interpretation, see Horowitz, *Mesopotamian Cosmic Geography*, 117.

76. The break at the end of line 48 is particularly annoying, because the object is lost in the break: 'Marduk created (*banu*). . .'.

and fog and with Marduk's appointing himself to control them. In short, it is here that the functions relating to the weather are created.

Finally, in lines 53–58, the waters of Tiamat are harnessed in order to provide the basis of agriculture. The piling up of dirt, releasing the Tigris and Euphrates, and digging holes to manage the catchwater are included.

What follows is the establishment of the three realms of ancient cosmic geography (lines 59–68) and then the transition into the enthronement of Marduk and the building of his temple and the city of Babylon—the grand climax. It is no surprise that a creation text should ultimately be about the god who controls the cosmos and the origin of his temple. We will see below that cosmic origins and temple origins are intricately intertwined.

In an older Sumerian debate text, *The Debate between Winter and Summer*, Enlil is involved in creation in these same three functional areas as Marduk in *Enuma Elish* (Marduk: basis for time, weather, agriculture; Enlil: day and night [time]; fertility [basis for agriculture]; sluices of heaven [basis for weather]):

> An lifted his head in pride and brought forth a good day. He laid plans for . . . and spread the population wide. Enlil set his foot upon the earth like a great bull. Enlil, the king of all lands, set his mind to increasing the good day of abundance, to making the . . . night resplendent in celebration, to making flax grow, to making barley proliferate, to guaranteeing the spring floods at the quay, to making . . . lengthen (?) their days in abundance, to making Summer close the sluices of heaven, and to making Winter guarantee plentiful water at the quay.[77]

In Mesopotamian sources, as in Egypt, when the texts report on the components of the cosmos, the building blocks overwhelmingly involve functional aspects of these components rather than treating them primarily as material objects. Even when material objects are mentioned, it is their functions, not the structures or substance of these material objects that are the focus of attention. Causation, likewise, was not thought of as involving material natural processes; instead, causation is always the prerogative of deity.

Summary and Conclusions regarding Ontology

We have seen in the above sections that the precosmic world was understood not as a world absent of matter but as a world absent of function, order, diversity, and identity. The before-and-after pictures, with the acts

---

77. http://etcsl.orinst.ox.ac.uk 5.3.3, lines 1–11.

of creation serving as a transition between them, focus on the origins of function and order. The verbs that are used operate in the same semantic realm. Cosmos and culture are related, and their components are listed as functions rather than as objects. Causation is entirely in the realm of the gods and is characterized by a teleological perspective that transcends and virtually ignores the material, physical, natural world. Reality and existence in the cognitive environment of ancient peoples can be understood as predominantly comprising function and order, not matter and objects.[78] The acts of creation involved naming, separating, and temple building. This coincides with what Eliade observed concerning the perspective prevalent in the ancient world: the "ontological thirst" of the ancients was the pursuit of a view of reality that could give meaning to life.[79] Modern material ontology offers no secure understanding of the meaning of life, but the functional ontology of ancient Near Eastern peoples gave meaning to the reality that they experienced in the way the world worked.

In the ancient cognitive environment, it was more important to determine who controlled functions than who or what gave something its physical form. We could therefore conclude that *in the ancient world something was created when it was given a function.* Allen captures this common ancient perspective when he summarizes Egyptian thinking by observing that "the Egyptian explanations are more *metaphysical* than physical."[80] Similarly, Assmann emphasizes the element of time as more determinative of ancient ontology than space or substance.

> Our consideration of the Egyptian concept of "cosmos as drama" has already made it clear that the Egyptians did not conceive of reality as primarily spatial and material, but as temporal and performative, as a

---

78. H. Renckens was already anticipating this direction in *Israel's Concept of the Beginning* ([New York: Herder and Herder, 1964], 82–85), when he noted that Israel never considered the question of creation to concern the origin of matter. He notes that "it must be remembered that our generally accepted definition of creation as 'to bring forth something out of nothing' presupposes a concept of being and of nonbeing which is simply not that of the Bible, or at any rate is there only as part of a much broader and more concrete way of looking at things" (p. 85). The interest in order rather than matter was also observed by R. Coote and D. Ord, *In the Beginning: Creation and the Priestly History* (Minneapolis: Fortress, 1991), 4.

79. M. Eliade, *Cosmos and History: The Myth of the Eternal Return* (New York: Harper, 1954). Of course, as important as Eliade's work was, philosophy and anthropology have developed further. We need not retain Eliade's assessment that this represents a mythical view of reality; it is simply a functional view of reality.

80. Allen, *Genesis in Egypt*, 56. See also V. A. Tobin, "Myths: Creation Myths," *OEAE* 2:469.

living process that was represented most impressively in the course of the sun. Cosmological thought and concepts centered on the sun's course were thus expressed principally in temporal terms. The Egyptians had no concept of "space" in the sense of a primary category of cosmic totality, but rather one of "time."[81]

The idea that the ancients did not have a material ontology of course does not mean that they had no interest in or awareness of the physical world around them. That is, it is not as if they had a mystical view of the world rather than paying attention to the real world they experienced every day. The point is, however, that to them the "real" world was a world of divine presence and activity. Their cosmological ontology reflects that it is the *functioning* of that ordered, real world that is of importance, not its physical makeup or the physical origins of the material objects. The "hardware" is incidental; it is the "software" that counts. This is reflected in V. Tobin's summary statement about ancient Egypt, which is just as true of the rest of the ancient world.

> When the Egyptians contemplated the created universe through their myths and rituals, they would have been aware that the world around them was not simply a collection of material things. The universe was for them an awesome system of living divine beings. The earth, the sky, and the Nile were all entities that had a distinct life-force and personality and drew their life from the original creative power, no matter what name that power may have borne. These living beings were arranged and ordered in a definite system, purposely conceived as in the Memphite tradition, and naturally produced through the process of regeneration as was stressed by the Heliopolitan system. Egyptian creation myth emphasized the fact that there was order and continuity in all things and thus gave the optimistic assurance that the natural, social, and political order would remain stable and secure.[82]

In a material ontology, the world is full of objects. To us moderns, a cow or a tree can be nothing more than an object to be exploited for its material value (milk and meat in the case of the cow, wood or maybe shade or even beauty in the case of the tree). But in some cultures, where cows or trees have religious significance, they do not serve as objects that function only in terms of their material components or offer only material for exploitation. Although giving milk or shade are functions, the cow and tree are

---

81. J. Assmann, *The Search for God in Ancient Egypt* (Ithaca, NY: Cornell University Press, 2001), 74.
82. Tobin, "Myths: Creation Myths," 471.

considered to have sacred functions that at times preclude the exploitation of their material functions. They have been personified (imbued with the divine) or at least sacralized. The personification or sacralization of material things was common in the ancient Near East. Israel's theology moved away from the sacralization of the surrounding world. Isaiah the prophet argues that the wood used to make an idol is nothing more than wood and cannot attain the sacralized status that was attributed to the wood through the image-making process. But though the world around them was desacralized by Israel, this does not mean that the material of the world was objectified. The function performed by anything in the world is a result of its having been assigned this function by deity. The physical properties of the thing are designed to facilitate this function rather than to determine it. [83] Israel's movement toward desacralization may have been the first step toward a material ontology, but the functional perspective continued to dominate its understanding of the world.

In our modern, material ontology, we are inclined to think of the cosmos as a machine—often with no one running it (that is, the modern perspective is dysteleological). When we moderns think about the ancient world (including the Bible), it is most natural for us to imagine that ancient peoples simply thought of the world as a machine with Someone running it, rather than seeing that they did not in any respect conceive of the world as a machine. [84] In the ancient functional ontology, the cosmos is more like a business. [85] In this metaphor, it is clear that a business only functions in relationship to people, both the company's employees and its customers.

Thus, I must observe that, in like manner, the functions of the cosmos and culture are all in relation to people (and at times in relation to the gods, insofar as they share the world with people). R. Clifford draws a similar conclusion when he observes that ancient cosmology accounts are interested in the emergence of a particular society rather than in the emergence

---

83. When a child uses a colander as a knight's helmet, the function is what she says it is or imagines it to be. The physical features are a convenience that facilitates this function, but the child has no idea what a colander is, nor does he objectify it as a colander.

84. Note this statement by F. Wiggermann: "If nature is defined as a machine lacking free will, there is no nature in Mesopotamian thought," in "Mythological Foundations of Nature," in *Natural Phenomena: Their Meaning, Depiction and Description in the Ancient Near East* (ed. D. J. W. Meijer; Amsterdam: Royal Netherlands Academy of Arts and Sciences, 1992), 279.

85. J. Stek, "What Says the Scripture," in *Portraits of Creation* (ed. H. J. van Till; Grand Rapids, MI: Eerdmans, 1990), 203–65; on p. 255, he draws a contrast between machine and kingdom.

of the physical cosmos.[86] As a result, they show how the world became an adequate place in which people could live: "And God saw that it was good."

Cosmic Governing Principles

Mesopotamia: Sumerian ME *and Decreeing Destinies*

As shown in the previous chapter, in a modern material ontology, the building blocks of the cosmos are material objects (atoms, molecules, cells, etc.), whereas in the ancient functional ontology, the building blocks are functional processes. The next aspect of the ancient Near Eastern cognitive environment that warrants investigation is what the ancients considered to be the foundational realities of the cosmos: the impersonal cosmic principles that make the cosmos what it is, which the Sumerians designate by the word ME. We will explore the origin of these realities and their administration as well as the relationship of deities to these realities. These have already been introduced above as building blocks in the functional ontology of the ancient world, identified by the Sumerian term ME, to which we now turn our attention.

The most important reflection of the fundamentally functional emphasis in the thinking of ancient peoples about their world is embodied in the conceptual spectrum framed by the terms *parṣu, uṣurtu,* and *šimtu* in Akkadian and ME, GIŠḪUR, and NAMTAR in Sumerian. The semantic notions expressed by these terms are at the heart of the functional cosmos and play a major role in the establishment and operation of both the cosmos and the temple, as well as, of course, human society.

There continues to be considerable debate regarding the best definition and translation of the Akkadian and Sumerian terms. The confusion was present early on, because most modern scholars have concluded that the Akkadian translation for ME, *parṣu,* itself was a misunderstanding.[87] Some of the translations suggested for ME include 'functions', 'decrees', 'ordinances', 'prescriptions', 'rules', 'attributes', 'divine powers', 'arts of civilization', and 'cultural norms', just to name a few. It becomes even more com-

---

86. R. Clifford, "The Hebrew Scriptures and the Theology of Creation," *JTS* 46 (1985): 507–23.

87. See for example Glassner's assertion that "Akkadian had no equivalent for the Sumerian ME" in "The Use of Knowledge in Ancient Mesopotamia," *CANE* 3.1820. "In its most common Akkadian use, *parṣu* refers to a cultic ritual or ceremony" and "is strongly associated with verbs of cultic performance, specifically dealing with ritual or ceremony." Joshua Walton, unpublished study of *parṣu,* Harvard University, 2010. In a small number of cases, *parṣu* is used simply as the Akkadian translation of ME, as is the case in *Enuma Elish* and *Anzu*.

plicated when *šimtu* enters the picture. The description provided by van Binsbergen and Wiggermann suffices as a starting point for our discussion:

> While NAMTAR (*šimtu*) connotes the governmental decisions made by Enlil, ME (*paršu*) evokes an impersonal and timeless order, the nonvolitional state of equilibrium to which the universe and its constituent parts are subjected. The ME are at home in the old religious center of Eridu and guarded by its god Enki/Ea. The ME are not created, but they are simply there as part of the universe; they are the rules of tradition, the unchanging ways in which the world of man and things is supposed to be organized; they can be disused or forgotten, but never destroyed. Together they constitute natural law, a guideline for behavior untainted by human or divine interference.[88]

A. Livingstone suggests that ME "denotes an abstract concept, 'archetype,'" an understanding that he derives from B. Alster.[89] Alster includes four items in the range of ME:[90]

- archetype or cultural norm
- visible manifestation of said archetype
- process relating to the actualisation of the archetype
- anything that symbolizes the capability of actualizing the archetype

H. Vanstiphout prefers 'first principles' or 'quintessences' and offers the following definition:

> The MES are the eternal and unchangeable first principles, or quintessences, of everything that exists. They are also the blueprints for everything that exists, in that they prescribe how it should exist."[91]

---

88. W. van Binsbergen, and F. Wiggermann, "Magic in History: A Theoretical Perspective, and Its Application to Ancient Mesopotamia," in *Mesopotamian Magic* (ed. T. Abusch and K. van der Toorn; Groningen: Styx, 1999), 21. As an aside, I am inclined to see some similarity between the control attributes in Akkadian and the concept of *tradition* in *Fiddler on the Roof* (van Binsbergen and Wiggermann even translate ME 'tradition' in "Magic in History," p. 20). In the village of Anatevka, the precarious stability and order is maintained only by the traditions that govern the lives of the people and the roles that they take as a result. Any disruption of roles and traditions threatens to bring upheaval and chaos. In modern parlance, we might use the term *fabric* as a metaphor, apply it to "the fabric of life," "the fabric of civilization," or "the fabric of the cosmos."

89. A. Livingstone, *Mystical and Mythological Explanatory Works of Assyrian and Babylonian Scholars* (Winona Lake, IN: Eisenbrauns, 2007), 58.

90. B. Alster, "On the Interpretation of 'Inanna and Enki'," *ZA* 64 (1975): 33–34 n. 33.

91. H. Vanstiphout, "Die Geschöpfe des Prometheus, Or How and Why Did the Sumerians Create Their Gods?" in *What Is a God?* (ed. B. N. Porter; TCBAI 2; Winona Lake: IN, Eisenbrauns, 2009), 15–40, quotation on p. 35.

In his analysis, the ME defines the gods, not the other way around; it is the god who is contingent, not the ME. He concludes that ME refers to the "abstract but no less real quintessence of all things, procedures, action, interrelations. . . . Without its ME, nothing can exist. And the point of any kind of existing 'thing' is to conform as closely as possible to its ideal, if unreachable, form, which is its ME."[92] In an attempt to synthesize these ideas, I have occasionally used the rendering 'archetypal quintessence' for the Sumerian ME; however, recognizing that the expression, as all the others, remains as cumbersome as it is arguable, I have usually just reverted to using the Sumerian term.

The third pair of terms, GIŠḪUR/*uṣurtu*, has been the subject of less controversy but also plays an important role. It is often translated 'design' or 'plans' (such as, for instance, architectural plans), referring to the actions that flow out of the MEs and produce the decrees. Perhaps the best way to understand these terms and their usage in ancient literature is to incorporate them into an extended metaphor. Y. Rosengarten attempts precisely this by suggesting that MEs should be understood in relation to "prescriptions" governing the cosmos.[93] The MEs themselves are like the descriptions of medications in a pharmaceutical dictionary. The gods are the doctors who prescribe the medications. The kings are the pharmacists who distribute the medications, and the rites then would be the instructions for use and dosage of the medication. Rosengarten's suggestion is useful, but I also offer a complementary metaphor (briefly suggested in the last section), which is to compare the cosmos with a business entity.[94]

In this metaphor, the ME would be the business or the industry and perhaps its expression in a mission statement. Execution and application of the ME would indicate levels of control in the business. The GIŠḪUR would be the articles of incorporation and the business's vision statement. The NAM would be the job descriptions, and the Tablet of Destinies would be equivalent to the corporate organizational chart. The main gods (Anu, Enlil, Enki) would be the officers of the company or the board of directors, and the lesser gods would have the role of vice-presidents. Kings would be something like department supervisors and priests similar to managers and, in some

---

92. Vanstiphout, "Die Geschöpfe des Prometheus," 34.

93. Y. Rosengarten, *Sumer et le Sacré* (Paris : Boccard, 1977), 5.

94. L. Handy also uses a company paradigm to discuss the roles of various gods within the divine hierarchy in the pantheon at Ugarit; see *Among the Host of Heaven* (Winona Lake, IN: Eisenbrauns, 1994).

senses, like union bosses. Temples and cities would be roughly equivalent to the departments of the company or, perhaps, franchises, and people would be the employees, whose rituals are akin to punching the clock and putting in their time to help the company run; their only lot in life is to work their fingers to the bone until they are fired or reach retirement, having given their blood, sweat, and tears in service to the company and its officers, with little to show for their efforts. If we apply this metaphor to *Enuma Elish*, the theogony with which the text opens pertains to the founding (birth) of the company. The account begins when there were no company, no employees, and no jobs. The organizational work of Marduk later in the text represents the incorporation of the company under his management. As we examine each of these pairs of terms in the literature, we will be able to connect them with this metaphor at the various levels on which they function.

Sumerian ME[95]

The MEs are both the most difficult to understand and the most important. At times, the MEs are quite nebulous, but they also can be quite specific; in addition, they operate at various levels as various aspects of the operation of the cosmos are delegated in increasing detail. Consequently, they function at the cosmic level first of all, under the supervision of the gods. At the next-lower level, the temples and cities are given MEs, as are kings and people. It is jurisdiction over the pertinent MEs ('divine powers', in the examples) that allow a deity to formulate designs and to decree destinies, as illustrated in the following excerpts from the hymnic literature.[96]

> A *šir-namgala* (?) *to Inana for Ur-Ninurta (Ur-Ninurta A)*: She made the king whom she took by the hand humbly enter into the . . . where destinies are determined, where the good divine powers are assigned to the

---

95. Significant discussions of the control attributes are found in Rosengarten, *Sumer et le Sacré*, and G. Farber-Flugge, *Der Mythos "Inanna und Enki" unter besonderer Berücksichtigung der Liste der me* (Studia Pohl 10; Rome: Pontifical Biblical Institute, 1973); briefer discussion and summary of the issue is found in J. Klein, "The Sumerian *me* as a Concrete Object," *AoF* 24 (1997): 211–18. Klein seems to be skeptical of the connection between the noun *me* and the verb 'to be', a connection that was first suggested by Farber-Flugge in *Mythos "Inanna und Enki"* but then reconsidered less positively in her *RlA* article (*RlA* 7: 611a). Klein likewise makes a case that the abstract noun is sometimes applied to a "two dimensional symbol or image, engraved or painted on a sign, banner or standard, representing the underlying abstract concept" ("The Sumerian *me*," p. 212).

96. Notice, for example, that in *Enki and the World Order* Enki recounts that the control attributes were given into his hand (line 65) and, among other things, this results in his ability to decree destinies (line 76).

great gods—the E-kur, the holy dwelling of An and Enlil that is endued with terrifying awe.[97]

A hymn to Enki for Išme-Dagan (Išme-Dagan X): Lord who among the gods makes the clever decisions, most prominent among them from the south to the uplands; who holding a staff in his hand determines their destinies as the Anuna gods come to him; who possessing all the divine powers is alone surpassing.[98]

An adab to Nanna (Nanna H): Your father, holy An, has bestowed upon you divine powers to which other gods cannot aspire. Enlil has decreed them to you in destiny.[99]

An adab to Nanna for Išme-Dagan (Išme-Dagan M): You have been assigned divine powers from the divine powers by lord Nunamnir. He has presented you with the capacity to determine fates, the role of a supreme deity.[100]

The most important myth for understanding the cosmic level of the Sumerian MEs is *Enki and the World Order (EWO)*.[101] In *EWO*, Enki is praised for his custody of the control attributes ('powers'):

> Lord who rides upon the great powers, the pure powers, who controls the great powers, the numberless powers, foremost in all the breadth of heaven and earth; who received the supreme powers in Eridug, the holy place, the most esteemed place, Enki, lord of heaven and earth—praise![102]

As the deity associated with the fresh underground waters (his home is in the Abzu), his fructifying powers are well known. But his control attributes (MEs) extend much farther. For example, he is also praised for his administration of time:

> Counting the days and putting the months in their houses, so as to complete the years and to submit the completed years to the assembly for a decision, taking decisions to regularise the days: father Enki, you are the king of the assembled people.[103]

---

97. http://etcsl.orinst.ox.ac.uk 2.5.6.1, line 11.

98. http://etcsl.orinst.ox.ac.uk 2.5.4.24, lines 1–3.

99. http://etcsl.orinst.ox.ac.uk 4.13.08, A.6–7.

100. http://etcsl.orinst.ox.ac.uk 2.5.4.13, 1.B.D.2–3.

101. No up-to-date critical edition is available for *EWO*. For significant studies, see R. E. Averbeck, "Myth, Ritual and Order in 'Enki and the World Order'," *JAOS* 123 (2003): 757–71; H. L. J. Vanstiphout, "Why Did Enki Organize the World?" in *Sumerian Gods and Their Representations* (ed. I. L. Finkel and M. J. Geller; Groningen: Styx, 1997), 117–34; and S. N. Kramer and J. Maier, *Myths of Enki, the Crafty God* (New York: Oxford, 1989), 38–56. Transliteration and translation can be found online at http://etcsl.orinst.ox.ac.uk.

102. http://etcsl.orinst.ox.ac.uk, lines 135–39.

103. http://etcsl.orinst.ox.ac.uk, lines 17–20.

There is no doubt that the MEs are functional in nature. The more significant question concerns how they relate to the cosmos and the creation of
the cosmos. A general association can be observed in *The Return of Ninurta
to Nibru*, in which the major regions of the cosmos are compared with the
MEs that are linked to them:

> Sovereign of all the lands, in your massive might, warrior of Enlil, in your
> great might, fierce warrior, you have taken up the divine powers which
> are like heaven, son of Enlil, you have taken up the divine powers which
> are like the earth, you have taken up the divine powers of the mountains,
> which are heavy as heaven, you have taken up the divine powers of Eri-
> dug, which are huge as the earth.[104]

One way to determine the relationship of the MEs to the cosmos would be
to examine a list of the cosmic MEs. The *Myth of Inanna and Enki* contains
just such an extensive list of what were considered to be control attributes
(80 of them preserved, with numerous breaks, listed in the section above;
see pp. 40–41), but these MEs relate to society and culture, with none
representing the larger cosmic arena.[105] Though no list of MEs relating directly to what we would call the natural world are preserved, the well-estab-
lished relationship between the MEs and the decree of destinies can provide
the information we want. Because possession of the appropriate MEs is the
basis for the decreeing of related destinies, lists of destinies in the cosmic
realm inform us indirectly about the MEs of the cosmic realm.

Thus, Enki's jurisdiction over the MEs allows him to delegate certain attributes to lower-level deities. In *EWO*, 12 MEs, most of them cosmic in
nature, are transferred to the administration of 12 deities, as follows:[106]

ME	Deity
twin rivers	Enbilulu
marshes	?
sea	Nanše
rains	Iškur
agricultural constructions	Enkimdu
growing of plants	Anšan

---

104. http://etcsl.orinst.ox.ac.uk, 1.6.1, lines 7–12.

105. This is appropriate, because this particular list concerns the areas of Inanna's prerogatives and the areas represented in her city of Uruk.

106. List from Vanstiphout, "Why Did Enki Organize the World?" 117–18, derived from
lines 260–386.

clay works	Kulla
architecture	Mušdama
animal life on the plains	Šakan
herding	Dumuzi
demarcation and judgment	Utu
weaving	Uttu

Another list can be derived from the *Lament over the Fall of Sumer and Urim:*

> May An not change the divine powers of heaven, the divine plans for treating the people with justice. May An not change the decisions and judgments to lead the people properly.

> To travel on the roads of the Land:
>> may An not change it. May An and Enlil not change it, may An not change it. May Enki and Ninmaḫ not change it, may An not change it.
>
> That the Tigris and Euphrates should again carry water:
>> may An not change it.
>
> That there should be rain in the skies and on the ground speckled barley:
>> may An not change it.
>
> That there should be watercourses with water and fields with grain:
>> may An not change it.
>
> That the marshes should support fish and fowl:
>> may An not change it.
>
> That old reeds and fresh reeds should grow in the reed-beds:
>> may An not change it. May An and Enlil not change it. May Enki and Ninmaḫ not change it.[107]

A third list can be derived from *The Exploits of Ninurta:*

> Lady, since you came to the Mountains, Ninmaḫ ('Great Lady'), since you entered the rebel lands for my sake, since you did not keep far from me when I was surrounded by the horrors of battle—let the name of the pile which I, the Hero, have piled up be Mountain (hursaĝ) and may you be its lady (nin): now that is the destiny decreed by Ninurta. Henceforth people shall speak of Ninhursaĝa. So be it.

> Let its meadows produce herbs for you.
> Let its slopes produce honey and wine for you.
> Let its hillsides grow cedars, cypress, juniper and box for you.
> Let it make abundant for you ripe fruits, as a garden.

---

107. http://etcsl.orinst.ox.ac.uk, 2.2.3, lines 493–504.

Let the mountain supply you richly with divine perfumes.
Let it mine gold and silver for you, make . . . for you.
Let it smelt copper and tin for you, make its tribute for you.
Let the Mountains make wild animals teem for you.
Let the mountain increase the fecundity of quadrupeds for you.

You, O Queen, become equal to An, wearing a terrifying splendour. Great goddess who detests boasting, good lady, maiden Ninhursaĝa, Nintur, . . . approach me. Lady, I have given you great powers: may you be exalted.[108]

Here, the destiny of Ninhursag is decreed (notice the association of destiny with the giving of a name) and this destiny is equated with giving her MES ('powers'). The list that is enumerated is cosmic in nature.

A fourth possible list is somewhat less certain, and I offer it tentatively. When reading Sumerian literature, one notices on a number of occasions that a certain deity is said to govern the 50 MES:

Ninisina and the gods (Ninisina F): This is what the Great Mountain, Enlil, determined as her fate for . . . perfect with the great divine powers, the fifty divine powers.[109]

An adab (?) to Ninurta for Išme-Dagan (Išme-Dagan O): Great hero, strongest in heaven and earth! Ninurta, who controls perfectly the fifty divine powers in the E-kur![110]

A hymn to Nisaba (Nisaba A): Perfectly endowed with fifty great divine powers, my lady, most powerful in E-kur![111]

Lugalbanda in the mountain cave: It is they, like Nanna, like Utu, like Inana of the fifty divine powers, . . . in heaven and earth;[112]

The building of Ninĝirsu's temple (Gudea, cylinders A and B): Because of his great love, my father who begot me called me "King, Enlil's flood, whose fierce stare is never lifted from the mountains, Ninĝirsu, warrior of Enlil," and endowed me with fifty powers.[113]

The number *50* is particularly interesting both for its rarity in the texts and for the very prominent place it holds in *Enuma Elish*, where Marduk is given 50 names (tablets VI–VII), apparently in fulfillment of the earlier promise made to him that he would become the one who decrees destinies.

---

108. http://etcsl.orinst.ox.ac.uk, 1.6.2, lines 390–410.
109. http://etcsl.orinst.ox.ac.uk, 4.22.6, line B.6.
110. http://etcsl.orinst.ox.ac.uk, 2.5.4.15, lines A.1–2.
111. http://etcsl.orinst.ox.ac.uk, 4.16.1, line 5.
112. http://etcsl.orinst.ox.ac.uk, 1.8.2.1, line A.490.
113. http://etcsl.orinst.ox.ac.uk, 2.1.7, line 253.

In tablets IV–V, the victorious Marduk decrees destinies for the cosmos (thus demonstrating his command of the MEs), and in tablets VI–VII, the assembly of the gods decrees Marduk's destiny by naming him and so transferring the 50 MEs to him.[114] If this interconnection between the destinies, the MEs, and the names can be sustained, the names of Marduk include a list of MEs that is helpful to us.[115]

Regardless of the status of the names of Marduk, the nature of the cosmic MEs is clarified in the text as pertaining to the functional level of the cosmos and as intimately involved with creation. The organizational aspect of creation, in contrast to the material aspect, is brought into high relief by Vanstiphout when he asks the question, "Why did Enki need to organize the world?" He answers his own question and in doing so makes an important observation that goes to the heart of the nature of the MEs: they deal with the infrastructure of the cosmos:

> The interest lies not so much in the material goods themselves—they were there anyway—but in the possibility of realizing their potential. The things themselves were already in existence: the need was for a system by which they could be used efficiently.[116]

Vanstiphout's observation points out again the fact that in the ancient Near East there is little interest in material cosmology and intense interest in functional cosmology, the latter being the context in which the MEs played a central role.

Design (GIŠḪUR)

In more than a dozen contexts throughout Sumerian literature, the MEs are paralleled by the designs or plans of the cosmos, a parallelism that demonstrates their close interrelationship. A few examples will suffice:[117]

---

114. The names of Marduk represent a complex exegetical analysis of the attributes and nature of the god based on scribal hermeneutics in terms of both semantics and orthography. See J. Bottéro, "Les Noms de Marduk, l'écriture et la logique en Mesopotamie ancienne," in *Essays on the Ancient Near East in Memory of Jacob Joel Finkelstein* (ed. M. deJ. Ellis; Hamden, CT: Archon, 1977), 5–28.

115. Bottéro ("Noms de Marduk," 26) goes so far as to associate the names with the destiny that is decreed for Marduk by the gods.

116. Vanstiphout, "Why Did Enki Organize the World?" 122.

117. Additional examples may be found in http://etcsl.orinst.ox.ac.uk in the following literary works: An adab to Suen for Ibbi-Suen (Ibbi-Suen C) 2.4.5.3, A.22; The Lament for Sumer and Urim 2.2.3, line G.448; A Praise Poem of Išme-Dagan (Išme-Dagan A + V) 2.5.4.01, lines A.33–34; A Hymn to Enki for Išme-Dagan (Išme-Dagan X) 2.5.4.24, lines 5–6; Sîn-iddinam and Iškur (Sîn-iddinam E) 2.6.6.5, line 73; Ninurta's Journey to Eridug: A šir-gida to Ninurta

A tigi to Enki for Ur-Ninurta (Ur-Ninurta B): August lord, you excel in heaven and earth, and you have made your name shine forth. Enki, you have gathered up all the divine powers that there are, and stored them in the *abzu*. You have made praiseworthy the divine powers, exceeding all other divine powers, of your holy dwelling which you have chosen in your heart—the *abzu*, the august shrine . . . —as well as its divine plans.[118]

Ninurta and the turtle: At his command your weapon struck me evilly. As I let the divine powers go out of my hand, these divine powers returned to the *abzu*. As I let the divine plan go out of my hand, this divine plan returned to the *abzu*. This Tablet of Destinies returned to the *abzu*. I was stripped of the divine powers.[119]

A hymn to Nibru and Išme-Dagan (Išme-Dagan W): You are the pillar (?) in the south and the uplands, the mooring post of all people. Your divine powers are supreme divine powers with which no divine powers can compare. Your plans are as if rooted in the *abzu*, endowed with great terrifying splendour. As if it were the lovely earth itself, no one can comprehend your eminence. Your pre-eminent destiny surpasses all praise. You are a lofty hill that no one can reach. Outstanding, with head high, you reach to the heavens.[120]

The last two excerpts illustrate the three-way interrelationship between the MEs, the design, and the destinies, and this leads us to the third member of the functional triad.

Destinies (NAM)

In conjunction with the business metaphor (see p. 48), the company's job descriptions (destinies) reflect the outworking of the nature of the business and the company's mission statement. The divine decrees, the destinies, and specifically the Tablet of Destinies have already been discussed at some length above, because they are intertwined with the MEs at many points. These destinies, however, differ from the MEs in that they play a more significant role in the cosmological literature and the activities of creation.

Presupposed in the cosmogonies is that destinies or characterizations were fixed on the day of creation. . . . The first time is the authority-filled moment, for then divine intent is freshest and most visible.[121]

(Ninurta B) 4.27.02, lines A.24–25; An *adab* to Enlil for Išme-Dagan (Išme-Dagan H) 2.5.4.08, line A.18; A Prayer to Marduk (?) for Hammu-rābi (Hammu-rābi B) 2.8.2.2, line 3.

118. http://etcsl.orinst.ox.ac.uk, 2.5.6.2, line C.25–28.
119. http://etcsl.orinst.ox.ac.uk, 1.6.3, line B.3.
120. http://etcsl.orinst.ox.ac.uk, 2.5.4.23, lines A.20–37.
121. Clifford, *Creation Accounts*, 72.

We will now take a brief look at some of the texts mentioning destinies and observe the specific role that the decrees/destinies have.

Hymn to E-engura

When the destinies had been fixed for all that had been engendered (by An),
When An had engendered the year of abundance,
When humans broke through earth's surface like plants,
Then built the Lord of Abzu, King Enki,
Enki, the Lord who decides destinies,
His house of silver and lapis lazuli[122]

Enki and Ninmaḫ

In those days, in the days when heaven and earth were created;
In those nights, in the nights when heaven and earth were created;
In those years, in the years when the fates were determined;
When the Anuna gods were born;
When the goddesses were taken in marriage;
When the goddesses were distributed in heaven and earth;[123]

In this text, the parallel between creation and decreeing destinies is seen in relationship both to cosmogony (lines 1–2) and theogony (lines 4–6).

Enuma Elish (Dalley)

The following summary statements identify some of the sections that feature the destinies.

I 8: Part of the "before" picture is that destinies had not yet been decreed.

I 148–62: Qingu is given the tablet of destinies by Tiamat and thus exercises authority and control in the assembly of the gods: "As for you, your command will not be changed, your utterance will be eternal." (line 158)

II 61–62: Ea extols his father Anshar as one who is the ordainer of destinies and who has the power to create and destroy.

II 159–63: Marduk states his conditions if he is to be champion: The Assembly is to decree his destiny over them, and then he will have the authority to decree destinies. "Whatever I create shall never be altered! The decree of my lips shall never be revoked, never changed!"[124]

---

122. Clifford, *Creation Accounts*, 29–30.
123. http://etcsl.orinst.ox.ac.uk.
124. Lines 162–63; S. Dalley, *Myths From Mesopotamia* (Oxford: Oxford University Press, 1991), 244; cf. IV 1–15.

IV 19–29: In this section, the destiny of Marduk is set as one who commands the destinies. Consequently, "Command destruction or creation, and may it be so." As an act of "creation," a constellation is destroyed and then created.

In these passages, it is evident that decreeing destinies is both functional in nature and an act of creation and rule. The exercise of control over the destinies and the rule of the world of the gods and eventually the world of humans takes place in the temple that is ordained as the control room of the cosmos. Just as the gods who are given destinies execute the MES, so the king executes the MES that have been decreed for him.[125]

Possession of the Tablet of Destinies gives the bearer the authority to assign roles throughout the cosmos.[126] 'Destiny' is not the same as 'fate' but includes some of the elements conventionally associated with fate. The following paragraphs and table 3.1 (p. 64) summarize the interrelated roles of the three terms (*parṣu*, *uṣurtu*, and *šimtu* in Akkadian; ME, GIŠHUR, and NAMTAR in Sumerian) across the spectrum of the functional cosmos.

The Heaven and Earth. The MES of which the cosmos consists are entrusted to Anu, Enlil, and Enki,[127] who are considered their administrators. But even these gods are bound by the MES. However, administering their MES allows destinies to be decreed lower on the hierarchy so that control in limited ways is delegated on other levels. The texts offer little information regarding the origins of the MES of heaven and earth. In *KAR* 4,[128] which recounts the organization of the cosmos preparatory to setting up an irrigation system, the term 'design' (*uṣurtu*) is used.[129] In another text, Nanna is described as someone "qui parfait les pouvoirs du ciel et de la terre."[130] Rosengarten's study suggests that 'accomplish' or 'activate' may be a better rendering of the verb here.[131] Consequently, one may conclude that the MES

---

125. Said of Rim-Sin; see *COS* 2.102C.

126. W. G. Lambert, "Destiny and Divine Intervention in Babylon and Israel," *OtSt* 17 (1972): 65–72; A. R. George, "Sennacherib and the Tablet of Destinies," *Iraq* 48 (1986): 133–46; J. Lawson, *The Concept of Fate in Ancient Mesopotamia of the First Millennium* (Wiesbaden: Harrassowitz, 1994).

127. Notice also the name of one of the ancestor deities, Enmešarra, "lord of the all the MES."

128. Clifford, *Creation Accounts*, 49 : "When the earth had been founded and set in place; after the gods had established the plan of the universe."

129. Lambert, "Destiny and Divine Intervention," 67.

130. E. Sollberger and J-M. Kupper, *Inscriptions Royales Sumeriennes et Akkadiennes* (Paris: Cerf, 1971), 194 IV B 13a.

131. Rosengarten, *Sumer et le Sacré*, 17 ('vollkommen machen', 'vollenden', 'accomplissent').

that most regularly describe the functional cosmos—time, weather, and fertility—are generally portrayed as organized and delegated by the gods and therefore typically appear in the context of the designs and destinies. The closest that Sumerian and Akkadian literature comes to addressing the *establishment* of MES at the macrocosmic level is in *Enuma Elish* V, when Marduk organizes the heavenly bodies, the functions of which are interwoven with the MES of the cosmic deities;[132] he then proceeds to establish the functions related to time, weather, and fertility (see pp. 41–42 above).

The Gods.   The gods are typically related to the destinies through the Tablet of Destinies (the tablet containing the decrees = *šimati*), which gives the holder some jurisdiction over the MES connected to the gods.[133] Possession of the tablet therefore allows one to make decrees. When Anzu (I 82, 109) steals the Tablet of Destinies, the MES are described as *nadu* = 'nonfunctional'.[134] In *Anzu* II 46, Ea is called the king of the decrees (*šar šimati*), even though Anzu possesses the tablet, so it is obvious that there is something that transcends the tablet's authority. The tablet functions as an emblem of authority that assigns MES and decrees to the gods. *Enuma Elish* I 8 refers to a time before the decrees of the gods were ordained. Thus, the destinies refer to divine attributes and powers as well as the gods' areas of jurisdiction and the activities related to these jursidictions.

The Temple/City.   Just as there is some degree of continuity between the cosmic level and the divine level, so there is continuity between the gods and their temples and cities. The MES and decrees of the temple are fixed when it is dedicated. So, for example, Utu established the destiny of the temple Ebabbar and had it equipped with MES.[135] The city, as an extension of the patron deity and the temple, shares the temple's destiny and MES. In *Inanna and Enki*,[136] the MES have often been treated (and the terms trans-

---

132. The noun *parṣi* in this context (*Enuma Elish* V 67) is consistently translated 'rites' or something similar (compare *CAD* P 196b; Horowitz, *Mesopotamian Cosmic Geography*, 119; 'the ceremonial', *CAD* B 138b; 'cult', Dalley, *Myths From Mesopotamia*, 257), despite the fact that everything in the context pertains to the organization of the cosmos. Foster modestly deviates from this consensus, or at least retains some ambiguity, by translating it 'prerogatives': *Before the Muses*, 465 (cf. *COS* 1.111).

133. Bonds/cables (*markas*) of heaven hold the cosmos together. The chief god is said to hold the cosmic bonds, and the temple serves as the cosmic bond. Holding the cables is comparable to possessing the Tablet of Destinies (worn at the breast as an emblem of power); A. R. George, "Sennacherib and the Tablet of Destinies," 138–39.

134. *COS*, 'suspended'; *CAD* N/1 78, 'disregarded'; *CAD* N/1 66–68, adjective (houses and lands uninhabited, fields uncultivated); N/1 68–104, verb.

135. Sollberger and Kupper, *Inscriptions Royales Sumeriennes et Akkadiennes*, 190, IV B 9b.

136. *COS* 1.161, 522–26.

lated) as cultural norms or arts of civilization. More recently, they have been understood as the specific MEs of Inanna that are honored and reflected in her city.[137]

In a Hymn to Nanše, the MEs of the city of Niĝin are stated and, on the basis of these MEs, the destiny of the city and its temple are decreed:

> There is a city, whose powers are apparent. Niĝin is the city whose powers are apparent. The holy city is the city whose powers are apparent. The mountain rising from the water is the city whose powers are apparent. Its light rises over the secure temple; its fate is determined.[138]

The King.   The link between the temple and the king is the city. The MEs and decrees of the temple are fixed at its dedication, not year by year; but fixing the decrees of the king and his people *is* an annual activity carried out in connection with the New Year Akitu festival. The Babylonian *Akitu* recalls the cosmic establishment of Marduk's kingship and temple building in connection with rituals that are intended to maintain and reenact enthronement.[139]

Humanity.   When we consider the human level, the MEs are less prominent than the decrees. The general destiny of mankind is death.[140] Individually, however, people show concern regarding what is decreed for them through their prayers. They can learn about what has been decreed through divination, and they can seek to avert its negative effects through *namburbi* rituals.

In this section, we have seen that the governing principles in Mesopotamia represent both the more static (MEs) and the more dynamic (designs, destinies). These elements relate to creation in different ways, but together they constitute the functional governance of the cosmos. In the functional ontology of the ancient world, the dyad of static versus dynamic is preferred over the dyad of material versus immaterial as a means of circumscribing reality. As we consider this preference, we might conclude that a thing's MEs are relatively static in the sense that they are determined without

---

137. E.g., Farber-Flugge, "*Inanna und Enki.*"

138. http://etcsl.orinst.ox.ac.uk; see also *COS* 1.162.

139. Nothing has been preserved regarding what the determining of the destinies during the *Akitu* entailed (J. Bidmead, *The Akitu Festival* [Piscataway, NJ: Gorgias, 2002], 92), and there is no written record of what the decrees actually were (ibid., p. 92 n. 164). Which day of the *Akitu* served as the time when the first decree of destinies was issued remains uncertain; but the text focuses primarily on Marduk's right to so issue the decree. The second act of decreeing was on the 11th day and focused on the king and the people.

140. See *CAD* Š/3 16–18.

being regularly rethought or readdressed. MEs are 'standing orders', do not change, and do not require reestablishment. In contrast, the decrees are much more dynamic and are reestablished periodically. Decrees are provisional. At the same time, the MES need to be perfected, executed, or activated.[141] When people execute MES, it is in the context of performance of rituals. In this sense, the MES need to be renewed or upheld, and the people do so by performing the appropriate rituals. So Rim-Sin "perfects the power and ordinances of Eridu."[142]

In Mesopotamia, it is logical to conclude that the gods did not create the MES, because if they did, they could not be bound by them. Nonetheless, these very MES governed the functions of the cosmos and culture. In this cognitive environment, the functions of the ordered cosmos were defined first and foremost by the MES. Just as the unbounded waters represented the starting point for creative activities, so the MES represented a specific foundation for the ordered cosmos that was brought into being. The MES neither existed prior to the creative activity, as did the waters, nor were they instituted by the gods. They were like gold or iron that must be mined in order to bring them into operation.[143] The mountain of the MES, apparently the place that functioned as their storehouse, is identified by Rosengarten as the heavenly mountain of An's residence.[144]

Egypt: Tefnut, Shu, and Maat

In Egypt, the governing principles are not as prominent in the literature as in Mesopotamia but are to some extent mirrored in the paradox of *Eternal Sameness* and *Eternal Recurrence*. The former, represented as 'Order' (*ma'at*, connected with Tefnut) is reflected in the unchanging, static aspects of the cosmos (such as, for example, sky above the earth, flow of the Nile, day following night). The latter is represented as 'Life' (connected

---

141. Various renderings of Sumerian *šu-du*, Akkadian *šuklulu*.

142. Rosengarten, *Sumer et le Sacré*, 21–22.

143. Notice some of the temple-names, which suggest a celestial mountain as the place of their origin: é.kur-me.sikil ('House, Mountain of the pure MES'), a sanctuary of Ištar, and é.kur me.šar.ra ('House, Mountain of all the MES'), the temple of Aššur built by Tukulti-Ninurta I at Kar-Tukulti Ninurta; see A. George, *House Most High: The Temples of Ancient Mesopotamia* (MC 5; Winona Lake, IN: Eisenbrauns, 1993), 117, ##686, 687. Other temples that refer to the MES in their names can be seen in ##746–60, 774–77, 788–92, and 1193. In Sumerian, see the reference to 'Kulab, Mountain of the Great MES' (Kur.me.gal.gal.la) in *Enmerkar and the Lord of Aratta*, lines 213 and 531; H. Vanstiphout, *Epics of Sumerian Kings* (SBLWAW 20; Atlanta: Society of Biblical Literature, 2003).

144. Rosengarten, *Sumer et le Sacré*, 56: "O Utu, lord (who possesses) the *me*, who lives on the 'mountain of *me*'," in a legend on Kassite seals.

with Shu) and is reflected in the rising and setting of the sun, the flooding and receding of the Nile, birth and death, and so on.[145] As in Mesopotamia, the operational oppositional pair is static versus dynamic. The static eternal sameness of order is similar to the MES in Mesopotamia. The dynamic eternal recurrence overlaps in part with the decreeing of destinies. Nonetheless, there are significant differences that need to be noted. In Egypt, these aspects of the cosmos came into being at the initiation of Atum. Tefnut, as a deity, does not exist outside of and separate from the gods in the way that the MES do in Mesopotamian. Shu, likewise a deity, is not a principle pursued or administered by the gods. These deities are aspects of creation but not governing principles. The nature of the dichotomy (static versus dynamic) shared with Mesopotamian civilization is more important than the diverse forms that it takes in the two regions.

If we examine the Egyptian cognitive environment for governing principles, the most likely candidate is Maat. But Maat is more the *goal* of the rule of gods and kings than the mechanism by which rule and function are established. Maat, as order, stands in contrast to Isfet, disorder, and either one can displace the other. Though all of these Egyptian concepts differ significantly from their putative Mesopotamian counterparts, all of the terms from both locations nevertheless convey the centrality of the concept of order and function within the cognitive environment of the ancient Near East against the background of a cosmos balanced between the static and the dynamic.

Several texts deal more specifically with gods' being assigned functions. For example, in a text found on the Tutankhamun shrine and in several 19th-Dynasty tombs, Re assigns functions to Thoth. The named functions include his role among the gods (he is a scribe), as well as his cosmological functions. He is therefore designated Re's "place-taker" during the night hours, when Re is passing through the netherworld; and, furthermore, this explains "how the moon of Thoth came into being."[146] Thus, in Egypt as well, it is clear that "coming into being" occurs when a function is assigned.

---

145. CT 80; Allen, *Genesis in Egypt*, 25–26; see also CT 1130 and comment by Assmann, *Search for God*, 178.

146. *ANET*, 8, "The Assignment of Functions to Thoth." See also Atum's assignment of role to Osiris in chap. 175 of the Book of the Dead (Papyrus of Ani).

Conclusion

In the cognitive environment of the ancient world, the cosmos was governed by the gods as they served as administrators of the MEs, delegating them throughout the cosmos by decreeing destinies. The MEs were not created by the gods but came into existence along with the cosmos and the gods themselves. These governing principles define existence, because they determine how the world functions. Creation is characterized by these MEs' coming into existence, being organized and delegated, and being exercised. If the governing principles pertain to the functional cosmos, and the governing principles define existence and creation, this confirms that ontology and cosmology in the ancient cognitive environment were fundamentally functional in nature.

Roles and Positions of the Players

Divine Place in the Cosmos

In the cognitive environment of the ancient Mesopotamian world (with echoes in Egypt), it could be said that deities were inside the cosmos, not outside it.[147] This statement is arguably more defensible on the basis of the Mesopotamian evidence than the Egyptian, though in Egypt the most notable potential exception occurs only at the very beginning of the "creation" process in the person of the primal deity who "became millions." This deity, however, as noted by Hornung, can only be encountered through the "millions" that he became, and all of this process of becoming occurs inside rather than outside the cosmos.

> For the Egyptians, the fact that their gods exist means that they are subject to the limitations and diversity that characterize all existence. The undifferentiated one of the beginning differentiated himself through his work of creation, he "made himself into millions"; mankind can experience him only in the multiplicity of the created, mortal, and changing gods.[148]

---

147. I am not addressing here, nor am I interested in addressing the once-popular "myth-versus-history" discussion that was prominent in the writings of Y. Kaufmann and B. Anderson, to name two authors. See the summary and critique of that approach in Simkins, *Creator and Creation*, 82–88. See also P. Machinist, "The Question of Distinctiveness in Ancient Israel: An Essay," in *Ah, Assyria!* (ed. M. Cogan and I. Eph'al; ScrHier 33; Jerusalem: Magnes, 1991), 196–212 (especially p. 200).

148. Hornung, *Conceptions*, 185.

If we accept the conclusion that the ontology of the ancient world was functional, it is logical also to conclude that the extent to which deities were made manifest in the components of the cosmos was the extent to which their existence was tied to these components. Their role was to maintain the functioning cosmos, and this role gave them life and defined their existence.

> In Egyptian religion the will of the gods was bound up with the maintenance of the cosmic process. The lot of the gods was to forever play their part in the daily drama of the cosmic process. The ritual reenactment of this process was designed not only to adapt the order of the human world to the order of the cosmos but also, and indeed primarily, to keep the cosmic process itself in good working order.[149]

This intrinsic correlation between deity and the cosmos is what leads inevitably to the close connection between cosmogony and theogony.

> The cosmic dimension of the divine was not confined to the sheer materiality of cosmic elements such as earth, air, water, and so forth, or to celestial bodies such as the sun and the moon, but rather that it referred to specific complexes of actions, traits, attitudes, and qualities that were interpreted as cosmic phenomena "in action" and in which humankind also participated. Nut was not so much the sky as what the sky did.[150]

J. Assmann has used the term "cosmotheism" to describe polytheistic religions that "worship the cosmos as the collective manifestation of various different deities."[151] He explains:

> Gods had names, genealogies, and a mythically revealed spectrum of roles; they had a "portfolio," a sphere of cosmic, vegetative, or cultural competencies; and finally they had cult locations from which they exercised their earthly rule.[152]

We thus see the interplay between cosmic roles and political roles. Even in the initial Ennead of the Heliopolitan cosmological tradition, the integration of the cosmological with the political can be seen:[153] both constitute representations of how the cosmos is ordered on the inside.

---

149. Assmann, *Mind of Egypt*, 205.
150. Assmann, *Search for God*, 81.
151. Assmann, *Mind of Egypt*, 204.
152. Assmann, *Mind of Egypt*, 205.
153. Tobin, "Myths: Creation Myths," *OEAE* 2:469. This is in contrast to the Hermopolitan Ogdoad, which represents pairs of contrasting principles, but in agreement with the *Memphite Theology* in which Ptah, as creator of all things, combines the cosmological and the political in his creative work.

Table 3.1. Hierarchy of the *parṣu* (ME) / *šimtu* (NAM) complex

Each level links to the level above and below it.

Level	Primary Texts	Comments
cosmic	*Enuma Elish* V (paths of stars; moon; precipitation; water sources; all described as *parṣu* in *Ee* V 67, parallel to *uṣurtu*)[a]; KAR 4 (*uṣurtu*)	*Ee* V 39–46 (time); *Ee* V 47–52 (weather); *Ee* V 53–58 (agriculture)
gods' attributes/offices (associated with cultural norms)	*Tale of Anzu* (Tablet of Destinies); *Enuma Elish* I, III (Tablet of Destinies); *Ee* VI 96 (Marduk's destiny); *Enki and World Order*; *Inanna and Enki*	ME controls *šimtu* ?; *Ee* VII 141; *Anzu* I 73–75; 94 items, connected with Inanna's attributes and the cultural norms she controls, extended to city
temple/city	Gudea A ix 12 ME possessed by temple; Gudea B vi 15; Gudea B vi 7–10; Gudea B xiii 6; *Enki and World Order* (shrine of Ur)	Declared at dedication; *šimtu* throne in the temple; Ningirsu designates roles of functionaries as result of his ME; Suen made its ME surpassing; Extended to city
king	Akitu; Sennacherib and the Tablet of Destinies; Substitute King Texts	
mankind	*Enki and Ninmah*; Connected to death (*šimat amelutim*)	Namtar: find a function in society for[b]
individuals	*šuilla* prayers[c]	Results learned through divination,[d] avoided through *namburbi*
inanimate objects	Hymn to Shamash[e]	House[f]
rituals	E.g., Hammurabi Prologue ii.64	

a. Horowitz, *Mesopotamian Cosmic Geography*, 117–19.
b. Lambert, "Destiny and Divine Intervention," 66.
c. Lawson, *Concept of Fate*, 58, BMS 19 rev. 21.
d. Lawson, *Concept of Fate*, 92.

e. P. A. Schollmeyer, *Sumerisch-babylonisch Hymnen und Gebete an Šamaš* (Paderborn: Schoningh, 1912), #13, 71–72.
f. Lawson, *Concept of Fate*, 59–60.

Nearly everything that has been observed above regarding Egypt is also true of Sumerian texts from Mesopotamia. The cosmic deities do not govern the cosmos from an independent existence outside the cosmos. The cosmos functions as a result of the gods' being who they are. The daily function of the cosmos is the story of the lives of the cosmic deities. They are not only manifest in the components of the cosmos; the cosmos is their very identity. Though mythology developed personalities for these deities in narrative contexts, the foundation of these personalities is grounded in their cosmic identity. Running the cosmos is not something they do; it is a result of who and what they are. It is from this cosmic identity that their portfolio of competencies is derived. Cosmic deities are those who are associated with the static aspects of the cosmos. Some deities, such as Enki, have a role both in the static and the dynamic aspects of the cosmos, but the relationship between the cosmos and the cosmic deities is inextricably intertwined.

A change can be observed, however, in the second millennium, when a new reigning paradigm emerged in the literature represented particularly by *Enuma Elish* in Mesopotamia and also, to a lesser degree, in New Kingdom Egypt and in Ugaritic literature. In this new paradigm, instead of ruling deities who are cosmic deities having primordial status, the ruling deities are given a rank higher than the cosmic deities. Consequently, the cosmos as well as the primordial cosmic deities are supervised by a ruling deity who is the arbitrator of roles and who resolves conflict. L. Handy has explored this ruling function in the mythology of Syria–Palestine and observes that the role of El involves running the cosmos by serving as the supervisor of the gods whose individual portfolios identified them with components of the cosmos.

> Keeping proper order among the deities appears to have been a major task for El. In this duty El was the organizer of the cosmos; it was his job to see that the universe functioned properly and that all of the deities properly filled their positions in the divine scheme. El did not do the work of running the universe but made certain that those who were supposed to do the work, both human and divine, functioned correctly.[154]

Handy proceeds to label "active deities" those who actually do the business of running the cosmos.

---

154. Handy, *Among the Host of Heaven*, 87.

Serving under the authority of those who actually owned the universe, the active gods were expected to perform in a way that would enable the cosmos to operate smoothly. Each of the gods at this level of the pantheon had a specific sphere of authority over which to exert his or her control. [155]

Recognition that there are competing paradigms for describing the way that the cosmos and the gods function (cosmogonic/theogonic model versus the political/bureaucratic model) draws our attention back to *Enuma Elish*. In this myth, we may actually be able to see the paradigm shift. The older Near Eastern view of the cosmos run by the primordial cosmic deities (cosmogonic/theogonic model) is represented briefly in the theogony of tablet I, though the text does not pause to develop the resulting cosmology that we know well from Sumerian texts. However, Marduk's ascension reflects the new paradigm (the political/bureaucratic model) in which a noncosmic deity [156] is elevated to a ruling position over the cosmic deities as arbitrator and supervisor of cosmic functions (as Handy observed at Ugarit). [157] In *Enuma Elish*, this shift occurs after theogony—the foundation of the reigning paradigm—has resulted in theomachy. [158] Resolving the conflict in the theomachy is what elevates the noncosmic ruling deity and necessitates his role. In this sense, theomachy can be seen as the mythological mechanism of the paradigm shift. [159] Theomachy only appears to take its place as a narrative element in cosmogony when the paradigm is shifting away from a cosmogonic/theogonic model of cosmic operations to a political/bureaucratic model (to be discussed in detail in the next section, pp. 68–74). Consequently, deities such as Marduk are associated nearly exclusively with the dynamic aspects of the cosmos, which is usually understood in relation to ruling functions.

---

155. Handy, *Among the Host of Heaven*, 97.

156. In his ascension, he is given cosmic powers; compare his 47th name, ADDU, identifying him as a storm-god.

157. Of course, in the case of El, the Ugaritic literature does not portray him as elevated to this position; instead, he always already has it in the literature that is extant.

158. The texts from Ugarit certainly feature theomachy prominently, but because the texts preserve very little that could be called cosmogony, an earlier paradigm (or the lack of one) cannot be posited, nor can theogony and cosmogony be linked in the literature left to us in this language.

159. In this regard, it is interesting to notice that there is barely a hint of *Chaoskampf* or theomachy in Sumerian and Egyptian sources. In Egypt, Amun/Re does daily battle with Apophis, who represents the forces of disorder (see, e.g., CT 160; *COS* 1.21), but this is only a personification of disorder, not a case of divine entities taking sides and engaging in warfare that needs to be resolved by action of the pantheon.

A similar paradigm shift can be seen in the Egyptian *Memphite Theology*, which recounts the transference of rule to Ptah, a god who is originally neither cosmic nor primordial,[160] a transfer that parallels the conferring of rulership on Marduk in *Enuma Elish*. However, instead of theomachy being the mechanism that triggers the paradigm shift, the *Memphite Theology* simply puts Ptah at the beginning of the theogonic process. In this case, then, the cosmogonic/theogonic model is not replaced by another (political/bureaucratic) model; instead, the deity in the theogonic model is replaced, because Ptah is portrayed as the one who made Atum and the Ennead. His rule over the cosmos is demonstrated as early as the Coffin Texts:

> I am the one who makes vegetation grow,
> > who makes green the banks of the Nile Valley,
> > lord of the highlands, who makes green the wadis;
> he who is over the Nubians, Asiatics, and Libyans,
> > for the Nine Bows have been gathered for me,
> > and totality has been given to me by the Sun, Lord to the Limit.
> I am South of His Wall, sovereign of the gods.
> I am King of the sky,
> > Distributor of *ka*s, who officiates over the Two Lands;
> > Distributor of *ka*s, who gives *ba*s, manifestations, *ka*s and beginnings.
> I am Distributor of *ka*s, and they live according to my action:
> > when I wish, I make it possible for them to live,
> there being none of them who can speak to me
> > except for the one who made that unique identity of mine,
> because I am Annunciation in his mouth
> > and Perception in his belly.[161]

Allen notes that, in this earliest portrayal of Ptah's ascension into a new role, the author "apparently perceived Ptah's function as the exact cosmic counterpart to Egyptian kingship,"[162] much like the role played by Marduk in *Enuma Elish*. Despite the many differences that exist between the roles of Ptah and Marduk and the complexities of each of their profiles and history, it is nonetheless clear that both are participants in a paradigm shift in which rule of the cosmos is transferred to a deity who previously had

---

160. Ptah is given a primordial role in the *Memphite Theology* and a cosmic role by being identified with Ta-tenen, who represents the primeval hillock. These developments appear to have taken place in the New Kingdom period. For a thorough summary of Ptah and his role, see the entry by J. van Dijk in *OEAE* 3:74–76. A similar role for Ptah is found in the Berlin Hymn to Ptah from the 22nd Dynasty (Allen, *Genesis in Egypt*, 39–40).

161. CT 647; see Allen, *Genesis in Egypt*, 39.

162. Allen, *Genesis in Egypt*, 41.

not been involved in a cosmogonic/theogonic system, having been neither primordial nor cosmic.

In the revised cognitive environment that results from this paradigm shift, the cosmos has a Divine Creator-King. Nonetheless, even without having been inserted into a cosmogonic/theogonic model, the newly empowered Marduk is still clearly inside rather than outside the cosmos. This is evident from some of the names (and their accompanying explanations) that Marduk is given in tablet VII of *Enuma Elish*.

VII 6: Who implements the decrees of Anu, Enlil, Ea
VII 11: devises a spell (is not the creator of magic)
VII 70–77: Did not create Tiamat, but defeats her and manipulates her
    corpse to set up functions
VII 106: Took charge of all commands

Even though he is designated the one who "created the firmament and fashioned the netherworld" (VII 134–35), Marduk is inside the cosmos and remains subject to the MES. He has been elevated to an executive position but is still part of the corporate system.

The roles of the gods may be summarized as follows:

- They are identified with components of the cosmos in cosmogonic/ theogonic models
- They fill an executive role in the "company" in the political/ bureaucratic model
- They exercise operational jurisdiction (through the destinies they decree)

These roles and models all concern functions, not material origins, and the functions all operate from within the system rather than acting on it from outside. The authority and jurisdiction of any god is circumscribed by his or her relationship to the components of the cosmos or to other deities.

Theomachy

In the cognitive environment of the ancient Near East, the gods become involved in conflict[163] under a variety of circumstances and at various levels: (1) they fight among themselves on an individual or corporate level, (2) they battle with entities or nonentities that represent a threat of some kind, and

---

163. Parts of this discussion were included verbatim in a journal article while this book was awaiting publication; see my "Creation in Genesis 1:1–2:3 and the Ancient Near East: Order out of Disorder after *Chaoskampf*," *CTJ* 43 (2008): 48–63.

(3) they enter into conflict with humans. I refer to all three of these potential scenarios by the term *theomachy*. The nature of the gods' adversary and determining what is at stake in the conflict must be considered, however, before we can decide what role theomachy plays in the cognitive environment and what relationship it might have to cosmogony in any specific culture or text. In the past, much confusion has resulted from the too-facile application of a term such as *Chaoskampf* to a wide variety of conflicts, as well as the frequent underlying assumption that theomachy, *Chaoskampf*, and cosmogony are all to be linked as a matter of course (i.e., if one was present, the others also were present).[164] In this book, I use *Chaoskampf* only to refer to macrocosmic disorder.[165]

At the beginning, then, it is helpful to lay out a more carefully nuanced classification of the categories of theomachy.

Categories of Theomachy

- class revolt and dissatisfaction with assigned roles among the divine proletariat
- order versus disorder in the macrocosmos (*Chaoskampf*), taking at least three different forms:
  initial establishment of order
  response to a one-time threat from a chaos monster
  renewal of order on a seasonal or daily basis
- a struggle for rule among the gods involving competing claimants
- a generational coup, with "younger" gods' seizing the rule from "older" deities

Class revolt among the divine proletariat who are dissatisfied with their roles. Theomachy of this kind occurs only in Mesopotamia in the ancient Near East and is most familiar from the major Akkadian epics, *Atrahasis* and *Enuma Elish*. In Sumerian literature, it is much rarer, occurring only briefly in *Enki and Ninmaḫ*, where the dissatisfaction takes the form of grumbling, and Enki responds before the tension comes to blows. In *Atrahasis*, the

---

164. The connection was introduced by Gunkel and has been affirmed by others who have been inclined to infer the presence of cosmogony when a *Chaoskampf* motif has been identified; cf. J. Day, *God's Conflict with the Dragon and the Sea* (Cambridge: Cambridge University Press, 1985); L. R. Fisher, "Creation at Ugarit and in the Old Testament," *VT* 15 (1965): 313–24; R. Clifford, "Cosmogonies in the Ugaritic Texts and in the Bible," *Or* 53 (1984): 183–201.

165. I use *macrocosmic* as a subcategory that refers to what we might call the "natural" world. I resist using the term *natural world* because it reflects a concept entirely foreign to the ancient cosmic environment. The term *macrocosmic* distinguishes between the operation of the elements included in cosmic geography and elements that are associated with human society (which the ancients would have considered to be cosmic as well).

tension erupts into an actual insurrection among the gods, resulting in the death of the ringleader. In *Enuma Elish*, the adversary and the ringleader, Kingu, must be defeated, as well as the champion, Tiamat (and her hordes). In all three situations, the result is that humans are created in order to take over the work of the gods. Thus, *Enuma Elish* includes a new category of adversary, the cosmic creature, Tiamat, thereby expanding the theomachy to a macrocosmic level. In all three of these examples, the role of the gods is what is at stake. But in *Enuma Elish*, it is not simply the roles of the gods in relation to their workload that then is imposed on humanity; the question of who is in charge among the gods is at stake, and, thus, the central role of the Tablet of Destinies comes into question. The class revolt element, however, has to do with the labor burden, while the Tablet of Destinies issue belongs to another category entirely. I therefore conclude that the class-revolt specie of theomachy does not of itself have anything to do with cosmogony, and the only chaos that is central to the plot is the chaos among the gods with regard to their social rank; thus, class revolt incidents do entail theomachy but should not be included in the *Chaoskampf* category.

Order versus disorder in the macrocosmos (Chaoskampf). In the ancient cognitive environment, disorder threatened on numerous fronts. The joint task of gods and humans was to contain and combat the inclination toward disorder or the incursion of it into the ordered world. Order was first established at some point in the past, but this by no means meant that the battle was over. Recurrent threats came both in the form of occasional attacks and in the seasonal and daily cycles of ordinary life. Although the legitimacy of applying the term *chaos* to these situations has been rightly contested, we can adopt it to describe this category of theomachy, with the important qualification that it pertains to elements representing macrocosmic disorder, whether they are personified or not. Having established this qualification, we can now discuss the three subcategories of *Chaoskampf.* And we note that all three subcategories have in common the feature that the adversary is macrocosmic disorder. It is this adversary that distinguishes *Chaoskampf* from the other categories.

One *Chaoskampf* subcategory comprises texts in which macrocosmic order is being initially established. The classic literary work in which this subcategory is found is *Enuma Elish*, but it must be recognized that this is nearly the only piece of ancient literature having this feature.[166] The *Chaos-*

---

166. D. Tsumura, *Creation and Destruction: A Reappraisal of the* Chaoskampf *Theory in the Old Testament* (Winona Lake, IN: Eisenbrauns, 2005), 190.

kampf subcategory is the second of three types of theomachy found in *Enuma Elish*. Here, Tiamat, the personified Sea, is the enemy, and cosmogony is the result of the conflict. The only other example I have been able to locate in ancient literature is in a single line in the (Egyptian) *Instruction of Merikare*: "He [Re] made sky and earth for their sake; he subdued the water monster."[167] The common ground in this subcategory is that the adversary is the representative of the Sea, and macrocosmic order is established as a result of the conflict.

Having said this, however, we must identify a significant caveat. As Alan Millard has pointed out, in *Enuma Elish* the cosmogony that results from the *Chaoskampf* is not an initial cosmogony.[168] The first three tablets clearly testify to a world already in existence. The cosmogony is presented as a re-organization of the cosmos under Marduk's control. In *Enuma Elish,* then, we find *Chaoskampf* related to macrocosmic order and to a cosmogony, but it is not an initial cosmogony. This leaves no remaining examples of *Chaoskampf* related to initial cosmogonies in ancient literature.

The difference in the second subcategory is that an adversary arises who threatens an already-established order among the gods and, therefore, at least indirectly, threatens the established order of the macrocosmos.[169] Examples include a couple of little-known Akkadian tales (Nergal/Labbu;[170] Tishpak/Lion-Serpent[171]), as well as the more famous Akkadian tale of *Ninurta and Anzu*.[172] Even though cosmic order is threatened by the beasts who serve as adversaries, the eventual victory over them does not

---

167. *COS* 1.35, line 131. This example may also need to be discarded, however, if Lesko's translation is preferred: 'He repelled the greed of the waters'. See L. H. Lesko, "Ancient Egyptian Cosmogonies and Cosmology," in *Religion in Ancient Egypt* (ed. B. E. Shafer; Ithaca, NY: Cornell University Press, 1991), 103. The alternate reading offered by Lesko reflects a suggestion originally made by Posener that the word translated 'monster' (*snk*, which occurs in all manuscripts of the work) is a metathesized form for *skn* ('greed'). See J. Hoffmeier, "Some Thoughts on Genesis 1 and 2 and Egyptian Cosmology," *JANES* 15 (1983): 39–49, especially p. 48 n. 90.

168. Private communication.

169. It is certainly possible also to view the threat from Tiamat in *Enuma Elish* in this category. The difference is that, in the examples cited here, cosmogony does not result.

170. Foster, *Before the Muses*, 579–80; see discussion in T. Lewis, "CT 13.33–34 and Ezekiel 32: Lion-Dragon Myths," *JAOS* 116 (1996): 28–47.

171. Foster, *Before the Muses*, 581–82.

172. Foster, *Before the Muses*, 555–78. Other minor Ninurta battles may be included here, such as, e.g., *Ninurta and Azag*. P. Machinist has drawn attention to the similarities in the plot lines of *Anzu, Enuma Elish* and the *Ishum and Erra Epic*, P. Machinist, "Order and Disorder: Some Mesopotamian Reflections," in *Genesis and Regeneration* (ed. S. Shaked; Jerusalem: Israel Academy of Sciences and Humanities, 2005), 31–61.

result in cosmogony, and thus we have an instance of *Chaoskampf* without cosmogony.[173]

In the third subcategory, the adversary threatens order in regular cycles, and this is usually associated with threats to seasonal fertility or the prospect of the loss of the daily appearance of the sun. The former is known from the Levant (Illuyanka or Mot's threat to Baal) and the latter from Egypt (where the threat is from Apophis). Throughout most of Egyptian literature, Apophis is considered part of that which is nonexistent and has no beginning or end.[174] One could conclude that he was initially defeated by the creator-god,[175] but this does not appear to be a significant element in the mythology. Apophis plays a more significant role in the daily recurrent creation than in the cosmogonic accounts. Apophis (not himself a god) engages in conflict with the gods throughout time—he represents the threat from the nonexistent; Seth (see below) represents the threat of political disorder within the realm of the gods on an ongoing basis—thus, the threat within the existent. Unlike the situation in *Enuma Elish*, neither of these threats results in a cosmogony.

Struggle for rule among the gods involving competing claimants. In this category of theomachy, the question to be resolved is which god is in charge. The adversary is an individual deity who challenges the current order, and what is at stake is control of the divine realm. Once again, *Enuma Elish* provides an example (the dispute between Kingu and Marduk), and there are examples from every literary culture in the ancient Near East: in Egypt, the challenge comes from Seth and Horus; in Syria–Palestine, the adversaries are Yamm and Baal; and then there are the protagonists in the Hittite *Kumarbi Cycle*. The adversary in these cases is positioned within the bureaucracy rather than within the cosmos per se. The conflicts do not always involve actual combat, and the defeated adversary is not necessarily destroyed. For instance, Horus attains kingship by being victorious over Seth, but then the two are reconciled and Seth continues to rule Upper Egypt. He becomes useful, because he is employed by the gods to defeat Apophis (riding on the prow of the sun-god's boat).[176] These examples rep-

---

173. See N. Forsyth, *The Old Enemy: Satan and the Combat Myth* (Princeton: Princeton University Press, 1987), 45.

174. In late texts, Apophis is said to have been "spat out," so he has a beginning (Hornung, *Conceptions of God*, 158–59).

175. Hornung says that this may be inferred because the *msw-bdšt*, closely associated with Apophis, are destroyed on the primeval hill (*Conceptions of God*, 159 n. 59).

176. H. Te Velde, "Seth," in *OEAE* 3:269–71.

resent political rather than cosmic conflict. Consequently, Assmann uses the label "cratogony" rather than "cosmogony" to describe them.[177] It is true that Seth is one of the Heliopolitan Ennead, but even in this context he is a threat to kingship and is eventually replaced in the Ennead by Horus in New Kingdom times. What has been called *Chaoskampf* at Ugarit is now widely recognized as having to do with political power rather than cosmology, and in terms of the classification system presented above, it obviously fits much more easily into this category.[178]

Generational coup, with "younger" gods seizing rule from "older" gods. In the *Theogony of Dunnu*, the combat takes place when one generation of deities seeks to supplant the previous one. This is not a case of the corporate younger generation pitted against the older ruling elites; instead, individual gods engage in acts of conquest that include "family crimes" such as incest, patricide, and matricide.

Conclusions regarding Theomachy

Now that we have articulated a system that classifies the various forms in which theomachy occurred in the literature of the ancient Near East, we are in a better position to identify the relevant features of the cognitive environment.

- Theomachy is a regular feature throughout the ancient Near East, but almost never is theomachy relegated to cosmogony
- The adversary, or opponent of the gods is never a nonpersonified representative of macrocosmic chaos/nonfunctionality; that is, the adversary is always a personified representative of some part of creation
- In three of the four categories discussed above, what is at stake is rule and role among the gods, not order in the cosmos
- Initial cosmogony is not characterized by theomachy in any known literature from the ancient Near East

---

177. Assmann, *Search for God*, 121.

178. N. Wyatt, *Myths of Power: A Study of Royal Myth and Ideology in Ugaritic and Biblical Tradition* (UBL 13; Münster: Ugarit-Verlag, 1996); idem, "Arms and the King: The Earliest Allusions to the *Chaoskampf* Motif and Their Implications for the Interpretation of the Ugaritic and Biblical Traditions," in *"Und Mose schrieb dieses Lied auf . . .": Studien zum Alten Testament und zum Alten Orient. Festschrift für O. Loretz* (AOAT 250; Münster: Ugarit-Verlag, 1998), 833–82. See the careful assessment of the *Chaoskampf* motif in Tsumura, *Creation and Destruction*, 143–97; and R. S. Watson, *Chaos Uncreated: The Reassessment of the Theme of "Chaos" in the Hebrew Bible* (BZAW 231; Berlin: de Gruyter, 2005).

These negative results succeed in defining for us primarily what are *not* standard ingredients in the cognitive environment. Neither the literature of Canaan nor the literature of Egypt testifies to a revolt of the gods; all we encounter is one god challenging another god. In neither literature, however, is there any reason to conclude that the conflict is related to cosmogony. *Enuma Elish*, as we have seen, provides examples of three categories of theomachy: dissatisfied class struggle is resolved by creating humankind; macrocosmic chaos, represented in Tiamat's rebellion, is resolved in cosmogony; and struggle for rule (represented in Kingu's possession of the Tablet of Destinies) is resolved by Marduk's ascension to the throne. In this respect, *Enuma Elish* should be viewed as idiosyncratic rather than paradigmatic. We have no reason to expect that an ancient Near Eastern cosmogony would feature theomachy.

The Role of Humanity

Less than a dozen accounts of or allusions to human origins are scattered throughout Sumerian, Akkadian, and Egyptian texts.[179] Most of the accounts are brief (a couple of lines), with the longest excerpts (*Enki and Ninmaḫ* and *Atrahasis*) extending for several dozen lines. What follows is a brief listing of ancient accounts of human origins.

Sumer

Song of the Hoe. As a result of Enlil's work with a hoe and a brick-mold, people sprout from the earth. After a model of a person is built, people are mass-produced and begin their work. The material they are made of is not mentioned, but clay can be inferred as the source because of the mention of the brick-mold. The account is, however, more interested in all of the things that the hoe does than in what humans do.[180]

Hymn to E-engura. In a passing comment reminiscent of the *Song of the Hoe*, this temple hymn mentions only that humans "broke through the earth's surface like plants."[181]

Enki and Ninmaḫ. The gods complain about their hard life, and Enki is finally aroused to respond. Instigated by Nammu, who conceived of the

---

179. In this section, I will largely confine the discussion to issues relevant to the aspects of humanity that are the focus of Genesis 1. For a fuller discussion of the cognitive environment as it relates to Genesis 2, see my *Ancient Near Eastern Thought and the Old Testament* (Grand Rapids, MI: Baker, 2007), 203–15.

180. *COS* 1.157. This text is also called *Praise of the Pickax*; see Clifford, *Creation Accounts*, 31.

181. Clifford, *Creation Accounts*, 29–30.

idea, and aided by a number of birth-goddesses (Ninmaḫ foremost among them), people are created from clay. Several stages are involved in the creation process: Nammu has the idea and mixes the "heart" of the clay on top of the Abzu. Then the birth-goddesses pinch off pieces of clay to form people, who are then given the work of the gods as their destiny. The account ends with Enki and Ninmaḫ in a drunken contest, creating human archetypes that are defective to see whether functions can be found for them.[182]

KAR 4. Available in both Sumerian and Akkadian, this account provides some details not available elsewhere in the literature. Here, people are created from the blood of some slaughtered gods (the gods are not rebels in this story) to do the work of the gods. This work includes not only irrigation (working *in place of* the gods) but also includes building and maintaining temples and performing the rituals (working *to serve* the gods). As in some of the other Sumerian accounts, humans spring forth from the earth once the prototype has been designed.[183]

Akkadian

Atrahasis. The epic of *Atrahasis* contains the most detailed account of human creation in ancient literature. The topic begins about halfway through column 1 and takes up more than 150 lines, though some portions of these lines are broken. The process is introduced through the character of Mami (= Belet-ili and Nintu), the mother-goddess, and contains many of the elements known from other accounts (e.g., humans take upon themselves the drudgery of the gods). The most important unique feature of the creation portion of this epic is that people are created from a combination of the blood of the deity who was the ringleader of the rebellion and clay that has been spat upon by the gods.[184] Mami, aided by Enki, creates seven

---

182. *COS* 1.159.

183. Clifford, *Creation Accounts*, 50–51; Foster, *Before the Muses*, 491–93 merges the Sumerian and Akkadian versions into a single translation.

184. *COS* 1.130. For discussion of various details, see T. Abusch, "Ghost and God: Some Observations on a Babylonian Understanding of Human Nature," in *Self, Soul and Body in Religious Experience* (ed. A. Baumgarten, J. Assmann, and G. Stroumsa; Leiden: Brill, 1998), 363–83; B. Batto, "Creation Theology in Genesis," in *Creation in the Biblical Traditions* (ed. R. J. Clifford and J. J. Collins; Washington, DC: Catholic Biblical Association, 1992). In *Atrahasis*, both flesh and blood are used, whereas in *Enuma Elish* and *KAR* 4, only the blood is mentioned. Only in *Atrahasis* is a combination of common and divine materials used. There is no indication in *KAR* 4 that the two slain deities are rebels. The bilingual version of *Enki and Ninmaḫ* suggests that some kind of mixture may also occur there. See Lambert, "The Relationship of Sumerian and Babylonian Myth as Seen in Accounts of Creation," in *La*

human pairs (though unfortunate breaks in the text obscure the details) who mature and then begin to reproduce.[185]

Enuma Elish.   In tablet VI, Marduk envisions humankind as comprised of blood and bones and names them, giving them the task of relieving the burden of the gods. Ea carries out Marduk's vision, using Kingu's blood in the process; there is, however, no mention of clay. The entire account takes up slightly more than 35 lines.[186]

Egypt[187]

Coffin Texts (Spell 80, CT 2.43).   In this spell, there is only a passing reference to breath, which is put in the throats of human beings, along with all other creatures.[188]

CT Spell 1130.   This spell includes references to a few functions in society, but in regard to human origins, it only offers an etymological play on words: people have their origin in the tears of the eye of the creator-god.[189]

Instruction of Merikare.   This piece of wisdom literature contains the most important and extensive treatment of human origins and roles:[190]

> Provide for people, the cattle of God, for he made heaven and earth for their liking. He repelled the greed of the waters; he made the winds in order that their nostrils might breathe; [for] they are likenesses of him that came forth from his flesh. He shines in the sky for their liking; he has made vegetation, small cattle, and fish for them to nourish them. He has killed his enemies and destroyed his own children, because they planned to make rebellion. He makes daylight for their liking, and he sails around in order to see them. He has raised up a shrine behind them, and when they weep he hears. He has made them rulers even from the egg, a lifter to lift [the load] from the back of the weak man. He has made for them magic to be weapons to oppose what may happen.[191]

Here, the station of people in the cosmos and their relationship to the gods are addressed. Other elements of the cosmos are identified as functioning

---

Circulation des biens, des personnes et des idées dans le Proche-Orient ancient (ed. D. Charpin and F. Joannès; Paris: Editions Recherche sur la Civilisations, 1992), 129–35.

185. See the translation and notes of Foster, *Before the Muses*, 236–37. The Assyrian version is explicit about the number.

186. *COS* 1.111.

187. Allen, *Genesis in Egypt*; E. Wasilewska, *Creation Stories of the Middle East* (London: Kingsley, 2000); Hoffmeier, "Thoughts on Genesis 1 and 2."

188. *COS* 1.8.

189. *COS* 1.17; see also 1.9. This source of the life of human beings is also referred to in passing in spell 80.

190. *COS* 1.35.

191. Translation from Lesko, "Ancient Egyptian Cosmogonies and Cosmology," 103.

for the sake of human beings (sky and earth, sun, daylight). Human beings are provisioned by deity with food, leadership, and magic. Deity disciplines rebellion and guards people from traitors. The text adds a reference to the provision of a shrine to house the god so that he can hear the people's weeping.

A variety of texts allude to people being fashioned by Khnum on a potter's wheel. Some scholars have identified these allusions as early as the Pyramid Texts, but the references become more obvious in the Coffin Texts and in pictorial representations.[192]

Neither Egyptian nor Sumerian accounts put human origins in the context of conflict among the gods, as do the Akkadian accounts, though two of the Sumerian accounts (*Enlil and Ninmaḫ*, *KAR* 4) specify that people are to take over the work of the gods.[193] The accounts typically mention the process involved and the materials used in creation and the roles or functions assigned to humankind. In Egypt, there is no reference to humans' taking up the labor that the gods had previously been doing: people are cattle who are cared for, not slaves who are driven. Similarly, in Egypt no hint of a prior scenario or circumstance that led to humans' being made is cited.

As can be seen from the above examples, very little commonality exists between the Egyptian accounts and Mesopotamian accounts of human origins, with the exception that clay as a source ingredient is mentioned in specific texts from both cultures. The variety of materials used in the creation of humanity reflect differences in the archetypal elements that each account wishes to emphasize and for which an explanation is provided. The commonality in the cognitive environment, therefore, is that people are conventionally portrayed as being created out of elements that will explain the archetypal roles assigned to the people.

Human Functions

In this section, I am not concerned with addressing all of the different functions that humans could serve in the cosmos but want to focus specifically on functions that they are said to have been created to fulfill and roles that they were given at creation. There are three major aspects of the role

---

192. Hoffmeier, "Thoughts on Genesis 1 and 2," 47. P. O'Rourke, "Khnum," *OEAE* 2:231; Morenz, *Egyptian Religion*, 183–84; Simkins, *Creator and Creation*, 70; See also a reference to similar ingredients (clay and straw) in *Amenemope* 25:13–14.

193. A broken line in *Enlil and Ninmaḫ* suggests that the gods smash their tools once human beings are created, but it is difficult to interpret this line with certainty.

and function of humanity that are identified in the texts; human beings are created in order to:

- take over the drudgery work of the gods
- serve the gods through the performance of rituals and through provisioning the deities in the temples
- be in the image of deity

The first of these roles has already been treated above and is attested only in Sumerian and Akkadian sources. The second has also been demonstrated previously in the context of the decreeing of destinies in Mesopotamian literature[194] and can be seen throughout Egyptian literature.[195] These two roles together compose what I call the "Great Symbiosis." The foundation of religion in Mesopotamia is that humanity has been created to serve the gods by meeting their needs for food (sacrifices), housing (temples), clothing, and in general giving them worship and privacy so that these gods can do the work of running the cosmos. The other side of the symbiosis is that the gods will protect their investment by protecting their worshipers and providing for them. Humans thus find dignity in the role that they have in this symbiosis to aid the gods (through their rituals) in running the cosmos.

It remains for us to treat the notion of the image of God in more detail.

Image of God. The concept that particular people, some people, or all people are in the image of God is not limited to creation texts.[196] The brief survey below will examine the extant data to understand how images (of god or in other contexts) were understood in the ancient Near East.

Mesopotamia: King in the Image (ṣalmu)[197] of God. Bahrani has suggested that ṣalmu, more than being a copy or representation of a person, "has the potential of becoming an entity in its own right."[198] It serves as a

---

194. For instance, in *KAR* 4.

195. See Assmann, *Search for God*, 3–6; he cites a hymn to Re that portrays the king as representing the gods by judging humankind and as representing humans by satisfying the gods. See the additional texts that Assmann refers to on pp. 174–77 (Coffin Texts 1130).

196. The most comprehensive analysis was carried out by E. Curtis, *Man as the Image of God in Genesis in Light of Ancient Near East Parallels*, a dissertation supervised by J. Tigay at the University of Pennsylvania (1984). Other important studies include W. R. Garr, *In His Own Image and Likeness* (CHANE 15; Leiden: Brill, 2003); and Z. Bahrani, *The Graven Image: Representation in Babylonia and Assyria* (Philadelphia: University of Pennsylvania, 2003).

197. Akkadian ṣalmu is cognate to the Hebrew ṣelem, one of the terms used in Genesis 1. Bahrani (*The Graven Image*) treats it extensively on pp. 123–48 and offers a convenient summary of her conclusions on p. 205.

198. Bahrani, *The Graven Image*, 123.

substitute through representation.[199] Beginning in the Middle Assyrian period, with occurrences peaking in the Neo-Assyrian period, Assyrian kings were at times envisioned as being the image of deity. The following are the only examples in the extant literature.

- *Epic of Tukulti-Ninurta I.* The epic compares the Assyrian king's fearsomeness in battle to gods such as Adad and Ninurta and then says: "He alone is the eternal image of Enlil as it describes him as attentive to the people."[200] Here, the image is presented in the context of divine sonship, the notion that the king is the son of the deity. Thus, the rhetorical "biological" connection is the premise for the idea that the king is in the image of the divine. This connection may have been fueled by the fact that the crown prince, the designated heir to the reigning king, could at times serve as the authorized agent or deputy of the king.
- *Letter to Esarhaddon from Adad-šumu-uṣur.* In this letter to the king from one of his prominent subjects, the king is flattered as being benevolent, a benevolence that marks him as the very image of Bel.[201]
- *Letter to Esarhaddon from Ašredu.* This letter compares the king to Marduk as being justly angry, punishing appropriately, and then relenting in mercy, just like the deity.[202]
- *Bit Meseri Incantation.* The *ašipu* priest, an officiant of the official cult, is identified as being in the image of Marduk.

These examples indicate that, by virtue of the king's close association to deity and the incarnation of certain attributes of deity in the king, he qualifies to be considered the image of deity.

The Neo-Assyrian royal titularies, narrative inscriptions, astrological prognostications and unctuously flattering correspondence hammer away at the theme of the unique proximity of the king to the divine realm and extol his god-like powers. The kings were summoned prenatally to kingship, suckled by goddesses, warned by eclipses and other portents of imminent personal hazards, and succored by upbeat, motherly prophecies uttered by goddesses. Kings, like the gods, strode into battle

---

199. Bahrani, *The Graven Image*, 133.

200. Foster, *Before the Muses*, 301.

201. S. Parpola, *Letters From Assyrian and Babylonian Scholars* (SAA 10; Helsinki: State Archives of Assyria, 1993), #228, lines 18–19. In another letter from this same scholar (#196, lines rev. 4–5), Esarhaddon is compared to Shamash.

202. H. Hunger, *Astrological Reports to Assyrian Kings* (SAA 8; Helsinki: State Archives of Assyria, 1992), #333, line rev. 2.

surrounded by the *melammu*, a radiant, terrifying nimbus devastating to foes . . . and kings embodied god-like wisdom and could be characterized as the very image of the gods. The kings were not members of the state pantheon, but they dwelt in closer physical and ontological proximity to the gods than any other mortals.[203]

Thus, the image of god in the king makes it clear that the king functions on behalf of the god.

Mesopotamia: The King Sets Up Images of Himself

In both Mesopotamia and Egypt, kings set up monuments of various sorts (statues, reliefs, standing stones) to mark their presence in (and control of) territory outside their kingdom. In Egypt, according to Hornung, these are apotropaic monuments that establish the pharaoh's presence and protection.[204] In Mesopotamia, they appear to be associated primarily with the king's authority over the region.[205] When kings set up their images in temples, the intention again was to mark the king's presence, sometimes in conquered regions, in order to receive divine honors alongside gods;[206] on other occasions, the placement of a statue of the king was perceived as an act of devotion to the king's own god. Votive images placed in a temple were often expressions of thanks for past conquests and petitions for continuing protection and victory.

Not only did the kings set up images of themselves in distant or conquered lands, in the Neo-Assyrian period, images of the king (ᵈ*ṣalam šarri*) were used in a variety of ritual and judicial contexts.[207] This practice was intended to represent the presence and authority of the king rather than to exercise his prerogatives per se. And this practice demonstrates that the role of images was to function on behalf of the one who is being represented by the image.

Mesopotamia: Images of the Gods (How Divine Images Functioned)

The images of deities functioned primarily to mediate the presence of the deity,[208] though they also mediated revelation *from* the deity (through

---

203. S. Holloway, *Aššur Is King! Aššur Is King!* (Leiden: Brill, 2002), 181–82.

204. Curtis, *Man as the Image of God*, 118.

205. Holloway, *Aššur Is King*, 401; M. Cogan, *Imperialism and Religion: Assyria, Judah and Israel in the Eighth and Seventh Centuries B.C.E.* (SBLMS 19; Missoula, MT: Scholars Press, 1974), 58–60.

206. Holloway, *Aššur Is King*, 178–93.

207. Holloway, *Aššur Is King*, 186–87.

208. Note that Bahrani (*The Graven Image*, 144) describes the image as a "mode of presence."

divination) and mediated worship given *to* the deity. These mediating roles are accomplished through the ritual processes that infuse the image with the essence of the deity, thus making it a "living" image.[209] As mediators, the images functioned in the role of the god, on behalf of the god.

Egypt: People in the Image of Deity

When the image of god is attributed to human beings in general in Egypt, it is either indicative of a station that people occupy (as in *Merikare*) or of an attribute that they possess.

- *Instruction of Merikare*: "They are his images (*snn*), who came from his body." This is the best-known and oldest example of human beings in general being described as in the image of god.
- *Instruction of Ani*: All people are the likenesses (*snw*) of god, not just wise men, in that they listen to a person who brings a plea.[210]
- People who are able to imitate the deeds or attributes of a god are in some way in the likeness (*mjtj*) of that god.[211]

Egypt: King in the Image of Deity

Many different terms for *image* are used in Egyptian literature, and there are many more occurrences than in other ancient Near Eastern literature, so only a few general categories that apply to the idea of *image* will be

---

209. The ideology of images has been much discussed in recent years, the following being among the most significant publications: A. Berlejung, "Washing the Mouth: The Consecration of Divine Images in Mesopotamia," in *The Image and the Book* (ed. K. van der Toorn; Leuven: Peeters, 1997), 45–72; E. M. Curtis, "Images in Mesopotamia and the Bible: A Comparative Study," in *The Bible in the Light of Cuneiform Literature, Scripture in Context III* (ed. W. W. Hallo, B. W. Jones, and G. L. Mattingly; Lewiston, NY: Edwin Mellen, 1990), 31–56; M. B. Dick, *Born In Heaven, Made On Earth* (Winona Lake, IN: Eisenbrauns, 1999); W. W. Hallo, "Cult Statue and Divine Image: A Preliminary Study," in *Scripture in Context II: More Essays on the Comparative Method* (ed. W. W. Hallo, J. C. Moyer, and L. G. Perdue; Winona Lake, IN: Eisenbrauns, 1983), 1–18; V. Hurowitz, "Picturing Imageless Deities: Iconography in the Ancient Near East," *BAR* 23/3 (1997): 46–48, 51; T. Mettinger, *No Graven Image?* (Stockholm: Almqvist & Wiksell, 1995); J. J. M. Roberts, "Divine Freedom and Cultic Manipulation in Israel and Mesopotamia," in *Unity and Diversity* (ed. H. Goedicke and J. J. M. Roberts; Baltimore: Johns Hopkins University Press, 1975), 181–90; J. M. Sasson, "On the Use of Images in Israel and the Ancient Near East: A Response to Karel van der Toorn," in *Sacred Time, Sacred Place: Archaeology and the Religion of Israel* (ed. B. M. Gittlen; Winona Lake, IN: Eisenbrauns, 2002), 63–70.

210. Hornung, *Conceptions of God*, 138. *COS* 1.46: "Man resembles the god in his way if he listens to a man's answer." There is considerable controversy about the translation and interpretation of this section; see the discussion in J. R. Middleton, *The Liberating Image* (Grand Rapids, MI: Brazos, 2005), 100–101.

211. This term could also apply to those who temporarily occupy the place of deity, for example, when performing a ritual; see Curtis, *Man as the Image of God*, 94–95.

presented here. [212] Normally, it is the king who is referred to as being in the image of god (using various terms), but this language was not a common way to refer to the king until the mid-second millennium B.C.E. and then primarily in the New Kingdom. [213]

The term *hntj* was used in early Egyptian literature to refer to images of people buried in graves, statues of kings deposited in temples, the image of a deity that was carried around in public processions in the festivals; but finally, beginning in the 17th Dynasty, it came to be used of kings who are said to have been set up on earth as the image of deity, as the deity's visible manifestation. Other terms such as *šsp*, *sšmw*, and *twt* were used primarily as a part of New Kingdom epithets that likened kings to the sun-god. A number of these terms had previously been used to refer to statues of the gods. The same term that is used to refer to humanity in general in the *Instruction of Merikare* (*snn*) is used to refer to pharaohs such as Thutmose III and Hatshepsut and, in the Greek and Roman periods, to other rulers much more generally. [214] The pharaoh, as the living image of deity, functioned as the instrument that carried out the will of the god as he ruled, because the king was thought to be imbued with the divine presence.

Egypt: Images of the Gods (How Divine Images Functioned)

Images of the deities were thought to contain the essence (*ba*) of the deity and to manifest the presence of the deity. As in the case of the king's being in the image of god, images were considered to function on behalf of the god.

> Thus it appears likely that the primary significance of the image of a deity in both Egypt and Mesopotamia lay in the fact that the god manifested himself and was thought to be actually present in the statue. At the same time there was a representational significance in the statue. The image attempted to describe not so much the appearance of the deity, however, as something about his nature and function. [215]

---

212. Summarized in Curtis, *Man as the Image of God*, 87–96; this section in Curtis's work is dependent on E. Hornung, "Der Mensch als 'Bild Gottes' in Ägypten," in *Die Gottebenbild-lichkeit des Menschen* (Munich: Schriften des deutschen Instituts für wissenschaftliche Pädagogik, 1967), 123–56; Hornung cites eight terms. This section of this chapter is summarized from Curtis's discussion.

213. For an extensive but not exhaustive listing, see Curtis, *Man as the Image of God*, 226–28 n. 62; and Middleton, *Liberating Image*, 108–9.

214. Curtis points out a few other examples where a nonroyal individual is said to be in the image of the deity: *Man as the Image of God*, 92.

215. Curtis, *Man as the Image of God*, 113.

The close association of the image of god with the king suggests that the image most naturally implies that the deity rules through his image. That is, the concept "image of god" in the ancient Near East is most prevalent as part of royal ideology. As Curtis succinctly puts it, "The king as the image of god did the work of god on earth; it was the functional presence of the god that was manifest in the king." [216] We noted earlier in this chapter that in the mid-second millennium there was a perceptible change in the understanding of the divine that elevated nonprimordial deities to a status higher than the ancient cosmic deities. The importation of the "image of god" into royal ideology for the most part follows the shift of dominion and rule away from what we referred to as the cosmogonic/theogonic model. The ideology of the "image of god" would not have been very practical when the gods were primarily cosmic deities: the role of deity in the cosmogonic/theogonic model was not something a king could easily represent. To put it another way, conceiving of the king as the image of the deity makes most sense when the role of deity is seen primarily as a ruler (the political/bureaucratic model). [217] When the ruling gods are associated primarily with the dynamic aspects of the cosmos instead of the static aspects, the king who is in the image of god is engaged in the dynamic rule in the cosmos.

What significance, then, do passages have that attribute the image of god to humanity in general? It is not easy to make the leap to the claim that the ruling function was extended to humankind as a whole—the so-called "democratization process." If all human beings are rulers, no one remains for them to rule. Furthermore, since *The Instruction of Merikare* was written centuries before the rhetoric of the image of God came to be applied to kings, it is difficult to see the latter as a development from the former: [218] a thing cannot be democratized if it was not previously autocratic or undemocratic. In *The Instruction of Merikare*, the image, when applied to all people, is based on the premise that humans came from the god's own body. This exhibits some similarity to the connection between divine sonship and divine image in the royal rhetoric. The purpose of this rhetoric tends to be

---

216. Curtis, *Man as the Image of God*, 150.

217. We need to be careful not to be reductionistic or simplistic when we formulate schemas or developmental models. Enlil certainly was considered a ruling god, and those who ruled under his auspices were considered little Enlils. My point is *not* that the image of god aspect of royal ideology could not have been present in earlier periods, only that it did not become fully operative until rulership among the deities shifted to those with little or no cosmic association.

218. See Middleton, *Liberating Image*, 100.

the establishment of the role or station of the one possessing the image first and foremost within the context of royal ideology (but not in *The Instruction of Merikare*) and then leads to that person's assuming divine functions and prerogatives.

The image of a deity could be located in a manufactured statue, in the king, in a ritual specialist, or in humanity. Though people, or certain people, were considered to be in the image of god or viewed as the image of god, it is not common for ancient Near Eastern accounts of the creation of human beings to make a connection between the act of creation and the image of god. The only possible exception (which nonetheless still falls just short of an incontestably explicit statement) is *The Instruction of Merikare*. Only in this text of all the literature of the ancient Near East is archetypal corporate humanity described as the image of god.

By way of summary conclusion, the concept of the image of god fits in all of the categories we have defined above is that the person holding the image of God is a container for the divine presence and represents the deity in the role or function of this deity.

Summary Conclusion regarding the Role of Humanity

The role of humanity is not an independent topic; in the ancient Near Eastern cognitive environment, it can only be understood in relationship to the role of deity. All of the ideology concerning the role of humanity in the cosmos—whether it addresses the circumstances under which people were created, the materials of which they were made (i.e., their composition), their functions, or their propagation—associates them with deity.

The conception of humanity focuses on two roles:

1. Humanity's role with regard to its place or station in the cosmos
2. Humanity's role with regard to its functions in the cosmos

The place or station assigned to humanity in the first role is often addressed through the material ingredients used in creation. Thus, the place of archetypal humanity in the cosmos is expressed in material terms: the tears of the god, the blood of the god, clay, or dust. *The Instruction of Merikare* also addresses the place of humanity, although in broader terms. Most of the Egyptian texts that concern the creation of humanity focus on this first role: humanity's place in the cosmos.

The second category, humanity's function in the cosmos, is evident in Mesopotamian accounts in which people are created to carry out functions *for* the gods and, in the process, replace the gods by doing the menial tasks that the gods previously did to care for themselves. It later became part of royal ideology throughout the ancient Near East that select individuals carried out the functions *of* the gods, in this case pertaining primarily to rulership. A variety of functions are evident in various texts and can be summarized in the following categories:

- Function *in place of* the gods (menial labor; Mesopotamia only)
- Function *in service to* the gods (performance of ritual, supply of temple; Mesopotamia, Egypt, and Gen 2:15)
- Function *on behalf of* the gods (rule, either over nonhuman creation or over other people; role of the image in Mesopotamia, Egypt, and Genesis 1)

We can therefore conclude that in the general ancient Near Eastern cognitive environment, the interest of all of the accounts currently available to us is to elucidate the role of humanity through archetypal depictions that fall into the few paradigmatic categories we have listed above. Notable as the most radical departure from this general perspective is the contention in *Merikare* that creation was for the sake of humankind;[219] and though this text deals with the station of humanity, as do other accounts, it nonetheless offers a unique perspective on humankind's place. Though not as remarkably radical, *Atrahasis* reveals another departure from the general understanding, in that the blood of the slain deity plays a part in defining the nature and role of humanity. These exceptional cases notwithstanding, the most common interest in humanity has to do with its role and function in the cosmos (animate or inanimate), not merely biological existence.[220]

Conclusions: The ANE Cognitive Environment and Its Relationship to Positions and Roles of Beings in the Cosmos

The following list summarizes the conclusions reached in this chapter:

- Gods are inside, not outside, the cosmos
- Gods are involved in cosmic origins primarily in relation to the functions of the cosmos, both in the cosmogonic/theogonic model and in the political/bureaucratic model
- The cosmogonic/theogonic model of origins gives way in the second millennium B.C.E. to the political/bureaucratic model

---

219. Assmann, *Search for God*, 173.
220. Van der Toorn, *Family Religion in Babylonia, Syria and Israel*, 96; cf. Clifford, *Creation Accounts*, 8–9.

- Theomachy is ancillary to cosmogony and appears only idiosyncratically
- Accounts of human origins focus on humans' role in the cosmos, whether in terms of station or function
- Materials mentioned in the creation of humans have archetypal significance not material significance
- Similarly, the image of god concerns role and is mostly found in royal ideology in the political/bureaucratic model, confirming that the king has divine functions
- People and gods work together to ensure the preservation of order in the cosmos and its smooth operation (Great Symbiosis)

Together, these observations confirm the assessment offered by J. Allen: "[The ancient Egyptians] are concerned primarily with what lies beyond physical reality."[221] Allen elaborates by providing the common denominator of the cognitive environment: gods driving the functions of the cosmos.[222]

The Egyptian documents reflect a subjective rather than objective view of reality: concepts are expressed not in terms of mechanical forces and physical elements but in human terms, as the wills and personalities of sentient beings (the gods). And none of the Egyptian sources is the record of scientific or philosophical speculation for its own sake. All serve some practical end, whether the worship of god or the attempt to secure a successful afterlife for the dead.[223]

Cosmic Geography

Cosmic geography is the term we apply to how people envision the shape and structure of the world around them.[224] In modern cosmic geography, we understand, as a result of the application of science during the past few hundred years, that we live on a sphere marked by land masses that we call continents that themselves are surrounded by bodies of water we call oceans. We believe that this sphere is part of a system of planets that revolve around the sun, which is just one of many stars. Our planet itself also rotates, and another, smaller sphere, the moon, revolves around our planet. Our solar system is part of a galaxy of many stars and perhaps many planets

---

221. Allen, *Genesis in Egypt*, 56.

222. This is a teleological and transcendent perspective in contrast to modern-day dysteleological, material, and empirical perspectives.

223. Allen, *Genesis in Egypt*, 56.

224. Much of this chapter is adapted from a chapter on the same topic in my *Ancient Near Eastern Thought and the Old Testament*.

that, along with many other galaxies, make up the universe. The stars are very far away, and some are components of other galaxies. The fact that this cosmic geography seems so elementary and basic reveals just how deeply it is rooted in our self-understanding. Everyone in every time and place has a cosmic geography and knows what it is—though it is "second nature": no one needs to think about it.

It is clear that a culture's cosmic geography plays a significant role in shaping its world view and offers a context for the explanation of the things that people of the culture observe and experience. To substantiate this point, notice a few of the implications of this modern Western cosmic geography:

- Earth and its inhabitants are relatively insignificant, given the vastness of the universe.
- Our understanding of weather and time is based on this understanding of our physical context.
- Human beings live in a physical and material context.
- The universe and our own planet's context operate with consistency and predictability, and we have deduced and can trust the properties of physical objects and the laws governing their motion.

This cosmic geography has been formed by centuries of observation, experimentation, and deduction. We are fully convinced that it is "true," even if minor adjustments to our perspective are needed on a regular basis. What we call *science* is based on and continues to form the cosmic geography that we share.

The people of the ancient world also had a cosmic geography that was just as deeply integrated into their thinking, just as fundamental to their world view, just as prevalent in their cosmology, just as influential in every aspect of their lives, and just as "true" in their minds. And it was radically different from ours. If we aspire to understand the cosmological cognitive environment of the ancient world—whether Canaanite, Babylonian, Egyptian, or Israelite—it is therefore essential that we understand their cosmic geography.[225] The cosmological accounts of the ancients naturally will

---

225. The most significant reference sources include W. Horowitz, *Mesopotamian Cosmic Geography* (MC 8; Winona Lake, IN: Eisenbrauns, 1998); B. Janowski and B. Ego, *Das biblische Weltbild und seine altorientalischen Kontexte* (FAT 32; Tübingen: Mohr Siebeck, 2001); O. Keel, *The Symbolism of the Biblical World: Ancient Near Eastern Iconography and the Book of Psalms* (New York: Seabury, 1978; repr., Winona Lake, IN: Eisenbrauns, 1997); L. Stadelmann, *The Hebrew Conception of the World* (AnBib 39; Rome: Pontifical Biblical Institute, 1970); P. Seely, "The Firmament and the Water Above," *WTJ* 54 (1992): 31–46; idem, "The

describe origins in terms of their understanding of the cosmos, and their cosmic geography is one component. Despite some variation from one ancient Near Eastern culture to another, certain elements characterize all of them.

A Three-Tiered Cosmos

What kept the sky suspended above the earth and held back the heavenly waters? What kept the sea from overwhelming the land? What prevented the earth from sinking into the cosmic waters? These were the questions that people in the ancient world asked, and the answers they arrived at are embodied in their cosmic geography. Egyptians, Mesopotamians, Canaanites, Hittites, and Israelites all thought of the cosmos as composed of tiers: the earth was in the middle, with the heavens above and the netherworld beneath.[226] In general, people believed that there was a single, disc-shaped continent. This continent had high mountains at the edges that some believed held up the sky, which they thought was not vapors or air but solid (some envisioned it as a tent, others as a more substantial dome). The heavens where deities lived were above the sky, and the netherworld was beneath the earth. In some of the Mesopotamian literature, the heavens were thought to be made up of three superimposed disks, and the pavement composing each disc was made of various materials.[227] What they observed led them to conclude that the sun and the moon moved in roughly the same plane and in similar ways. The sun moved through the sky during the day and then moved into the netherworld during the night, traversing under the earth to its place of rising the next day. The stars were thought to be engraved on the sky and followed tracks as they moved through their ordained stations. Flowing all around this cosmos were the cosmic waters that were held back by the sky and on which the earth floated, even though it was conceived of as supported on pillars. Precipitation originated from

Geographical Meaning of 'Earth' and 'Seas' in Genesis 1:10," *WTJ* 59 (1997): 231–55; I. Cornelius, "The Visual Representation of the World in the Ancient Near East and the Hebrew Bible," *JNSL* 20 (1994): 193–218; J. E.Wright, "Biblical versus Israelite Images of the Heavenly Realm," *JSOT* 93 (2001): 59–75; C. Blacker and M. Loewe, *Ancient Cosmologies* (London: Allen and Unwin, 1975); Tsumura, *Creation and Destruction*.

226. Some scholars now propose that the netherworld was just another section of the earth and that, therefore, there were only two tiers. For a discussion of both formulations, see Keel, *Symbolism of the Biblical World*, 26–47. Determining whether there were two or three tiers does not contribute to the discussion of this chapter, so I will not attempt to address the arguments for each view here..

227. Details in Horowitz, *Mesopotamian Cosmic Geography*; brief treatment in Cornelius, "Visual Representation," 198, with citations.

the waters held back by the sky and fell to the earth through openings in the sky.

Similar views of the structure of the cosmos were common throughout the ancient world and persisted in popular perception until the Copernican revolution and the Enlightenment.[228] These ancient perceptions were not derived from scientific study (modern scientific techniques, of course, were not available to the ancients) but expressed their perception of the physical world.

However, in addition to the physical description sketched above, it is important to realize that the cosmic geography of ancient peoples was predominantly metaphysical and only secondarily physical and material: the roles and manifestations of the gods in the cosmic geography were primary. So, for example, in Mesopotamian thinking, cables held by the gods connected the heaven and earth and held the sun in the sky.[229] In Egypt, the sun-god sailed in his barque across the heavens during the day and through the netherworld at night. The stars of the Egyptian sky were portrayed as emblazoned across the arched body of the sky goddess, who was held up by the god of the air. In another Egyptian depiction, the Cow of Heaven was supported by four gods who each held one of her legs. She gave birth to the sun every day, and the sun traveled across her belly and was swallowed by her at night.[230] Egyptian art is more explicit than Mesopotamian art when it portrays the divine powers behind what we would describe as natural phenomena.[231]

Structure versus Function

In previous chapters, we have already presented the concept that ontology in the ancient world was more connected to function and role than to material substance. The apparent neglect of curiosity about the physical structure of the cosmos is therefore not simply a consequence of the ancients' inability to investigate their physical world. In their thinking, the physical aspects of the cosmos did not define its existence or its importance; physical realities were merely the tools that the gods used for carrying out

---

228. Seely, "Geographical Meaning."

229. Horowitz, *Mesopotamian Cosmic Geography*, 120, 265; W. G. Lambert, "The Cosmology of Sumer and Babylon," in *Ancient Cosmologies* (ed. C. Blacker and M. Loewe; London: Allen and Unwin, 1975), 62; see *Enuma Elish* V 59–68.

230. Lesko, "Ancient Egyptian Cosmogonies and Cosmology," 118.

231. Cornelius, "Visual Representation," 196–97.

their own purposes. The purposes of the gods were of prime interest to the ancients.

Egyptian literature and iconography are most obvious in their depiction of this concept. The gods are portrayed as standing in for the physical elements of the cosmos—that is, the components of ancient cosmic geography are gods, not inanimate objects. Mesopotamian iconography is less consistent in this regard, though the *kudurru*s and the Shamash plaque both clearly portray the interrelationship of deities and physical realities. Even when the Mesopotamian texts discuss issues such as the structure of the heavens and speak of the three levels' having three pavements of different sorts of stone (an obviously material statement), the primary focus is on which gods occupy each level.

Structure of the Heavens

The heavens were first of all the place where the gods lived. In Mesopotamian literature, Adapa ascends to heaven to meet with Anu. The heavenly temples of the great gods were located in heaven. There is some variation in the descriptions of heaven, with sometimes one, sometimes three, and sometimes seven levels of heaven,[232] the variations usually having the purpose of portraying distinct levels as the habitation of various deities, with the levels defining the hierarchical position of the deity within the pantheon.[233] Mesopotamian literature reflects various theories regarding the distances within the heavens[234] and the shape of the heavens. In the Levant, the gods are portrayed as living at the tops of mountains, but this is not a contradiction of the Mesopotamian portrayal because the mountains were thought to intersect with the heavens and, therefore, the heavens are at the tops of the mountains.

The Shamash plaque is particularly informative, because it shows worshipers who, though physically in the earthly temple, view themselves as present before Shamash's heavenly throne.[235] The cosmic waters of the Apsu are beneath Shamash's feet, and the stars are shown in the sky across the

---

232. Current also in rabbinic literature (*Midr. Deuteronomy Rabbah*); cf. Stadelmann, *Hebrew Conception of the World*, 41.

233. Horowitz, *Mesopotamian Cosmic Geography*, 244–52.

234. Horowitz, *Mesopotamian Cosmic Geography*, 177–88.

235. Sometimes referred to as the "Sun-God Tablet," this plaque is a Neo-Babylonian royal inscription related to the Ebabbar *lubuštu* ceremony now dated to the reign of Nabu-apla-iddina (888–855).

bottom of the portrayal.[236] On a Babylonian *kudurru* (boundary marker) of Kassite king Melishipak (sometimes Melishishu), the symbols of the primary celestial gods are portrayed in the top register, which represents the heaven sphere.[237]

Sky

The boundary between the heavens and the earth we will call the *sky*.[238] The sky's main function is to hold back the waters above. Occasionally, mountains are identified as intersecting the sky and perhaps holding it up. In other contexts (e.g., *Enuma Elish*), there is no mention of what holds up the sky. In addition to the sky's being portrayed as a pavement of blue (Mesopotamian *saggilmud*-stone = blue/lapis/sapphire),[239] Mesopotamian literature at times suggests that it is some sort of skin.[240] In Egyptian iconography, the sky is represented by Nut. In Pyramid Text 1040c, the mountains hold up the sky, which only makes sense if it is considered to be solid.[241]

An Egyptian word for "firmaments," *bia*, is clearly related to the words for "marvels" or "wonders," *biau*, and "iron," *biat*. Apparently the Egyptians made a connection between the marvelous meteoric iron that they used for ritual purposes and the material of which the sky's canopy was thought to be made. This idea would be consistent with the reflection of the sun's glory as it passed from east to west beneath the polished canopy, and perhaps also with its passage from west to east *above* this canopy. In the latter case, the sun's glory would be glimpsed through the stars, the holes left in the canopy when meteorites fell.[242]

---

236. C. Woods, "The Sun-God Tablet of Nabu-apla-iddina Revisited," *JCS* 56 (2004): 23–103.

237. Photograph, description, and discussion may be found in P. O. Harper, J. Aruz, and S. Tallon, *The Royal City of Susa* (New York: Metropolitan Museum of Art, 1992), 178–80 (article by Harper). See additional discussion in T. Ornan, *The Triumph of Symbol* (OBO 213; Fribourg: Academic Press / Göttingen: Vandenhoeck & Ruprecht, 2005), 46.

238. This terminology is difficult to define precisely, because the sky often refers to the space created between heaven and earth when they were separated, rather than the boundary for the waters. The space between is ruled by gods (e.g., Enlil) and is personified by gods (e.g., Shu). The boundary is never personified in Mesopotamian literature, unless one counts the corpse of Tiamat in *Enuma Elish* as functioning to personify it. In Egypt, the boundary is represented by Nut.

239. Horowitz, *Mesopotamian Cosmic Geography*, 263; cf. Exod 24:10.

240. *Ee* IV 139–40; cf. Horowitz, *Mesopotamian Cosmic Geography*, 262 with support from *CAD* Š/1 22a but contrary to *CAD* M/1 342a.

241. Seely, "Geographical Meaning," 233; see also PT 299a. If wordplays are to be taken seriously, the Egyptians may have believed that the heavens were made of meteoric iron, since pieces of it occasionally fell to earth; see Lesko, "Cosmogonies and Cosmology," 117.

242. Lesko, "Cosmogonies and Cosmology," 117.

Hoffmeier notes that the predominant view in Egyptian cosmology is that poles or staves hold up the sky over the earth.[243]

Weather and the Waters Above

The waters above (held back by the sky) may be represented iconographically in the Mesopotamian Shamash plaque but more unarguably on a number of Egyptian paintings, especially on sarcophagi.[244] In Mesopotamia, Marduk assigns guards to keep the heavenly waters from flooding the earth.[245] These waters are the remnants of Tiamat's body, which was split to form the waters above and the waters below after Tiamat was defeated by Marduk. Egyptian texts refer to the heavenly ocean as *kdbhdw-Hdr*, the cool or upper waters of Horus.[246] The sun-god's barque travels from horizon to horizon across this heavenly ocean.

The concept of heavenly waters is clearly a natural deduction drawn from experiencing precipitation.[247] If moisture comes from the sky, there must be moisture up there. This obvious association of the sky with weather will take on additional significance when we discuss Genesis 1. Mesopotamian imagery refers to "breasts of heaven" through which rain comes.[248] Ugaritic texts portray clouds as serving as buckets for the delivery of rain.[249] In both Egyptian and Mesopotamian thinking, entrance through the vault of the sky was made through gates. Sun, moon, stars, constellations, planets, and clouds all become visible by entering the realm of human perception through these gates.[250] All precipitation, including dew, comes from above, and thus all sources of moisture are regulated by the sky.

Celestial Bodies

Sun, moon, stars, and planets[251] were all considered to belong to the same category and were believed to occupy the same region—the air—because they could be seen beneath the sky. In Mesopotamia, the stars were thought to have been engraved on the underside of the sky and were assigned paths

---

243. Hoffmeier, "Thoughts on Genesis 1 and 2," 45–46. He points to PT §§348, 360, 1456, 1510, 1559; CT 1 2641; BD 450, 14.

244. Keel, *Symbolism*, 35–47.

245. *Enuma Elish* IV 139–40; see Horowitz, *Mesopotamian Cosmic Geography*, 262.

246. Keel, *Symbolism*, 37.

247. Horowitz, *Mesopotamian Cosmic Geography*, 262.

248. Horowitz, *Mesopotamian Cosmic Geography*, 262–63.

249. Stadelmann, *Hebrew Conception of the World*, 132.

250. Horowitz (*Mesopotamian Cosmic Geography*, 266) summarizes and provides bibliography (266 n. 33).

251. Mercury, Mars, Venus, Jupiter, and Saturn were the planets that they had identified.

of movement (3 tracks: the paths of Anu, Enlil, and Ea), with the heavens divided into 36 zones.[252] Constellations were identified and named, including the zodiacal constellations, though the concept of the zodiac itself was a later development.[253]

In Egypt, Mesopotamia, and the Levant, when the sun set in the west, it entered the netherworld and passed from west to east, to rise again in the morning. Shamash (the Babylonian sun-god) traveled through the netherworld, dispensing food and light to its denizens. Egyptian thinking about the night-time involved greater trauma: as Ra traveled on his barque, with stars serving as his oarsmen, he was threatened by various demons.

The main significance of the moon was its cycle, which regulated the calendar. All of the ancient cultures operated on a lunar-based calendar that periodically was adjusted by calculations of the solar or sidereal year. The planets and stars had less significance in ancient cosmic geography, though their movements were tracked, and they were the source of omens.[254]

Structure of the Earth

Diagrams and texts that convey how the ancients thought about the world around them have survived both in Mesopotamia (Babylonian world map) and Egypt (Egyptian Sarcophagi).[255] These sources confirm that all ancient Near Eastern cultures considered the earth to be a flat disk.[256] The sarcophagus stylized political, theological, and cosmic concepts. The Babylonian world map on the other hand, stylized political, cosmic, and topographical concepts.[257] Concepts expressed by both can be summarized as follows:

Political. Both sources see their own geographical region as the center of the earth. On the sarcophagus, the Duat (world of the dead) is in the center of a number of concentric rings, surrounded by the standards of the 41 nomes of Egypt. As one moves outward, the next ring identifies foreign lands. On the world map, Babylon is in the center, with a few other geographical locations placed around it (Susa, Assyria, Urartu, Habban, Bit

---

252. Horowitz, *Mesopotamian Cosmic Geography*, 256.

253. Stadelmann, *Hebrew Conception of the World*, 87.

254. Hunger, *Astrological Reports to Assyrian Kings*.

255. Of particular interest is the stone engraving on the top of the lid of the Ptolemaic sarcophagus of Wefernesheph from the necropolis of Sakkara. For discussion, see Keel, *Symbolism*, 37–39; Cornelius, "Visual Representation," 196–98, fig. 2.

256. Egypt: Keel, *Symbolism*, 37; Mesopotamia: Horowitz, *Mesopotamian Cosmic Geography*, 334: Israel: Seely, "Geographical Meaning," 238, and see Isa 40:22;

257. Horowitz, *Mesopotamian Cosmic Geography*, 20–42.

Yakin). Five triangular areas are identified as *nagu*—that is, islands of the sea.[258]

Cosmic.   Both sources see the cosmic waters as disc-shaped and surrounding a single disc-shaped landmass. The sarcophagus includes representations of the other realms (heavens and netherworld), while the world map shows only the terrestrial features.

Topographical.   There are no topographical indications on the sarcophagus (Egypt), but the world map (Mesopotamia) shows mountains at the top, the Euphrates, a canal, and a swamp, and they are correctly though not precisely located.[259]

Divinities.   The sarcophagus includes a number of features: deities represented include Anubis, Nun, Nut, and Ra, but they are all connected to cosmic rather than specifically terrestrial features. No religious features appear on the world map.

Some of the most helpful speculative information about the middle level of the cosmos comes from the *Epic of Etana*, where the hero is carried up to heaven on the back of an eagle. This literary work attempts to portray the land and the sea as they would appear at different altitudes.[260] Horowitz summarizes the two images used in this description.

> First, the sea is described as encircling the land just as the cosmic ocean *marratu* encircles the central continent on the World Map. Second, the author describes the land and sea in terms of agricultural features (gardener's ditch, garden, animal pen, irrigation ditch, trough) as the earth's surface appears to decrease in size when viewed from the heights of three, four, and five leagues.[261]

These images suggest that the sea was not understood as having an extent as great as the land because it is compared to a boundary ditch that surrounds a plot of land or a fence that surrounds an animal pen. Akkadian texts estimate the land surface of the earth to be equivalent to a disc having a diameter of about 3,000 miles, stretching from the mountains of southern Turkey in the north, where the sources of the Tigris and Euphrates were, to southeastern Iran in the south (just beyond Susa). To the east, it extended to the Zagros Mountains and the Iranian Plateau, but the sources are less

---

258. All of these are areas reached only by travel over water, though they could still be what we call continents. See the discussion in Horowitz, *Mesopotamian Cosmic Geography*, 30–33.

259. See Horowitz, *Mesopotamian Cosmic Geography*, 29, for adjustments.

260. Horowitz, *Mesopotamian Cosmic Geography*, 43–66.

261. Horowitz, *Mesopotamian Cosmic Geography*, 60–61.

clear about the western boundaries. The map's creators were certainly aware of the Mediterranean and considered it the primary western boundary.[262]

Mountains at the edges of the known world were viewed as intersecting the sky, perhaps as supporting it, and were thought to have roots in the netherworld. In some cases, mountains were viewed as a boundary of the cosmic waters.[263] One example of some of these perspectives is the description of Mount Simirria in one of Sargon II's inscriptions as follows:

> Mount Simirria, a mighty mountain-peak, which spikes upward like the cutting-edge of a spear, on top of the mountain-range, the dwelling of Belet-ili, rears its head. Above, its peak leans on the heavens, below, its roots reach into the netherworld.[264]

The Egyptians also sometimes thought of mountains as holding up the sky, though other opinions of what held up the sky can be found.

> Above the earth was the expanse of the sky, separated from the earth by the air, and held aloft like a great flat plate by four supports at the corners of the earth. In some representations these supports are shown as poles or forked branches, such as might be used for holding up the corners of an awning. In other instances they were spoken of as being four great mountains.[265]

When we turn our attention from the edges of the known world to the center, we also find several different images. As previously mentioned, from a sociopolitical perspective, it was commonplace for peoples of any area to see themselves and their land or their capital city as being located at the center of the earth.[266] In cosmic terms, the center of the earth was often

---

262. Much of this is derived from the "Sargon Geography"; see Horowitz, *Mesopotamian Cosmic Geography*, 67–95.

263. For discussion, see Horowitz, *Mesopotamian Cosmic Geography*, 331–32. Cf. F. Wiggermann, "Mythological Foundations of Nature," in *Natural Phenomena: Their Meaning, Depiction and Description in the Ancient Near East* (ed. D. J. W. Meijer; Amsterdam: Royal Netherlands Academy of Arts and Sciences, 1992), 286.

264. Translation from Horowitz, *Mesopotamian Cosmic Geography*, 98; see also the description of Mt. Mašu in *Gilgamesh* IX.

265. J. M. Plumley, "The Cosmology of Ancient Egypt," in *Ancient Cosmologies* (ed. C. Blacker and M. Loewe; London: Allen and Unwin, 1975), 20–21; see also Hoffmeier, "Thoughts on Genesis 1 and 2," 39–49.

266. For Jerusalem as the center of the Israelite world, see Ezek 5:5, 38:12. Cf. D. Bodi, *The Book of Ezekiel and the Poem of Erra* (OBO 104; Freiburg: Universitätsverlag / Göttingen: Vandenhoeck & Ruprecht, 1991), 219–30; Stadelmann, *Hebrew Conception of the World*, 147; Clifford, *Creation Accounts*, 135, 183.

conceived of either as a world tree or as a cosmic mountain.[267] The latter is
more prominent in Ugaritic literature, probably because the topography of
Syria is mountainous. The central mountain concept is less prominent in
Egypt and Mesopotamia, because these civilizations were centered on the
plains and in the river basins.[268] In Mesopotamia and Egypt, the cosmic
center was located in the temple,[269] which in Egypt at times contained the
primeval hillock that first emerged from the cosmic waters.[270]

Another perception in the ancient world is that a great tree stands in the
center of the world, sometimes referred to as a "World Tree" or a "Tree of
Life."[271] The idea that a cosmic tree is at the center of the world is a common
motif in the ancient Near East. The tree's roots are fed by the great subterranean ocean, and its top merges with the clouds, thus binding together
the heavens, the earth, and the netherworld. In the *Epic of Erra and Ishum*,
Marduk speaks of the *mesu* tree, the roots of which reach down through the
oceans to the netherworld and the top is which is above the heavens.

> Where is the *mesu*-wood, flesh of the gods,
> The proper insignia of the King of the World,
> The pure timber, tall youth, who is made into a lord,
> Whose roots reach down into the vast ocean
> Through a hundred miles of water, to the base of Arallu,
> Whose topknot above rests on the heaven of Anu?[272]

In the Sumerian epic *Lugalbanda and Enmerkar*, the "eagle-tree" has a
similar role. In Assyrian contexts, the motif of a sacred tree is also well
known. Some scholars have called it a tree of life, and some also associate
it with the world tree. The tree is often flanked by animals or by human or
divine figures. A winged disk is typically located centrally over the top of

---

267. In the Sumerian myth "Lugalbanda and Anzu," these two images are combined; see
H. Vanstiphout, *Epics of Sumerian Kings* (SBLWAW 20; Atlanta: Society of Biblical Literature,
2003), 136–39; R. S. Falkowitz, "Notes on 'Lugalbanda and Enmerkar,'" in *Studies in Literature
from the Ancient Near East* (ed. J. M. Sasson; New Haven, CT: American Oriental Society,
1984), 105. Wiggermann ("Mythological Foundations," 285–86) discusses the "holy mound"
(du$_6$-kù) in Sumerian sources.

268. Clifford, *Cosmic Mountain*, 9–10.

269. Clifford, *Cosmic Mountain*, 25.

270. Clifford, *Cosmic Mountain*, 27–29. See also Keel, *Symbolism*, 113.

271. Several scholarly treatments are more interested in the tree as a symbol of divine order and as representing the king; see S. Parpola, "The Assyrian Tree of Life," *JNES* 52 (1993):
161–208; P. Lapinkivi, *The Sumerian Sacred Marriage in Light of Comparative Evidence* (SAAS
15; Helsinki: Neo-Assyrian Text Corpus Project, 2004), 111–18; M. Henze, *The Madness of Ne-
buchadnezzar: The Ancient Near Eastern Origins and Early History of Interpretation of Daniel
4* (JSJSup 61; Leiden: Brill, 1999), 75–90. Biblical texts that share some of these ideas are Daniel 4 and Ezekiel 31.

272. *Erra and Ishum* (Dalley, *Myths From Mesopotamia*, 291).

the tree. The king is presented as the human personification of this tree. The tree is thought by some to represent the divine world order, but discussion of the tree is absent from ancient Near Eastern texts.[273]

Finally, the earth was believed to be undergirded by pillars but to be supported by the roots of the mountains that reached down into the netherworld. These images must be integrated with the idea that the earth floated on the underground waters.

The Sea

The three kinds of water that were known in ancient thought—the cosmic sea that encircles the land,[274] the waters beneath the earth, and the waters above the earth—were not considered separate, distinct bodies of water.[275] The fact that fresh water and salt water existed was known, but this distinction did not require separation of the bodies of water (after all, fresh water rivers flowed into the salt water seas). Metaphors such as locks, bolts, bars, nets, and so on were used to express the means by which the sea was kept in its place. All of these control features were established and maintained by a deity or deities, who ultimately set the boundaries.[276]

Egyptians viewed the cosmos as "a limitless ocean of dark and motionless water, within which the world of life floats as a sphere of air and light. The texts describe this ocean as existing above the sky."[277]

In the flood traditions of the ancient Near East, the waters that flooded the earth came from a variety of sources.

Atrahasis

Anzu tore the sky with his talons and the flood (*abubu*)[278] came out.[279]
Torrent (*radu*),[280] storm (*mehru*)[281] and flood (*abubu*) came on.[282]

---

273. Parpola, "Assyrian Tree of Life."

274. Seely, "Geographical Meaning," 243; Egyptians at times referred to the Mediterranean as *shenwer*, the "great encircler" (Lesko, "Cosmogonies and Cosmology," 117).

275. Seely, "Geographical Meaning," 253; Horowitz, *Mesopotamian Cosmic Geography*, 325ff.; Tsumura, *Earth and the Waters*, 61. In Mesopotamian literature, Adad was considered the god associated with the flow of water from both above and below. See Weinfeld, "Gen. 7:11," 244–45.

276. Horowitz, *Mesopotamian Cosmic Geography*, 326–27.

277. Allen, *Genesis in Egypt*, 4.

278. Here *abubu* comes from the sky, whereas in other texts it rises from the bowels of the earth; see *CAD* A/1 80.

279. Dalley, *Myths From Mesopotamia*, 31, Atrahasis III iii 7–11.

280. The standard word for rainstorm or cloudburst is *radu*; see *CAD* R 60–61.

281. The term *mehru* is generally associated with wind, dust, and fire, rather than water; see *CAD* M/2 4–6.

282. Dalley, *Myths From Mesopotamia*, 33, Atrahasis III iv 25

Gilgamesh

Erakal pulled out the mooring poles; Ninurta marched on and made the
weirs overflow. [283]

Flood (*abubu*) and tempest (*meḫru*) overwhelmed the land. [284]

In all of these texts, it is the cosmic waters of every sort and from every
source that are involved in the flood. The act of creation had involved setting boundaries for the cosmic waters; in the flood, the restraints were re-
moved, bringing about destruction.

Structure of the Netherworld

In this category, we find the most notable distinctions between Egypt
and the rest of the ancient world, so we will discuss the various geographical regions separately. In Egypt, the place of the dead, Duat, was subterranean and was entered from the western horizon. The Duat was inhabited
by numerous gods, the most important being Anubis and Osiris. The Book
of Nut says: "Every place void of sky and void of land, that is the entire
Duat." [285] This netherworld needed to be crossed at death by every human,
and the eventual goal was to travel with the sun-god to the Field of Reeds
or the Field of Offerings.

The journey of the dead began in the west when each individual entered the netherworld with the sun-god as the sun set. In the New Kingdom
book titled *Amduat*, the netherworld is referred to as the "Great City," and
the gate into it is called the "Swallower of all." [286] The netherworld is first
encountered because it is crossed in the barque of the sun-god. Next, a desert area is encountered, complete with obstacles, including various gates
through which one must pass, darkness, a lake of flames, and serpents. The
middle portion of the netherworld features a water-hole filled with the primeval waters. The barque's movement is threatened by the great chaos serpent, Apophis.

The rest of the ancient world shared a view of the netherworld at variance
with Egypt's perspective; in its broad outlines, the outlook of the remainder of the ancient Near East was fairly homogeneous. In Mesopotamia, the
terms used are KUR when people are involved and ARALI when evil spirits

---

283. *Gilgamesh* XI 102–3; see Dalley, *Myths From Mesopotamia*, 112.
284. *Gilgamesh* XI 129; see Dalley, *Myths From Mesopotamia*, 113.
285. *COS* 1.1.
286. E. Hornung, *The Ancient Egyptian Books of the Afterlife* (Ithaca, NY: Cornell University Press 1999), 34.

are discussed.[287] A Babylonian *kudurru* (boundary marker) from the Kassite period portrays the netherworld as a city. In this city were the palaces of the netherworld deities. Like any other city, it had a sociopolitical hierarchy.[288] Myths such as the *Descent of Ishtar* and the *Gilgamesh Epic* provide information concerning the seven gates through which the dead must pass and describe the treatment of the inhabitants. Entry into the netherworld was through the grave, which explains why proper burial was so important.

Cosmic Geography Conclusions

Modern cosmic geography addresses four general concerns:

1. How the cosmos is arranged (e.g., the position of the solar system in the galaxy, planets in the solar system, continents on the earth's surface)
2. How the cosmos works (e.g., physics: gravity and other forces, laws of motion)
3. How the cosmos originated (e.g., various theories: "big bang," continental drift)
4. What it is made of (e.g., gases of the atmosphere, earth's core, dark matter)

Ancient cosmic geography overlapped with these in some ways, but of course entailed very different conclusions:

1. How the cosmos is arranged (e.g., cosmic waters surrounding land, sun, moon, and stars in the space between sky and earth)
2. How the cosmos works (e.g., sky holding back waters, pillars holding up earth)
3. How it originated (much less on this than modern cosmic geography but factors frequently expressed are the separation of heaven and earth and the emergence of dry land from water)
4. What it is made of (almost no discussion of this; exception: the stone that makes up the pavements of the various levels of heaven; however, this shows more interest in colors than in the material composition of the stone)
5. Corresponding to the modern interest in composition was the ancients' interest in jurisdiction—that is, who was responsible.

---

287. D. Katz, *The Image of the Netherworld in the Sumerian Sources* (Bethesda, MD: CDL, 2003), 58–59.
288. Katz, *Image of the Netherworld*, 113–96.

Interest in the responsible party is absent from modern cosmic geography but was paramount in ancient cosmic geography.

Today, function is the primary focus of architectural design. But whereas our interest in functions is concerned with the mechanics, in the ancient world, the interest was in who is maintaining control. To recite the example adduced above, there is a difference between identifying how a machine works and identifying how a company works. To observe that someone's office is on the top floor is not so much a reflection of the building's physical architecture as it is a statement about the person's position in the company.

To summarize: cosmic geography is concerned with physical arrangement, architectural design, and jurisdiction of the various components of the cosmos. The basic design of ancient Near Eastern cosmic geography shows only minor variations across time and culture, and the interest in jurisdiction is a common denominator. The only variations are which gods are associated with which components. What comment there is on the *origins* of the cosmic architecture speaks to the separation of heaven from earth (not the manufacturing of either) and the emergence of earth from the cosmic waters. These events along with Marduk's splitting of Tiamat are concerned with the establishment of the functional cosmos.

Cosmos, Temple, and Rest

The Cosmic Role of the Temple in the Ancient World

Throughout the ancient world, the temple was a significant part of the cosmic landscape. It was considered to be at the center of the cosmos, the place from which the cosmos was controlled, and a small model of the cosmos—a microcosm. L. Fisher captures many of the relevant issues in his summary of Baal's temple.

> Even as Baal's temple is a microcosm of the world so the temple of Baal in Ugarit was a replica of his temple on Ṣapan and a microcosm (at least according to Ugaritic belief). . . . Hence the new king has a temple which is a microcosm, and the ordering of this temple resembles the creation of the cosmos.[289]

These ideas persist in the cognitive environments of the ancient Near East and will be explored below.

---

289. Fisher, "Creation at Ugarit and in the Old Testament," quotation from p. 318.

The Building of the Temple Is Described in Cosmic Terms

The cosmic role of the temple is consistently identified by its position in the cosmos as described in building accounts: it represents the cosmic mountain that has its head in the heavens and its roots in the netherworld. Examples of this representation have been gathered by V. Hurowitz and demonstrate that this motif extended across all time periods.[290] The earliest surviving example is in the Keš temple hymn, one of the oldest pieces of literature known.[291]

> House Keš, platform of the Land, important fierce bull!
> Growing as high as the hills, embracing the heavens,
> Growing as high as E-kur, lifting its head among the mountains!
> Rooted in the Abzu, verdant like the mountains!

The most extensive temple-building text known from the ancient world is contained in the two cylinders of Gudea, from the early second millennium B.C.E. In the Gudea account, the cosmic positioning of the temple is clear, for example, in cylinder A XXI 19–23:

> They make the house grow like a mountain range,
> Let it soar into the midst of heaven like a cloud.
> They make it lift (its) horns like a bull,
> Make it raise (its) head over all lands like the *gišgana* tree of the Abzu.[292]

An example of the same idea from the Old Babylonian period can be found in the Epilogue to the Code of Hammurapi, where Esagila, the Babylonian Temple of Marduk, is described as a temple with firm foundations like heaven and earth. In the Neo-Assyrian period, a millennium later, Esarhaddon applies the same traditional descriptions with regard to the temple of Assur:

> I raised to heaven the head of Ešarra, my lord Assur's dwelling.
> Above, heavenward, I raised high its head.
> Below, in the underworld I made firm its foundations.[293]

---

290. V. Hurowitz, *I Have Built You an Exalted House: Temple Building in the Bible in Light of Mesopotamia and Northwest Semitic Writings* (JSOTSup 115; Sheffield: Sheffield Academic Press, 1992), 335–37.

291. J. Black et al., *The Literature of Ancient Sumer* (Oxford: Oxford University Press, 2004), 325–30; lines 13–16 are cited here, but the ideas are repeated throughout the piece.

292. D. O. Edzard, *Gudea and His Dynasty* (RIME 3/1; Toronto: University of Toronto Press, 1997), 82. There are numerous other cosmic references throughout. See *COS* 2.155.

293. Hurowitz, *I Have Built*, 245.

A few hundred years later, the tradition is continued in Nabopolassar's Neo-Babylonian account of the rebuilding of Etemenanki, the Temple of Marduk at Babylon:

> To found its foundations
> In the bosom of the netherworld
> And cause its head
> To rival heaven[294]

Finally, Hurowitz observes the relationship in *Enuma Elish* between temples that are built and the various cosmic regions.

> *Enuma Elish* relates how Ea built Apsu—his own (cosmic) temple (I 71–78), how Marduk built Ešarra (IV 141–146), and how all the gods built Babylon and Esagila for Marduk (V 113–VI 75). The temples referred to in these passages are simultaneously earthly temples and cosmic regions associated with various gods.[295]

In cosmic space, the temple is at the center. In cosmic time, it precedes everything else. Thus, J. Levenson terms the temple "protological."[296] This protological role is further attested in the functions that are associated with the temple.

Temples Are Described as Having Cosmic Functions

The cosmic functions of the temple are most often indicated by the names that they are given. Not only are temples built touching the heavens above and the netherworld below (as demonstrated in the last section), which is a matter of cosmic positioning, but they also serve as the foundation for the cosmos or even function as the bond that holds the cosmos together. This concept is expressed in the first line of Gudea Cylinder B, where the temple Gudea builds to Ningirsu in Lagash is identified as the "mooring pole of the land."[297] Toward the end of cylinder B, Ningirsu, speaking to Gudea, suggests that it is the temple that separates heaven and earth, thus associating it with that most primordial act of creation:

> [Gu]dea, you were building my [house] for me,
> And were having [the offices] performed to perfection [for me],
> You had [my house] shine for me
> Like Utu in [heaven's midst],

---

294. Hurowitz, *I Have Built*, 336.
295. Hurowitz, *I Have Built*, 333.
296. J. Levenson, "The Temple and the World," *JR* 64 (1984): 275–98; see p. 283.
297. Edzard, *Gudea and His Dynasty*, 89.

Separating. Like a lofty foothill range,
Heaven from earth.[298]

A variety of cosmic functions are expressed by the names of temples/
ziggurats, as the following list shows:[299]

É.a.ra.li 'House, Netherworld' (13)
É.ab.ša.ga.la 'House which stretches over the midst of the sea' (28)
É.abzu 'House of the Apsu' (30)
É.an.ki 'House of Heaven and the Underworld' (69; see 71)
É.dim.an.ki 'House, Bond/Pole of Heaven and the Underworld' (158)
É.dim.gal.an.na 'House of the great bond of heaven' (161; see 166)
É.du₆.[kalam?].ma 'House, mound of the Land(?)' (176)
É.dur.an.ki 'House, bond of heaven and underworld' (218)
É.giš.hur.an.ki 'House of the ordinances of heaven and underworld'
    (409)
É.giš.lam.šar.šar 'House where heaven and underworld mingle' (417)
É.hur.sag.an.ki.a 'House, mountain of heaven and underworld' (475)
É.ᵍⁱˢkiri₆.mah 'House, grand garden' (649)
É.kun₄.an.kù.ga 'House, pure stairway of heaven' (672)
É.kur 'House, mountain' (677)
É.kur.me.sikil 'House, mountain of pure MES' (686; see 687, 'all MES')
É.lam.ma 'House of the netherworld' (702)
É.me.an.na 'House of the MES of heaven' (747)
É.me.huš.gal.an.ki 'House of the great awesome MES of heaven and
    underworld' (755; see 753–60)
É.me.ur₄.an.na 'House which gathers the MES of heaven' (789)
É.sag.abzu.ta.an.ús 'Foremost house, supporting heaven from apsu'
    (955; see 973, 'supporting from land')
É.šár.ra 'House of the Universe' (1034)
É.te.me.en.an.ki 'House, foundation platform of heaven and
    underworld' (1088)
É.ur₄.(me).imin.an.ki 'House which gathers the seven (MES) of heaven
    and underworld' (1193)

In addition to its role in cosmic geography, the temple also plays a cosmic
role as the source of fertility and provision for the land. A variety of temple
names allude to this: temples are identified as houses of grain, goat's milk,
barley, a sheep-pen, and so on. Three images confirm the central role of the
temple in the way that people experienced their sustenance in the cosmos:

298. Gudea B xx 8–11, translated by T. Jacobsen, *The Harps That Once...* (New Haven, CT:
Yale University Press, 1987), 441–42.
299. Culled from George, *House Most High*; the number of the entry in George's catalog is
given in parentheses.

- The temple is associated with the first land to emerge from the cosmic waters.
- The temple is identified as the place from which fertile waters flow.
- The temple is identified as the place from which the sun rises.

The association with the first dry land to emerge from the cosmic waters is most evident in Egyptian literature.

> The temple recalled a mythical place, the primeval mound. It stood on the first soil that emerged from the primeval waters, on which the creator god stood to begin his work of creation. Through a long chain of ongoing renewals, the present temple was the direct descendant of the original sanctuary that the creator god himself had erected on the primeval mound. An origin myth connecting the structure with creation is associated with each of the larger late temples.[300]

Second, though temples were at times actually built over springs, at other times they simply adopted the motif of being the source of flowing, life-giving waters.

> The temple is often associated with the waters of life which flow forth from a spring within the building itself—or, rather, the temple is viewed as incorporating within itself or as having been built upon such a spring. The reason such springs exist in temples is that they are perceived as the primeval waters of creation, Nun in Egypt, Abzu in Mesopotamia. The temple is thus founded on and stands in contact with the primeval waters.[301]

This ideology is illustrated in the Sumerian myth of *Enki and Ninḫursaǧa*:

> At that moment, on that day, and under that sun, when Utu stepped up into heaven, from the standing vessels (?) on Ezen's (?) shore, from Nanna's radiant high temple, from the mouth of the waters running underground, fresh waters ran out of the ground for her.[302]

In Ugaritic literature, the dwelling place of El is portrayed as being at the source of the waters. This location gives him control of the earth's fertility.

---

300. Assmann, *Search for God*, 38; Compare with Clifford, *Creation Accounts*, 105–6; See also John Lundquist, "What Is a Temple? A Preliminary Typology," in *The Quest for the Kingdom of God* (ed. H. B. Huffmon, F. A. Spina, and A. R. W. Green; Winona Lake, IN: Eisenbrauns, 1983), 206–19, esp. p. 208; Keel (*Symbolism*, 113) demonstrates that this is true of both Egypt and Mesopotamia.

301. Lundquist, "What Is a Temple?" 208.

302. http://etcsl.orinst.ox.ac.uk, *Enki and Ninḫursaǧa* 1.1.1.

The importance of El for the maintenance of order in the cosmos is also displayed in the description of his abode. El was pictured in the Ugaritic texts as dwelling at the center of the universe, where waters merged, authority resided, and order was preserved. The nebulous location and the description of El's house, characteristic of descriptions of the cosmic center, symbolically set it apart as the center of order around which the earth's existence was dependent.[303]

Thus, we can see that these cosmic associations are not merely superficial or metaphorical—they communicate that the central functions of the cosmos are carried out from the temple, the control room of the cosmos from which order in the cosmos is maintained. Fertility flows from this cosmic center to the surrounding territory.[304] This idea is frequently represented iconographically in the portrayal of a deity holding a jar from which waters flow.[305]

Finally, the temple is also sometimes viewed as the place from which the sun rises as in this example from the Sumerian temple hymns:

> O primeval place, deep mountain founded in an artful fashion, shrine, terrifying place lying in a pasture, a dread whose lofty ways none can fathom, Ĝišbanda, neck-stock, meshed net, shackles of the great underworld from which none can escape, your exterior is raised up, prominent like a snare, your interior is where the sun rises, endowed with widespreading plenty.[306]

This idea is even more evident in Egyptian literature, for which the sun is more central than is the case in Mesopotamian literature.

> The *naos* in which the cult statue rests is the remotest part of the sky, where the gods and the goddesses dwell. The doors of the shrine are the celestial gates through which the sun god passes in the morning.[307]

---

303. Handy, *Among the Host of Heaven*, 90. Handy cites Ugaritic text KTU 1.4 IV 20–22.

304. Hurowitz, *I Have Built You an Exalted House*, 322–23.

305. Many of these are represented in the sketches in the back of T. Ornan, *The Triumph of the Symbol* (OBO 213; Fribourg: Academic Press / Göttingen: Vandenhoeck & Ruprecht, 2005), ##1, 10, 11, 17, 18, 82, 102; in addition, see the fresco from the Mari palace and several other examples illustrated in L. Stager, "Jerusalem as Eden," *BAR* 26/3 (2000): 38–41; Keel, *Symbolism*, 140–44; see also the façade of the Kassite-period Inanna Temple at Uruk, which features gods in niches that are separated by the flowing water motif: P. Amiet, *Art of the Ancient Near East* (New York: Abrams, 1980), #84. Though this is usually a divine motif, Gudea is sometimes portrayed in the same way (pp. 52, 376).

306. http://etcsl.orinst.ox.ac.uk, Temple Hymns, 4.80.1

307. Assmann, *Search for God*, 36.

As these examples make quite clear, the central functions of the cosmos are associated with the temple.[308]

Temple as a Model of the Cosmos with Cosmic Symbolism

One of the most significant evidences of the intrinsic relationship between cosmos and temple is the fact that temples were designed to be models of the cosmos. Given their central role in the cosmos and their cosmic functions, this is no surprise.[309] Thus, for example, C. Meyers notes that "It is axiomatic that every sanctuary is constituted as an *imago mundi*, with the cosmos as paradigmatic model."[310]

> Sanctuaries are structures which, in attempting to render permanent the experience of the holy, are characterized by the homologizing of their architectural features to the cosmos. The space enclosed by the structure thus shares the same sacred reality as the primeval world structure.[311]

This same symbolism is also evident in Egypt: Assmann affirms that the cosmological significance, especially of late Egyptian temples, is "the best known of all their aspects and functions."[312]

> Essentially, the floor of these later temples represented the earth, and the ceiling the sky. Columns took the form of plants rising from the earth, and the dados of the walls were decorated with marsh plants or with processions of "fecundity figures," personifications of telluric fruitfulness that always face the inner part of the temple, bearing offerings. As the sky, the ceilings were decorated with stars or with astronomical representations. Between the floor and the ceiling, between earth and sky, stretched the decorations on the walls with their endless cult scenes filling this stony cosmos *in effigie* with action and life.[313]

He concludes that the temple "*was* the world that the omnipresent god filled to its limits."[314] Indeed, the temple is, for all intents and purposes, the

---

308. Note that the same is true of Baal's Temple at Ugarit: "Baal's temple and kingship will bring fertility and cosmic harmony. If this is the function of the heavenly temple it is also the function of the earthly shrine which represents the heavenly sphere" (Clifford, *Cosmic Mountain*, 106).

309. G. W. Ahlström, "Heaven on Earth—At Hazor and Arad," in *Religious Syncretism in Antiquity* (ed. B. A. Pearson; Missoula, MT: Scholars Press, 1975), 67–69; Clifford, *Cosmic Mountain*, 27.

310. C. L. Meyers, *The Tabernacle Menorah* (ASOR Diss 2; Missoula, MT: Scholars Press, 1976), 171.

311. Meyers, *The Tabernacle Menorah*, 171.

312. Assmann, *Search for God*, 35. He indicates that cosmological connection of the divine and the temple first becomes evident in the Ramesside period (p. 37).

313. Assmann, *Search for God*, 35.

314. Assmann, *Search for God*, 37.

cosmos.[315] This interrelationship makes it possible for the temple to be the center from which order in the cosmos is maintained.[316]

Cosmic Origins Are Connected to Temple Building

The interrelationship between cosmos and temple is also evidenced by the fact that accounts of origins often include accounts of temple building, with temple building at times being at the climax of the origin account or even serving as the purpose for creation. Assmann goes so far as to assert that "each temple was not only the center, but also the origin of the world."[317] Clifford similarly declares that the temple is "the concrete expression of the finality of creation."[318] And Coote and Ord make the observation that the connection between temple and cosmos is based on the ancients' view of reality.

> The whole idea of creating a "world" depends on the scope of the world as a person conceives of it. Since creation in the ancient Near East is viewed from a particular cult setting, by far the most common concept of creation is the creation of the world with the urban temple at its center and as its most important element. The temple is the focal point of creation in nearly every account available to us.[319]

Early evidence may be found in the Sumerian Hymn to E-engura, Enki's Temple at Eridu dating to the Ur III period.

> When the destinies had been fixed for all that had been engendered (by An),
> When An had engendered the year of abundance,
> When humans broke through the earth's surface like plants,
> Then built the Lord of Abzu, King Enki,
> Enki, the Lord who decides destinies,
> His house of silver and lapis lazuli.[320]

---

315. Assmann, *Search for God*, 35–36.

316. Fisher, "Creation at Ugarit and in the Old Testament," 320

317. Assmann, *Search for God*, 39. Assmann's generalization is valid despite the fact that temple building is not usually a part of cosmogonic texts in Egypt. *The Instruction of Merikare* mentions shrine building in connection to creation (line 135), but with a different focus.

318. Clifford, *Creation Accounts*, 61.

319. Coote and Ord, *In the Beginning*, 6. Even if the last sentence is an overstatement, the connection between temple and creation is a commonplace. It should also be noted that Coote and Ord attribute the account of Genesis 1 specifically to the cult of the late-sixth-century Aaronids in Persian Babylon and in Jerusalem (p. 49; but this conclusion derives from literary-critical analysis that has little bearing on our discussion here, and in any case I do not find this specific conclusion particularly persuasive).

320. Clifford. *Creation Accounts*, 29–30.

Here, the building of the temple coincides with the activities of creation. The absence of a temple is sometimes noted as part of the description of the precreation condition. This is clearest in the preamble to a prayer that concerns the founding of Eridu:[321]

> No holy house, no house of the gods, had been built in a pure place;
> No reed had come forth, no tree had been created;
> No brick had been laid, no brickmold had been created;
> No house had been built, no city had been created;
> No city had been built, no settlement had been founded;
> Nippur had not been built, Ekur had not been created;
> Uruk had not been built, Eanna had not been created;
> The depths had not been built, Eridu had not been created;
> No holy house, no house of the gods, no dwelling for them had been created.
> All the world was sea,
> The spring in the midst of the sea was only a channel,
> Then was Eridu built, Esagila was created.[322]

The poem proceeds to describe Marduk's settling the gods into their dwelling places and then creating people and animals and creating the courses of the Tigris and Euphrates. Lest this description be thought only a late development, one need only consult *Enuma Elish*, where temple building is clearly the climax and perhaps even the purpose of creation.[323] Here again, the building of Marduk's Temple is sandwiched between the organization of the macrocosm and the remainder of the creative acts.[324]

In another text, a prayer inscribed on a foundation brick memorializing the founding of a temple, it is obvious that the cosmos and temple were considered to be inseparable parts of a single whole and have origins that are virtually simultaneous.

> When Anu, Enlil, and Ea had a (first) idea of heaven and earth,
> They found a wise means of providing support of the gods:
> They prepared, in the land, a pleasant dwelling,
> And the gods were installed (?) in this dwelling:
> Their principal temple.[325]

---

321. It is difficult to date the prayer. The copy we have is Seleucid (Clifford, *Creation Accounts*, 62), but Horowitz thinks it derives from a Sumerian original (*Mesopotamian Cosmic Geography*, 129–31), so it is likely that the text is much older than the extant copy.

322. Foster, *Before the Muses*, 488.

323. Hurowitz, *I Have Built*, 94; Hurowitz also notes that the connection between creation and temple building is also present in Egyptian texts.

324. Clifford. *Creation Accounts*, 64.

325. Clifford, *Creation Accounts*, 61.

This close connection between cosmogony and temple building is present throughout the ancient Near East: temples were considered primordial, and descriptions of cosmic origins frequently included a description of or reference to temple building.

The Cosmos as a Temple

We have seen that the temple is equated with the cosmos in the ancient world in a variety of ways. The next question to consider is whether the reverse is also true: is the cosmos as a whole ever portrayed as a temple? J. Levenson has drawn a distinction between the priestly theology reflected in Genesis 1, which sees the temple as the world, and the perspective of Third Isaiah, which sees the world as a sanctuary.[326] Is the latter concept—the created world as sanctuary—found in the ancient world in general? Levenson has argued that cosmos and temple are congeneric and homologized concepts in the ancient world. His conclusions have been shown to be true of the ancient Near East in the above discussions. The two are congeneric in that their origins are linked (e.g., Marduk creates the world then builds his temple). They are homologized[327] in that the temple can be considered a microcosm or a model that is described using cosmic symbolism, with the result that the divine presence and activity in the cosmos is equivalent to the divine presence and activity in the temple.

Thus, the temple may be central to the structure and origins of the cosmos and may be constructed at the time when the cosmos is created, but these data fall short of suggesting that the cosmos itself, as a whole, *is* a temple. Various temples represent different parts of the cosmos (E-apsu, Esharra) and thus could be referred to as cosmic temples; however, this fact does not establish the conclusion that the cosmos is viewed as a temple in the ancient world.

In Egypt, we might go so far as to suggest that the entire land of Egypt in some sense was viewed as a temple.

> As lords of the cities and proprietors of huge landed estates, the deities dwelled in castles on their "primeval mounds," determining the

---

326. Levenson, "Temple and World," 296.

327. The distinction between homology and metaphor is an important one. A metaphor is built on an arbitrary point of comparison that generally only goes one direction. Love could be a river, or a rock, or a rainbow depending on what point was to be made. But a river is not love. Homology identifies an element that is essential rather than arbitrary, and the identification goes both ways. The cosmos *is* a temple; the temple *is* the cosmos. For this important distinction, see E. N. Ortlund, *Theophany and Chaoskampf: The Interpretation of Theophanic Imagery in the Baal Epic, Isaiah, and the Twelve* (Piscataway, NJ: Gorgias Press, 2010), 29–30.

appearance of the land so exclusively that it was possible to conceive of Egypt as a single huge temple, the "temple of the entire world."[328]

But this comment only refers to the centrality and significance of the land as temple for Egypt rather than encompassing the entire world. In the ancient Near East, the concept of temple universal was not a likely scenario for several reasons. First, any god who claimed the entire cosmos as his temple would have left no temple for any other god. Such an extreme level of imperialism among the gods would not have been acceptable. In *Enuma Elish*, Marduk's Temple could be central but not universal. Second, in the ancient Near East, the temple was understood as the world of the gods, and people were always intended to serve the gods, from their domain, outside. This understanding requires that there be an "outside."

Despite these objections, it nonetheless can be affirmed that creation texts do follow the model of temple-building texts and, in this way, at least, they imply that the cosmos is conceived to be a temple.[329]

Divine Rest and Temples in Cosmogonies

Divine rest is portrayed as occurring in a number of different contexts in ancient Near Eastern cosmogonies.[330] Aside from the occasional text in which rest refers to an inactive stupor,[331] divine rest generally represents a state that has been achieved through a particular action that was undertaken as a response to a condition or situation that prior to the divine action was usually viewed as unacceptable. The condition in each case represents something that prevents rest. The action indicates how rest is achieved, and the state describes the type of rest anticipated or enjoyed. The common denominator in most of these cases is that divine rest provides a sense of security. When the situation among the gods or in the larger cosmos is secure, deity may rest—regardless of whether the rest means that he/she is thereby free to do nothing, to socialize, to enjoy life, or to do the work of running the cosmos unimpeded. The location where this rest will be experienced is, of course, the temple, the palace home of the god, where the deity

---

328. Assmann, *Search for God*, 27.

329. Hurowitz, *I Have Built*, 242.

330. B. F. Batto, "The Sleeping God: An Ancient Near Eastern Motif of Divine Sovereignty," *Bib* 68 (1987): 153–77. Cf. A. Mrozek, "The Motif of the Sleeping Divinity," *Bib* 80 (1999): 415–19.

331. For example, Ea's imposition of a stupor on Apsu and Mummu, *Enuma Elish* I 63–72.

Table 3.2.

	Condition	Mechanism	State
1.	General activity	Go to bed	Sleep
2.	Exile, unsettled	Build temple	Home
3.	Cosmic disorder	Organize cosmos	Cosmic rule from temple
4.	Hard labor; social disorder	Create people or punish people	Peace, leisure, downtime
5.	Battle	Warfare and victory	Social rule from temple

may enjoy leisure, social activity, and rule.[332] The typical combinations of condition—mechanism—state can be represented as in table 3.2 (above).[333] Before discussing each category, we must look at rest in *Enuma Elish* as a whole, because it has such a wide representation of these categories.

Deities already at rest (category 1) become disturbed

- Tiamat (I 19–28) is disturbed by the uproar of other gods, preventing her sleep
- Apsu and Mummu (I 37–38, 50) are upset by the uproar of other gods, preventing sleep
- Tiamat and her cohorts (I 108–10, 116, 120, 122) are disturbed by Marduk's playing with four winds

Deities are given rest (category 4) from hard labor

- Through creation of people (VI 8, 12–14, 34–36; VI 133–34)

Deities on whom rest is imposed (by death or imprisonment)

- Apsu and Mummu (I 63–72), by Ea
- Tiamat (anticipated in II 150), by Marduk with Ea's help

Deities anticipate rest for themselves and being able to provide rest for Marduk (combination of 3 and 4) in temples in the aftermath of victory, organization of cosmos, and Marduk's kingship

- V 138 a stopping place
- VI 51–54 stopping place to visit

332. A modern analogy is, perhaps, the U.S. White House, which has both living quarters and office space but most importantly, the Oval Office, the seat of executive functions in the American government (in Mesopotamian terms, the place from which destinies are decreed).

333. Some texts feature several of these categories and at times even mingle them. *Enuma Elish*, for example, evidences five of the six categories.

- VI 57–64 Marduk's shrine built
- VI 64–65 Marduk dwells in sublimity
- VI 68 Anunna gods' shrines
- VII 10 purification of shrines

Deities seek rest (categories 3 and/or 5) through conflict

- Ea defeats Apsu and Mummu (I 67–70, 72–74), founds temple (I 71, 75–78)
- Marduk, on behalf of the council, defeats Tiamat and Qingu (IV 95–140), founds Esharra temple for Enlil (IV 142–46) and Esagila for himself (V 122), from which he rules (V 124) and where the other gods can visit, relax, and socialize (V 125–30)

We will now consider each category and texts in addition to *Enuma Elish* that illustrate it.

General Activity → Sleep.   In Egyptian texts, the sleep of the gods is part of their daily routine and is attested primarily in ritual rather than narrative contexts.[334] In narrative contexts in Mesopotamia, this category of rest is seen as an initial state of disengagement that is disturbed by some sort of unrest, from complaints to outright revolt. In these initial situations, the gods can be described as negligent or unresponsive at best and lazy or comatose at worst.

> a. *Enki and Ninmaḫ.*   In this Sumerian myth, Enki is so deeply asleep in his temple in the *apsu* that he is not only undisturbed by the loud complaints of the gods but cannot be aroused to deal with the situation.

> a. *Atrahasis.*   Early in the epic, the overworked gods conspire to rebel and come to Enlil in the middle of the night, when it is no surprise that he is sleeping.[335] This is neither neglect nor laziness, since it is the normal time for sleep.

Exile, Unsettled → Home.   In some texts, the god has no temple (either because it has fallen into ruin, been destroyed, or never was built) and

---

334. The focus of this section will be on Mesopotamia, because in Egyptian literature this motif is nearly absent. In Egypt, the gods are awakened each morning, and there are liturgies for this process, such as the *Daily Ritual of the Temple of Amun-Re at Karnak* (see COS 1.34). See also the general acknowledgment of the Egyptian motif of divine rest in temples, referred to by M. Weinfeld ("Sabbath, Temple and the Enthronement of the Lord: The Problem of the Sitz im Leben of Genesis 1:1–2:3," in *Mélanges bibliques et orientaux en l'honneur de M. Henri Cazelles* [ed. A. Caquot and M. Delcor; Neukirchen-Vluyn: Neukirchener Verlag / Kevelaer: Butzon & Bercker, 1981], 501–12, esp. p. 502).

335. Lambert and Millard, *Atra-Hasis*, I ii 70–73 (p. 47).

therefore is without creature comforts, but, more importantly, he is without a palace that would identify his status and authenticate his rule.[336] Temple building provides a place of rest and is often referred to in hymnic literature. Some of the most famous temple-building texts, such as the Ugaritic *Baal Epic* and Gudea's building of a temple for Ningirsu focus on precisely this kind of divine rest.

Cosmic Disorder → Orderly Operation, Cosmic Rule. After cosmic order is achieved, the next natural step is to build a temple as a place from which this order may be sustained. N.-E. Andreasen summarizes the connection between temple and cosmic stability.

> We can say then that the gods seek rest, and that their rest implies stability for the world order. The gods rest because they want to see the world ordered. A chaotic world brings chaos into the pantheon itself and vice versa.[337]

The temple is a perquisite of the deity who has achieved ruling status. Marduk's defeat of Tiamat and the subsequent building of his temple referred to in the treatment of *Enuma Elish* above is the most prominent example of this motif, but allusions to it can be seen throughout ancient Near Eastern literature. So, for example, in Athirat's hymnic response to El's decree that a temple be built for Baal, she states that in the temple Baal will continue his work of imposing the order that was initiated by Baal's defeat of his enemies.[338]

In this category is one of the only indications of divine rest in Egyptian literature (aside from the ritual awakening of the gods mentioned earlier), in the *Memphite Theology:*

> So has Ptah come to rest after his making everything and every divine
>   speech as well,
> Having given birth to the gods,
> Having made their villages,

---

336. It is often difficult to distinguish whether the deity has no home at all or simply lacks one appropriate for his standing. See the discussion in M. Tsevat, "A Window for Baal's House: The Maturing of a God," in *Studies in the Bible and the Ancient Near East: Presented to Samuel E. Loewenstamm on His Seventieth Birthday* (ed. Y. Avishur and J. Blau; Jerusalem: Rubenstein, 1978), 151–61.

337. N.-E. Andreasen, *The Old Testament Sabbath: A Tradition-Historical Investigation* (SBLDS; Missoula, MT: Society of Biblical Literature, 1972), 182.

338. CAT 4 V 6–9. S. B. Parker, *Ugaritic Narrative Poetry* (SBLWAW 9; Atlanta: Scholars Press, 1997), 129; see R. Clifford, "The Temple in the Ugaritic Myth of Baal," in *Symposia Celebrating the 75th Anniversary of the American Schools of Oriental Research* (ed. F. M. Cross; Cambridge: American Schools of Oriental Research, 1979), 137–45.

Having founded their nomes,
Having set the gods in their cult places,
Having made sure their bread-offerings,
Having founded their shrines,
Having made their bodies resemble what contents them. [339]

In Sumerian literature, the idea is found in the Kesh Temple Hymn.

House . . . inspiring great awe, called with a mighty name by An; house . . . whose fate is grandly determined by the Great Mountain Enlil! House of the Anuna gods possessing great power, which gives wisdom to the people; house, reposeful dwelling of the great gods! House, which was planned together with the plans of heaven and earth, . . . with the pure divine powers; house which underpins the Land and supports the shrines! [340]

This sort of rest is associated not with disengagement but with engagement in the primary work that each deity must do.

Hard Labor, Social Disorder → Leisure, Relaxation Time, and Peace. When we think of the temple in terms of providing living quarters for the deity, we can understand divine rest in terms of leisure time, personal time (e.g., with the god's consort), social time (with other visiting gods), and sleeping time. These are private activities of the gods during which subordinates should be reluctant to intrude. This sort of rest is characterized by disengagement in the form of "down time"—that is, time not engaged in the deity's primary work. In several of the myths, this rest is disrupted by complaint or rebellion or is impossible to experience because of the god's heavy work load. Thus, in *Atrahasis*, the working gods cannot experience any rest because of the hard labor with which they are burdened. Their rest is achieved when people, who take on the workload previously shouldered by the gods, are created. Later in *Atrahasis*, the social disorder is not among the gods but among people and eventuates in the flood.

The [land] was bellowing [like a bull],
The gods got disturbed with [their uproar].
[Enlil heard] their noise
[and addressed] the great gods,
"The noise of mankind [had become too intense for me],
[With their uproar] I am deprived of sleep." [341]

---

339. Allen, *Genesis in Egypt*, 44. Cf. *COS* 1.15; column 59.
340. http://etcsl.orinst.ox.ac.uk, 4.80.2, D.58A–F.
341. Lambert and Millard, *Atra-Hasis*, 67, 73 (I vii 354–59 and II i 3–8).

The *Poem of Erra and Ishum* likewise cites human noise as disrupting the rest of the gods.

> Do a favour to the Anunnaki who love silence!
> Sleep no longer pours over the Anunnaki, because of people's noise.
> Cattle are trampling down the pastureland, the life of the country.
> The farmer weeps bitterly over his [yield].
> The lion and the wolf lay low Shakkan's cattle.
> The shepherd prays to you for his sheep, he cannot sleep by day nor by
>   night. [342]

Battle → Victory, Social Rule.   The last category deals with cases in which social disorder among the gods actually leads to armed conflict. Aside from *Enuma Elish*, the only extant ancient Near Eastern text that connects temple rest and combat is the Ugaritic Baal cycle.

Categories 1, 2, and 4 assume that gods live more or less as humans and have needs as humans do. Categories 4 and 5 assume a system that includes multiple gods in relationship with one another and at times in conflict with one another over jobs and over who is in charge among the gods. Categories 3 and 5 are sometimes connected to cosmogonies, but category 4 is most often connected to anthropogeny.

We can see from these examples that gods rest in temples and that the temples are considered the control room of the cosmos. Rest is *not* engagement in the control of the cosmos but it provides for the life of the gods so that they can maintain the order that has been established. In this way, 'rest' is multifaceted: it provides opportunity for both disengagement from labor or activity and for engagement in the activities connected with ritual and rule. Rest can be in the deity's private chambers or on his dais or throne. [343] Rest while on the dais/throne is illustrated in the following hymn.

> When in your precinct and shrine the Ibgal you regulate the divine or-
> dinances like the divine powers of An, when you regulate the heavenly
> ordinances like the divine powers of Enki and cause awe of you to reach
> up to the heavens, then your seat is on the . . . dais on the terrace by your
> Gate of Four Faces. [344]

---

342. S. Dalley, *Myths from Mesopotamia* (*I 81–86 on 288).

343. Hurowitz, *I Have Built*, 330. Note Hurowitz's citation of a prayer by *kalu* priests during a building ritual that refers to the time "when Anu built in the land a dais for the rest of their heart."

344. http://etcsl.orinst.ox.ac.uk: A hymn to Inana as Ninegala (Inana D) (4.07.4), line 48.

It is from this throne in the temple that the deity issues decrees and judgments.

> In the E-tar-sirsir, founded for you by An, you decide the fate of all the countries; you, my lady, render verdicts and decree judgments. Bau, in the E-tar-sirsir, founded for you by An, you decide the fate of all the countries; you, Bau, render verdicts and decree judgments.[345]

Texts such as these two illustrate the fact that, in the ancient Near Eastern cognitive environment, rest can be combined with cosmic rule. When a modern candidate for political office ambitiously anticipates residing in the governor's mansion or the White House (or their equivalents in other political systems), he or she might think about sleeping there, residing there, hosting and presiding over banquets, and receiving important guests—all of these are the trappings and prerogatives of rule, and the same is true of temples in the ancient world. Sleeping and entertaining are not the goals of having the job; they are simply the perquisites of office.

A final note: in both historical and mythological contexts, the focal point of temple building is the moment when the temple becomes functional. In several key contexts, the number seven is prominent in temple building. In the Baal cycle, the temple becomes increasingly functional over the course of the seven days during which it is built. Fire does the work of fashioning Baal's house for six days.

> [Quickly] he builds his house,
> [Quickly] he erects his palace,
> He [se]ends to Lebanon for its wood,
> To [Sir]yon for its choicest cedar.
> A fire is set in the house,
> A f[l]ame in the palace
> There! For a day and a second,
> A fire burns in the house,
> A flame in the palace.
> For a third and a fourth,
> [A f]ire burns in the house,
> A flame in the palace.
> For a fifth and a si[x]th,
> A fire burns [in] the house,
> A flame a[mid the pa]lace.
> Then on the seventh d[ay],
> The fire leaves the house,
> The f[lam]e, the palace.

---

345. http://etcsl.orinst.ox.ac.uk: an *adab* to Bau for Luma (Luma A) from Lagash.

The silver had turned to plates,
The gold had turned to bricks.
Mightiest Baal rejoices:
"My house I have built of silver,
My palace of gold."[346]

A lavish banquet is then prepared to celebrate the building's completion. Some interpreters have concluded that the Baal cycle implies a cosmogony, because the text includes this temple-building scene.[347] This conclusion remains controversial, but a conclusion on the matter does not seriously affect our discussion here. However, it is safe to conclude that, regardless of whether the initiation of temple functions is connected with cosmogony or not, seven days is an appropriate period of time for temple building or inauguration.[348]

In most temple-building texts, the temple becomes functional by means of a dedication ceremony. Prior to the dedication, it is nothing but timber, masonry, cloth, precious metals, and so on, that craftsmen have prepared. The temple becomes operational at the time of dedication by virtue of the fact that its functions are named (and thus come into existence), its accessories (functional furniture and trappings) are put in place, the priests are vested and commissioned (installed to begin the rituals), and, most importantly, at the climax, the deity is brought into his/her residence in the central cella. Only then is the temple functional; only then is it real; only then is it a temple. It is at this point that the deity is able to settle into his/her new home and is able to begin the job of ruling the cosmos and maintaining order.[349] V. Hurowitz has conveniently gathered all the information on temple dedications in the ancient world, so there is no need to repeat the details here that he provides.[350] We can be content to summarize the most significant of his findings, especially in terms of their pertinence to this study.

---

346. CAT 1.4 VI 16–38; translation by M. Smith in Parker, *Ugaritic Narrative Poetry*, 133–34.

347. Fisher, "Creation at Ugarit," 319.

348. Hurowitz lists other temple dedications, and the number *seven* is prevalent, though there are variations (e.g., Esarhaddon's dedication of a temple in Assur in the course of 3 days and Assurnasirpal's dedication of Kalhu, which took 10 days; see *I Have Built*, 275–76. His appendix on pp. 280–82 provides the entire list of more than 40 dedications. Another striking 7-day festival is an Old Babylonian ritual from Larsa: see E. C. Kingsbury, "A Seven Day Ritual in the Old Babylonian Cult at Larsa," *HUCA* 34 (1963): 1–34. There is no evidence that this is a temple-dedication ritual; in fact, each day focuses on a different god. Intriguingly, the rituals for each new day also begin in the evening (p. 26). On p. 27, Kingsbury lists several other 7-day rituals.

349. Hurowitz, *I Have Built*, 267.

350. This section assumes the data that Hurowitz presents throughout his study.

By far the most extensive temple-building account in ancient literature is inscribed on the two cylinders of Gudea; it describes the entire process of his founding of Eninnu, the Temple of Ningirsu at Lagash, from conception to dedication.[351] The seven-day dedication ceremony that Gudea undertakes[352] primarily features rituals and prayers, but it has significance here because it recounts the transformation of the temple as it becomes the place of divine rest and the place from which the cosmos is controlled. The inscription alludes (primarily in the opening hymn, B i 1–11) to the cosmic functions of the temple. Much more time is spent on the installation of the functionaries, whose presence allows the temple to be operational (the concern here is at the ritual level).[353]

> (Proudly) he [Ningirsu] lifted the head in great office,
> And ranged the gods, housekeepers, and (estate) functionaries,
> His court and household,
> One after the other, for the Eninnu close.[354]

The list begins with key staff members (B vi 11–xii 25), then proceeds to accoutrements and furniture (B xiii 11–xiv 24). The next section refers to the fish filling the rivers and lakes (B xiv 25–xv 3) and the animals filling the land B xv 5–12) and concludes with the entrance of the prince, Gudea (B xvi 1). Then attention turns to Ningirsu, in the throne room:

> Its throne set up in the assembly of the administrators
> Was (like) An's holy throne resting among the stars. (B xvi 18)

The 7-day dedication ceremony thus proclaims the functions of the temple, inducts the personnel, installs the furniture, and has the human ruler enter and meet with the deity, who has taken up his rest on the dais in order to begin ruling from the temple.

---

351. See translations by R. Averbeck, *COS* 2.155; D. O. Edzard, *Gudea and His Dynasty* (RIME 3/1; Toronto: University of Toronto Press, 1997), 69–101; Jacobsen, *The Harps That Once . . .* , 386–444; and on Oxford's Sumerian literature Web site, http://etcsl.orinst.ox.ac.uk, 2.1.7. Extended treatment can be found in Hurowitz, *I Have Built*, 33–57.

352. B xvii 19; Hurowitz, *I Have Built*, 271.

353. It should be noted that dedication texts are not the only ones to address the functions and functionaries of a temple. The Sumerian *Hymn to Keš* also begins with the functions of the temple (through the fourth section), then moves on to the functionaries (in this case, the various personnel that serve the temple).

354. B vi 7–10, translated by Jacobsen, *The Harps That Once . . .* , 430.

Conclusions

We have seen that one of the roles that the ancient Near Eastern temple played was to take a significant functional part in cosmology. Individual temples were designed as models of the cosmos, but in addition, and more importantly, the temple was viewed as the hub of the cosmos. It was built in conjunction with the creation of the cosmos. Gods took up their rest in the temple for a variety of reasons, one of which was the ruling of the cosmos as they continued to maintain the order that had been established and to exercise control of destinies.

The association among the temple, the installation of the god in the temple, and the god's control of the cosmos from the temple is nowhere more dramatically presented than in the Akitu festival, which celebrates the renewal of rule and order through the ceremonial reinstallation of the deity in the temple.[355]

> The Babylonian Akitu does exemplify a cosmogonic New Year's festival: through its rites, the Esagila temple, and hence the world, are symbolically razed, purified, and re-created; kingship, and hence cosmic order, are abolished and renewed. Thus the Akitu festival also effects a return to the time of creation, which culminated in the enthronement of Marduk and the construction by the gods of Marduk's temple in Babylon, the Esagila.[356]

The Akitu is thus a testimony to the centrality of the temple and the rest of the deity in the temple, and the rest of the deity symbolizes that the order initially established in the cosmos by the deity is regularly renewed and constantly maintained.

Summary of the Cosmological Cognitive Environment of the Ancient Near East

- The precosmic world was understood not as a world absent of matter but a world absent of function, order, diversity, and identity.

---

355. Even though 11 days of activities are prescribed for the Akitu, several scholars indicate that the first 3 days are preliminary to the actual festival, which begins on day 4, and is therefore an 8-day festival. See K. van der Toorn, "The Babylonian New Year Festival: New Insights from the Cuneiform Texts and Their Bearing on Old Testament Study," in *Congress Volume: Leuven, 1989* (VTSup 43; Leiden: Brill, 1991): 332 n. 7.

356. B. Sommer, "The Babylonian Akitu Festival: Rectifying the King or Renewing the Cosmos?" *JANES* 27 (2000): 81–95; quotation, p. 85. Note that not all agree with this assessment of the Akitu; see van der Toorn, "Babylonian New Year Festival," 331–44, although van der Toorn's main objection is to the reenactment of the cosmic battle motif, which, however, does not need to be assumed in order for cosmic order to be addressed.

- Depictions of the state of things before and after creation, between which the acts of creation serve as transition, focus on origins of function and order, and the verbs used to describe creation operate in the same semantic realm.
- The things created in the related realms of cosmos and culture are *functions*, not objects.
- In the context of creation, causes are entirely in the realm of the gods and are characterized by a teleological perspective that transcends and virtually ignores the material, physical, natural world.
- Reality and existence in the ancient cognitive environment are best described as comprising function and order, not matter and objects.
- The acts of creation were naming, separating, and temple building.
- In the ancient world, something was created when it was given a function.
- The functions of the cosmos and culture are all relative to people.
- The functions of the ordered cosmos were defined first and foremost by the MES, which, unlike the cosmic waters, did not exist prior to the gods' creative activity; on the other hand, these functions were not instituted by the gods.
- The operational dichotomy was static (the MES) versus dynamic (the destinies).
- Decreeing destinies was both functional in nature and at the same time an act of creation and rule.
- Exercise of control over the destinies and the rule of the world, including both the gods and eventually humans, originates in the temple, which is ordained as the control room of the cosmos.
- The MES that most frequently describe the functional cosmos—time, weather, and fertility—are generally portrayed as being organized and delegated by the gods.
- The gods were inside the cosmos, not outside it.
- Gods are involved in cosmic origins in relation to the functions of the cosmos both in the cosmogonic/theogonic model and in the political/bureaucratic model.
- Theomachy is ancillary to cosmogony and appears only idiosyncratically in ancient Near Eastern texts.
- Accounts of human origins focus on their role in the cosmos, whether in terms of their status or their function.
- Physical materials mentioned in the creation of humans have archetypal, not material significance.

- The image of a god is related to the deity's role and is mostly found in the royal ideology of the political/bureaucratic model, where it confirms the king as having divine functions.
- People and gods work together to ensure the preservation of the order and smooth operation of the cosmos (Great Symbiosis).
- Cosmic geography is concerned with physical arrangement, architectural design, and jurisdiction over the various areas.
- The description of the origins of the architecture of the cosmos focuses on separating heaven from earth (not manufacturing either of them) and on earth's emerging from the cosmic waters.
- Individual temples are designed to be models of the cosmos.
- The temple is viewed as the hub of the cosmos.
- The temple is built in conjunction with and parallel to the creation of the cosmos.
- Gods take up their rest in the temple for a variety of reasons, one of which is to permit the rule of the cosmos as they continue to maintain the order that has been established and continue to exercise control of the destinies.

Chapter 4

Genesis 1

Now that I have established that that there was a common cosmological cognitive environment throughout the ancient Near East that provided a common context for ancient peoples' ideas of cosmology and creation, I can turn our attention to Genesis 1 to examine just how much of the ancient Near Eastern cognitive environment is also observable in this core Israelite text. In what follows, I will investigate the text of Genesis 1 systematically, identifying the ground that it holds in common with other ancient Near Eastern literature as well as its distinctives.

In A. Heidel's groundbreaking comparative analysis of the relationship between Genesis and Babylonian literature, he cites a clear distinction between the two: the biblical account actually gives account of material creation but the Babylonian account only offers details of organization.

> Moreover, a comparison of the Babylonian creation story with the first chapter of Genesis makes the sublime character of the latter stand out in even bolder relief. *Enuma Elish* refers to a multitude of divinities emanating from the elementary world-matter; the universe has its origin in the generation of numerous gods and goddesses personifying cosmic spheres or forces in nature, and in the orderly and purposeful arrangement of pre-existent matter; the world is not *created* in the biblical sense of the term but *fashioned* after the manner of human craftsmen.[1]

This distinction between what we might call material origins and functional origins has been repeated in the literature many times in the 60-plus years since Heidel's work. We should note, however, that though there continue to be many evidences of what Heidel refers to as the "sublime character of the Genesis narrative" (including some that were alluded to in the above quotation), it is debatable that the distinction between "creation in the biblical sense" and "fashioning" can be considered one of them. Heidel carried with him into his analysis the presupposition (born of the post-Enlightenment period) that the biblical account was characterized by an underlying

---

1. A. Heidel, *The Babylonian Genesis* (Chicago: University of Chicago Press, 1951), 139.

material ontology and an accompanying interest in material origins of the cosmos. In what follows, I will attempt to demonstrate that this presupposition is unwarranted and that the Israelite mental framework was just as focused on "orderly and purposeful arrangement" (though we will choose other wording) as the Babylonian literature was, even if the biblical author did reject the theogony that was integrated into the Babylonian cosmogony.

Genesis 1:1

Some specific issues need to be addressed as part of our reexamination of the setting provided by Gen 1:1. These matters have often been the focus of commentary, so the topics are familiar; nonetheless, they deserve fresh investigation. The first two, the literary function of the verse and the meaning of (*bĕrē'šît*), will be considered together; a separate section will be devoted to a study of the Hebrew verb (*bārā'*).

Literary Function of Genesis 1:1 and the Meaning of Bĕrē'šît

Ever since the first modern analyses of *Enuma Elish* in the 19th century, it has been common to suggest that the syntax of Gen 1:1 is comparable to the opening line of the Babylonian cosmogony.[2] A minor adjustment in the pointing of the verb in the sentence, changing it from a finite verb to an infinitive, would result in a reading in which v. 1 would be understood as a dependent temporal clause ('When God began to create the cosmos . . .'), with its main clause found in either v. 2 or v. 3. Objections to this interpretation have focused either on grammatical/syntactical discussions on the one hand or on theological concerns on the other.

Although those who favor reading v. 1 as a dependent clause have argued that the temporal adverb as it stands would logically be followed by an infinitive construct, others have pointed out that Biblical Hebrew syntax of temporal adverbs does not require a following infinitive verbal form, nor do temporal adverbs require the definite article, thus permitting the treatment of the opening phrase as an independent temporal clause. The technicalities are thoroughly treated in a number of technical commentaries[3]

---

2. *Enuma Elish* begins "When on high. . . ." It should be pointed out, however, that the suggestion that v. 1 is a dependent clause was made as early as the medieval Jewish commentator Rashi.

3. See especially G. Wenham, *Genesis 1–15* (WBC; Dallas: Word, 1987), 11–13; V. Hamilton, *Genesis 1–17* (NICOT; Grand Rapids, MI: Eerdmans, 1990), 103–8; K. Mathews, *Genesis 1–11* (NAC; Nashville: Broadman/Holman, 1996), 136–44; J. Sailhamer, "Genesis," in the *Expositor's Bible Commentary* (ed. F. E. Gaebelein; Grand Rapids, MI: Zondervan, 1990), 21–23;

and extensive investigation of this specific grammatical feature has further shown that time designations in adverbial expressions do not require the definite article.[4] Rules of syntax and usage therefore do not necessitate translating the phrase 'When God began . . .'.

From the theological perspective, some scholars (particularly conservatives) believed that the comparison with *Enuma Elish* and revised translation was entirely due to the influence of pan-Babylonianism and was an overzealous attempt to bring the text into conformity with the Babylonian version, thus diminishing the uniqueness of the biblical book and reducing Genesis to mythology. Though some proponents of the revised translation may have been motivated by a willingness or even a desire to diminish the traditional reputation of the biblical text, this reading does not necessarily lead to that conclusion. The objections to the revised translation (i.e., as a dependent clause) were raised primarily by scholars who believed that the traditional translation of Gen 1:1 supported the idea of creation *ex nihilo*— that is, an absolute beginning that presumes a material ontology. As I have shown in the previous chapters, however, it is inappropriate to impose our modern ontology onto the mental constructs of the ancient world. Nevertheless, the methodology lying behind the revised translation, which seems to be motivated in modern interpretation primarily by the similar syntax of a single Babylonian cosmological text, a text that is in itself idiosyncratic in the ancient world at many levels, seems questionable. Consequently, I do not believe that there is good reason to alter the Masoretic pointing, and I think that there are several advantages to retaining the pointing and the traditional translation of the opening phrase of Genesis 1 as an independent clause: "In the beginning, God created. . . ."

The first advantage that results from retaining the traditional understanding is found within Genesis itself. The well-known structure of the book of Genesis features eleven divisions, each introduced by the use of the phrase *'ēlleh hattôlĕdôt* 'This is the account of . . .'). The first of these occurs in Gen 2:4, leaving the 7-day cosmogony outside the "account" structure and making Gen 1:1–2:3 something akin to a preamble. It should be noticed, however, that the (*tôlĕdôt*) phrase is a transitionary phrase, linking what has come before to what is to come next in the book. Regardless of what follows, whether genealogical information or additional narrative, the

---

A. Ross, *Creation and Blessing* (Grand Rapids, MI: Baker, 1987), 18–23; C. Westermann, *Genesis 1–11* (Continental; Minneapolis: Fortress, 1984), 93–98.

4. G. Hasel, "Recent Translations of Genesis 1:1," *The Bible Translator* 22 (1971): 156–7.

introductory word also leads to a presentation of what eventuated from the person to whom the *tôlĕdôt* refers (e.g., "What came of Terah's son?" or "What became of Esau?"). Consequently, it is not possible to begin the book with this phrase: there is nothing earlier to which to refer.

In contrast, *bĕrē'šît* is a strikingly appropriate term to introduce a sequence that will be carried on by the *tôlĕdôt* transitions. It marks the very first period, with the *tôlĕdôt* phrases introducing each of the successive periods. If this be the case, the book would now have 12 formally marked sections (a number that is much more logical than 11). If the *bĕrē'šît* clause is a marker comparable to the *tôlĕdôt* clauses, it could easily be seen as functioning in an independent clause, just like the *tôlĕdôt* clauses. The conclusion then is that it is an independent clause that functions as a literary marker to introduce the seven-day account,[5] just as the *tôlĕdôt* phrase is a literary marker that introduces the passage that follows.

The second reason for retaining the Masoretic pointing and the traditional reading of *bĕrē'šît* as an independent clause is the observation that the wording of this clause shows much more affinity with Egyptian phrasing than with *Enuma Elish*. The Egyptian concept of the 'first occasion' (*sp tpy*) is important to consider: it is a concept that, as Morenz notes, refers to an initial period set off from what follows.

> This does not just mean the beginning. It only means the beginning of an event. For "time" means an event: "First time defeat of the east", we read in a First-Dynasty source, describing an outstanding event. On the other hand "time" does not exclude the period after the event; on the contrary, it implies that other "times" followed, in principle, times without number. Indeed, Egyptians did at first measure the passage of time by regularly recurring events, especially the taking of the census, i.e., "time" was a paradigm to denote periodicity.[6]

5. Note that E. van Wolde offers the same interpretation of Gen 1:1 without relating it to the *tôlĕdôt* clauses: *Reframing Biblical Studies: When Language and Text Meet Culture, Cognition, and Context* (Winona Lake, IN:, Eisenbrauns, 2009), 185.

6. S. Morenz, *Egyptian Religion* (Ithaca, NY: Cornell University Press, 1973), 166. In Egyptian thinking, the "first time" referred to the period during which "the pattern of existence was both established and first enacted" (Allen, *Genesis in Egypt*, 57). This "first time" is repeated over and over in nature and history (Morenz, *Egyptian Religion*, 168; Assmann, *Mind of Egypt*, 206). Repetition of this sort is not reflected in the Israelite or Mesopotamian perspectives. Despite this periodicity, the Egyptian ideology is not an ancient conception akin to that of Jürgen Moltmann, who put forth a perspective of dynamic creation and eschatological time (*God in Creation: An Ecological Doctrine of Creation* [London: SCM, 1985]; and the assessment of Moltmann in F. Watson, *Text and Truth* [Grand Rapids, MI: Eerdmans, 1997], 225–75), because in Egyptian thinking there is a beginning, a middle, and an end, despite the continual reiteration of creation (Morenz, *Egyptian Religion*, 169). At the same time, only

The Egyptian concept is somewhat different from the Biblical Hebrew sense in that its usage is tied closely to the idea of reiterated creation. That is, what happened on the "first occasion" is repeated daily, as creation, in some sense, takes place all over again. In the Hebrew Bible, Yahweh's ongoing role as creator is presented as his maintenance of the order initially established in Genesis 1. This is quite different from the daily reiterations of creation that occur according to the Egyptian cosmology. Nevertheless, the idea that there was an initial period of time during which the cosmos was created forms a strong link between Genesis and Egypt and makes the similarity between Genesis and *Enuma Elish* pale in comparison. The most significant Egyptian examples occur in Papyrus Leiden 1 350.[7]

> You began evolution with nothing, without the world being empty of you on the first occasion. (80th chapter)
>
> Light was his evolution on the first occasion with all that exists in stillness for awe of him. (90th chapter)
>
> Who began evolution on the first occasion. Amun, who evolved in the beginning, with its emanation unknown. (100th chapter)

J. Sailhamer has pointed out the unique function of the Hebrew term *běrē'šît*: he argues that it refers to an initial period or duration of time rather than to a specific point in time.[8] His case is supported most convincingly by passages such as Job 8:7, which refers to the early part of Job's life, and Jer 28:1, which refers to the beginning period of Zedekiah's reign. In Hebrew, a

---

pedantically can creation be restricted to a one-time event in Egyptian thought. The order that exists in the cosmos is constantly threatened with being undone. Whether the threat derives from the cosmic waters, from what we would term "natural" occurrences, from supernatural beings, from human behavior, or simply from the darkness of each night, the gods are responsible for reestablishing order day by day and moment by moment.

7. *COS* 1.16. For additional uses of the phrase in cosmological texts, see the following: *COS* 1.1, Book of Nut: "Then the incarnation of this god comes forth on earth again, having come into the world, young, his physical strength growing great again, like the first occasion of his original state." *COS* 1.1, Book of Nut: "Then he is evolved, like his original evolving in the world on the first occasion." *COS* 1.13, Ramesside Stela: "Noble god of the first occasion, who built people and gave birth to the gods, original one who made it possible for all to live; in whose heart it was spoken, who saw them evolve." Hymn to Amun-Re (J. Foster, *Hymns, Prayers, and Songs* [SBLWAW 8; Atlanta: Society of Biblical Literature, 1995], 65, text 32): "Splendid Soul who came to be in the Beginning, great God who dwells in Truth, Primordial God who engendered the first gods, through whom every god came to be, Most unique of the unique, who made all that is, who began the world back in the first time."

8. J. Sailhamer, *Genesis Unbound: A Provocative New Look at the Creation Account* (Sisters, OR: Multnomah, 1996), 38. Detailed discussion may be found in Sailhamer, "Genesis," at Gen 2:20–23; and a summary appears in an article by B. Arnold on *re'shith* in *NIDOTTE* 3:1025–26.

king's accession year was referred to as the *rē'šît* of his reign, and this is an initial period of time, not a point in time (such as the day of his enthronement). The semantics of the term *rē'šît* therefore offers an alternative way of understanding the 'beginning', even if none of the verses cited is an exact syntactical equivalent of Gen 1:1.[9]

In Genesis, the 'beginning' (*rē'šît*) refers to a preliminary period of time rather than a first point in time.[10] This is comparable with the Akkadian term *reštu*, which means 'the first part' or 'the first installment';[11] as well as with the Egyptian phrase introduced (above, p. 126), a term that plays a significant role in cosmological texts.[12] In these texts, the Egyptian phrase refers to "when the pattern of existence was established and first enacted."[13] In English, we might refer to an initial period such as this as the primordial period.[14] All of this information leads us to conclude that the 'beginning' is a way of labeling the seven-day *period* of creation described in the remainder of Genesis 1 rather than a *point* in time prior to the seven days. As an independent clause, it offers no description of creative acts but provides a literary introduction to the period of creative activity that then flows into the *tôlĕdôt* sections that characterize the remainder of the book. The next task is to understand the nature of this creative activity.

Creative Activity: Bārā'

The discussion of the ancient Near Eastern cognitive environment alerted us to the danger of imposing modern concepts of cosmological ontology onto the ancient world. Bearing this caution in mind, it is imperative that we next reexamine the semantic range of the verb *bārā'*, without being swayed by our common modern, material ontological understanding, in order to discover what sort of creative activity the term actually conveys.

---

9. Distinct syntactical features in Gen 1:1 that differentiate it from these other texts include the use of the preposition without the definite article; the sequence of a verbal form following *rē'šît* rather than a nominal form; and the use of the Masoretic disjunctive cantillation to separate this first word from the remainder of the verse. For discussion of these technical points, see the commentaries, especially Wenham (pp. 13–14) and Hamilton (pp. 106–7). Compare also W. Wifall, "God's Accession Year according to P," *Bib* 62 (1981): 527–34.

10. The distinction between *rē'šît* and *tĕhillâ* is noted by S. Rattray and J. Milgrom, "*rē'šît*," *TDOT* 13:269–70.

11. *CAD* R 272.

12. Morenz, *Egyptian Religion*, 168–71.

13. Allen, *Genesis in Egypt*, 57.

14. It is the opposite of the 'eschaton' or the 'latter days', the term for which in Hebrew is *'aḥărît*.

Summary of the Lexical Base

It has commonly been observed that the verb only appears with deity as its subject (or as an implicit agent when the verb occurs in the Niphal) in the approximately 50 times it occurs in the Hebrew Bible. This is an important observation: it has led to the common conclusion that the activity denoted by *bārāʾ* is a prerogative only of deity and not an activity that humans can undertake or even in which they can participate.

What is most important for the present study, however, is observing what direct objects the verb can take. Table 4.1 is a comprehensive listing.[15]

The grammatical objects of the verb can be summarized according to the following categories:

- Cosmos (10, including New Cosmos)
- People in general (10)
- Specific groups of people (6)
- Specific individuals or types of individuals (5)
- Creatures (2)
- Natural Phenomena (10)
- Components of cosmic geography (3)
- Condition (1: a pure heart)

What is obvious from this listing is that grammatical objects of the verb are not easily identified as material items, and even when they are, it is questionable that the context permits objectifying them.[16]

Discussion of the Semantic Range of bārāʾ

From a diachronic perspective, our data are too limited to arrive at firm etymological conclusions. *Bārāʾ* has no universally recognized cognates in contemporary Semitic languages, nor is there a sufficient variety of derivative forms to allow confident identification of a root meaning. It is intriguing, however, that when an etymology is suggested, it is usually derived from the few occurrences of the Piel of *bārāʾ* (not included in table 4.1) that modern lexicons have usually listed as a distinct though homonymous root.

---

15. Direct objects in the Dead Sea Scrolls include: vault, light, morning, evening, age, spirit, spice, treasury, sanctuary, people, deed, righteous one, wicked one, flesh, evil, and shame. See full citations in *DCH* 2:258–59; and discussion in H. Ringgren, "ברא *Bārāʾ*," *TDOT* 2:249.

16. See J. Stek, "What Says the Scripture?" in *Portraits of Creation: Biblical and Scientific Perspectives on the World's Formation* (ed. H. J. Van Till; Grand Rapids, MI: Eerdmans, 1990), 203–65 (especially p. 208).

Table 4.1. Objects of the Verb *Bārā'*

Reference	Object	Comments
Gen 1:1	heavens and earth	
Gen 1:21	creatures of the sea	
Gen 1:27	people	male and female
Gen 1:27 (2)	people	in his image
Gen 2:3	X	
Gen 2:4	heavens and earth	
Gen 5:1	people	likeness of God
Gen 5:2	people	male and female
Gen 5:2	people	
Gen 6:7	people	
Exod 34:10	wonders	// *'āśâ* (made/did)
Num 16:30	something new (debatable)	earth swallowing rebels
Deut 4:32	people	
Ps 102:18	people not yet created	to praise the Lord
Ps 104:30	creatures	renewing the face of the earth
Ps 148:5	celestial inhabitants	to praise the Lord
Ps 51:10	pure heart	
Ps 89:12	north and south	
Ps 89:47	people	for futility
Ecc 12:1	you	
Isa 4:5	cloud of smoke	
Isa 40:26	starry host	called by name, kept track of
Isa 40:28	ends of the earth	
Isa 41:20	rivers flowing in desert	to meet needs of his people
Isa 42:5	heavens	stretched out
Isa 43:1	Jacob	= Israel
Isa 43:15	Israel	
Isa 43:7	everyone called by my name	for my glory
Isa 45:12	people	
Isa 45:18	earth	did not create it to be *tōhû*
Isa 45:18	heavens	to be inhabited
Isa 45:7	darkness	// to form light
Isa 45:7	disaster	// bring prosperity
Isa 45:8	heavens and earth	to produce salvation and righteousness
Isa 48:7	new things, hidden things	
Isa 54:16	blacksmith	to forge a weapon
Isa 54:16	destroyer	to work havoc
Isa 57:19	praise	
Isa 65:17	new heavens and new earth	
Isa 65:18	new heavens and new earth	
Isa 65:18	Jerusalem	to be a delight
Jer 31:22	new thing	woman to surround a man
Ezek 21:30	Ammonites	
Ezek 28:13	king of Tyre	
Ezek 28:15	king of Tyre	
Amos 4:13	wind	
Mal 2:10	covenant people	

This suggests that we need to reconsider the relationship between the Piel occurrences and the Qal and Niphal forms of *bārā'* already discussed.

The Piel occurs five times:

- Josh 17:15, 18, referring to the tribes of Ephraim and Manesseh, about separating land for themselves
- Ezek 21:19[24] 2x, referring to distinguishing between two routes of travel
- Ezek 23:47, separate them [Oholah and Oholibah] with swords

The occurrences in Joshua are regularly translated as if the verb means 'to clear forested land'. But this conclusion is not necessary in the context, where Joshua simply refers to Ephraim and Manasseh's enlarging their holdings. In fact, he may be advising them to take action that would give them control of the forested hill country—that they should *distinguish* it as theirs. This sense fits more logically with the usage of the Piel in the two Ezekiel passages. On the basis of this meaning for the Piel, it is commonly concluded that the etymological base of the root *bārā'* is 'to separate'. [17] This conclusion runs contrary to the decisions of the lexicons to classify the Piel as a distinct homonymous root but is supported, if not confirmed, by one of the Qal occurrences, where this same meaning obtains. In Num 16:30, the Qal of *bārā'* is used with a cognate accusative (a construction in which the object of the verb is a noun derived from the verbal root) to introduce the opening up of the earth to swallow the rebels Korah, Dathan, Abiram, and their families. The NIV presents a typical translation:

> NIV: But if the Lord brings about (*bārā'*) something totally new (*bĕrî'â*), and the earth opens its mouth and swallows them, with everything that belongs to them, and they go down alive into the grave, then you will know that these men have treated the Lord with contempt.

> NRSV: But if the LORD creates something new. . . .

> NJPSV: But if the Lord brings about something unheard-of. . . .

That the noun ought to be translated 'something new' is, however, debatable. J. Milgrom notes the generally proposed etymology of the root and

---

17. C. Westermann indicates that the etymological base of the root *bārā'* is found in the idea of cutting or separating (*Genesis 1–11*, 99); R. van Leeuwen, "ברא" in *NIDOTTE* 1:731; Ringgren, "ברא," 245; and W. H. Schmidt, "ברא," *TLOT* 1:253. This is affirmed in general by E. van Wolde, *Reframing*, 185–200, though she opts for the translation 'distinguish' to differentiate it from *hibdîl*. It should also be noted that she does not arrive at this conclusion through analysis of the Piel forms (which she does not mention).

then specifies the cognate accusative in the same semantic vein, arriving at the translation: 'makes a great chasm' (that is, a separation, in this case, of land from land).[18] The result is a rendering that suits the context of the passage much better. If we accept this conclusion for interpreting the Qal here—and I see no reason not to—then there is no reason to continue to see the Piel occurrences as derived from a different root. One of the results of this conclusion is that there now would be occurrences of the verb with humans as the subject (at least in the Piel).

The analysis of the Hebrew verbal system by Waltke and O'Connor notes that, in fientive verbs (such as this one), the distinction between Qal (G) and Piel (D) is that the latter has a passive undersubject, while the former has no undersubject at all.[19] The activity of the subject in the D stem can actually establish the verbal activity as a reality or simply reflect someone's declaration or opinion that it is a reality. Thus, the tribes of Ephraim and Manasseh could either see to it that the forested land was distinguished as belonging to them or they could consider it to be so and begin working to make it a reality. Similarly, in Ezek 21:19[24], the prophet is instructed to see to it that roads are distinguished (marked off); he does not actually bring the roads into being, for they already exist.

Finally, in Ezek 23:47, the verb must be analyzed in relationship to the D stem of *btq*, which is used instead of *bārā'* in the almost identical phrase in Ezek 16:40. *Btq* is a hapax legomenon in Biblical Hebrew but is well represented in the Akkadian cognate *batāqu*.[20] The Akkadian D stem of this verb is used for cutting off parts of the anatomy of people captured in war, and this suits the context of Ezekiel well. Interestingly, it is also the verb used when Marduk cuts Tiamat in half (*Enuma Elish* IV 102). Given the bulk of the cognate evidence, it is likely that *btq* (D) in Ezek 16:40 and *bārā'* (D) in Ezek 23:47 both mean 'to separate or cut off', particular limbs/appendages rather than to dismember or hack to pieces. Thus, the notion that the verb *bārā'* indicates separation (here by cutting) is supported by the Ezekiel examples.

Synchronically, the verb in the Qal has generally been treated as a specialized cosmological term, in which case its etymology is largely irrelevant.

---

18. J. Milgrom, *Numbers* (JPS Torah Commentary; Philadelphia: Jewish Publication Society, 1990), 137. None of these commentators recognizes that the ancient Near Eastern background regarding ideas of *creation* makes a progression from "separating" to "creating" quite logical.

19. *IBHS* §21.2.2; cf. §24.2f–g.

20. *CAD* B 161–65.

Nevertheless, even as a technical term, it is not likely that its meaning can be totally divorced from its etymology. Commentaries and the dictionaries have not noted, however, how closely the diachronic analysis positions the root relative to the notion of creation in the ancient world, particularly as we have discussed it above.[21] It is impossible to ignore the fact that, in both Genesis and in the ancient Near Eastern cosmogonies, creation involves first and foremost an act of separation. At the same time, cosmological separation is not simply a spatial or temporal distinction, as implied by van Wolde.[22] Rather, it is one of the primary activities involved in bringing order to the cosmos.[23]

Given all of the above information, it is still best to consider the verb *bārā'* as meaning 'to bring something into existence'.[24] But a few refinements are necessary.

1. This analysis leaves unsettled the question how *existence* is defined. If we examine the range of things that are brought into existence in contexts that use this word, it is highly unlikely that *material* existence is in view. Instead, the definition of existence that easily encompasses the wide variety of objects we find associated with this verb is the very definition that we found dominating the ancient Near Eastern cognitive environment. If the Israelite ontology is functional rather than material, then to bring something into existence means to give it a function and a distinguishable role in an ordered system. This understanding of Israelite ontology best accounts for the semantic data.

2. From the fact that one of the primary means of bringing something into existence in ancient cosmogonies is separation, we may conclude that Hebrew *bārā'* was a remarkably apt term to choose to describe this process. This does not mean, however, that the verb should be translated 'to separate, distinguish'; it only suggests that the verb may at times carry within it the latent idea of separation, which makes it uniquely suited to cosmological contexts.[25]

---

21. An exception is É. Dantinne, "Création et Séparation," *Muséon* 74 (1961): 441–51.

22. Van Wolde, *Reframing*, 199.

23. Recall the Egyptian idea expressed in the idea of Atum as the singularity (e.g., COS 1.8). At the beginning, there were not two things, and then the god differentiated himself into millions in the acts of creation. See E. Hornung, *Conceptions of God in Ancient Egypt* (Ithaca, NY: Cornell University Press, 1982), 170, 176.

24. This idea is echoed in J. Stek's conclusion that "*bārā'* affirms of some existent reality *only that God conceived, willed and effected it*" ("What Says the Scripture?" 213; italics his).

25. At the same time, I am conscious of the need to avoid the semantic fallacy that builds the etymological history of a word into its usage at every turn. This fallacy is dubbed

Thus, the nuanced meaning of *bārā'* that best suits the data is that it means 'to bring something into (functional) existence'. It suggests the establishment of order often accomplished by making distinctions as roles, status, and identity are distinguished. In contexts where it may retain some of its latent etymology, it may even concern giving something a distinct (functional) existence. Nothing suggests that it should be considered an act of manufacturing something material. Thus, Gen 1:1 becomes, "In the initial period, God brought cosmic functions into existence."

It is not on the basis of the semantic sense of *bārā'* that we draw the conclusion that Israel's ontology was functional. The main evidence for this conclusion will be brought out in subsequent chapters. However, it is clear that the synchronic analysis of the verb *bārā'* becomes much simpler when the factor of Israelite ontology is brought into the investigation.

Excursus on ʿāśâ

Can the word *ʿāśâ*, especially in contexts dealing with cosmology, refer to anything other than a material manufacturing process? If we can show that functions or actions are sufficiently attested as objects of *ʿāśâ*, a variety of possibilities for the meaning of this common verb may present themselves, meanings that stretch beyond a simplistic conclusion that the word *means* 'to make' and therefore must refer to an act of material manufacturing. What, for example, would an Israelite be thinking when he/she referred to Yahweh as "Maker of heaven and earth"?

The data are much more complex than in the case of *bārā'*, because of both the high frequency of uses (more than 2,600) and the wide variety of ways in which the verb is translated into English. The verb has been identified as a multifaceted, general-use verb that simply is used of an activity of whatever sort the context dictates.[26]

1. *Categories within the semantic range.*   Traditionally, the lexicons offer the meaning 'to do' or 'to make', then list all the other variations that arise out of different contexts and collocations. There is no shortage of examples of both "do" and "make," but in English, these are two very different sorts of activities. "Doing" as a reference to activity and behavior is primarily a

---

"Semantic Obsolescence" by D. A. Carson, *Exegetical Fallacies* (Grand Rapids, MI: Baker, 1996), 35–37. If the notion of "separation" lingers in the history of the word, this may be why the author of Genesis chose to use *ʿāśâ* in 1:7 rather than risk using a verb that reminded his readers of Tiamat's divided corpse, which became the waters above and below in *Enuma Elish*.

26. Carpenter, "עשה," *NIDOTTE* 3:547: "It is a marker with almost no intrinsic restrictions placed upon what it might mean in all possible contexts."

functional category, whereas "making" is commonly product-oriented and is more likely to include a manufacturing or construction process.[27] It may be that the very reason that the verb *ʿāśâ* extends across the range of English 'to do' and 'to make' is because these two activities are much more closely interconnected in ancient thinking.[28]

It is also interesting that there are some contexts where English translations incline toward 'make' despite contextual evidence that suggests that 'do' would be a better choice. Perhaps most notable in this regard is the very significant statement in Exod 20:8–11, which is often invoked in support of the idea that God's manufacture (*ʿāśâ*) of the cosmos took place in seven solar days. A consideration of the context and of the use of the verb throughout the context, however, offer a different understanding. Verse 9 states that on six days the Israelites may *do* (*ʿāśâ*) their work but that on the seventh (v. 10), none of them should *do* work. In this context, it would be entirely justifiable to understand v. 11 as discussing God *doing* his work. The same Hebrew word used in these verses for 'work' is in fact used of God's creative activities in Gen 2:2: "On the seventh day God finished the work which he had *done*." Gen 2:2 is the verse that Exod 20:11 is referring to, and it would therefore be correct to conclude that the creative activities of the six days are better classified as "doing work" rather than as "making things." Gen 1:31, which on its own would be ambiguous, gains its meaning from 2:2 and should therefore be rendered 'God saw all that he had done'.

Akkadian *epešu* has a semantic range quite comparable to Hebrew *ʿāśâ*. The many transitive occurrences of *epešu*, which have to do with 'making', focus, as would be expected, on (1) the construction of structures such as buildings, walls, boats, bridges, and canals; (2) the making of equipment or garments; and (3) the making of images.[29] The verb is used only three times in contexts involving cosmology. In the first case, *Enuma Elish* I 126 refers

---

27. I readily acknowledge that these categories are generalizations that are so reductionistic as to be almost meaningless. It is not my intention here to establish rigid semantic categories but to identify the general directions that the meanings take.

28. Note the observation of H. Te Velde concerning Egypt: "The creation theology that was practiced or performed in the cult did not simply commemorate the great mythological deeds of the gods or express the coherence and process of the created world; it was, in effect, creation itself. An Egyptian term for performing rituals is 'doing things.' The priest had to 'do things' to make sure that the order of the cosmos would be maintained and that the universe, the state and the individual would continue their ordered existence" (*CANE* 1744).

29. *CAD* E 197–201; see also G. Pettinato, *Das altorientalische Menschenbild und die sumerischen und akkadischen Schöpfungsmythen* (Heidelberg: Carl Winter, 1971), 59.

to Tiamat and her cohorts making a "tempest."[30] In *Enuma Elish* VII 89–90, it is used in the interpretation of the 35th name of Marduk, describing his making first the world regions and then his making people out of parts of the gods.

2. *Comparison of ʿāśâ and bārāʾ.*   When these verbs are used in the same context, do they both have a functional element or a material element? Gen 1:26–27 shows that both verbs can be used to express the same action. They are also used in combination in Gen 2:3.

3. *Material and functional contexts.*   When ʿāśâ refers to God's creative activity, the objects of the verb, as is true of bārāʾ, range beyond material products to include functions. The objects appear that we expect: earth, sea, dry land, heaven, firmament, heavenly bodies, sun and moon, animals, and people. But also in the list are the windows of heaven (2 Kgs 7:2, 19), Moses and Aaron (1 Sam 12:6), and the nations (Deut 26:19; Ps 86:9).[31] Compare the obvious functional direction evident in the combination object in Job 10:12, where Job affirms that *ḥayyîm wāḥesed ʿāśîtā ʿimmādî* 'You gave me life and showed me kindness' (NIV).[32] The variety of direct objects used with ʿāśâ suggests that there is no clear distinction between the material and the functional aspects of meaning in this verb.

When God is the subject of the verb, approximately 80 occurrences have direct objects that are part of the created order. For the moment, we will set these aside as being ambiguous with regard to the question of whether they reflect a material or functional focus. What is of immediate interest is that there are approximately 370 other occurrences where God is subject of the verb, and in these cases, only 2 even hint at a material process or a material object:

> Gen 3:21: The Lord God *made* garments of skin for Adam and his wife.

> Isa 25:6: The Lord Almighty will *prepare* a feast of rich food for all peoples.

The remaining examples concern dealing with people, acting in a way that is in accordance with his nature (justly, righteously, etc.; these examples involve objects that in English we consider abstract nouns), doing signs and wonders, doing something in nature, or acting in ways that remain true

---

30. *u₄-mu* is read in several different ways. Foster suggests in a footnote that it perhaps should be translated 'monster' to agree with the sense of line 127 (Foster, *Before the Muses*, 443 n. 3). Note that this word often refers to a storm demon.

31. See the extensive but partial list in H. Ringgren, "עשׂה," *TDOT* 11:392; Vollmer, "עשׂה," *TLOT* 2:949–50.

32. The only verb here is ʿāśâ.

to his promises/words/name. Consequently, it could be concluded that in many cases the verb *'āśâ* focuses on God's actions rather than on his material projects.[33]

As has already been mentioned, it is typical in English to draw a distinction between the verb 'to do', which takes as its direct object *activities* performed by the subject, while the verb 'to make' usually takes material *things* as its grammatical direct objects. As a result, when we encounter a Hebrew text in which *'āśâ* has cosmic direct objects, and given that our basic modern ontology is material, we assume that *material things being made* are the objects of *'āśâ* rather than *activities being done*, and thus we translate 'make' rather than 'do'. But if the creation of the cosmos is an *activity* of organizing or ordering, the work identified with the word *'āśâ* must have to do with establishing its functions.

It is true that there are many contexts in which human subjects are engaged in producing material objects (approximately 365 occurrences).[34] But it is also interesting that, in a significant number of cases (approximately 25%), the individual who is subject of the verb is the one who supervises, delegates, or commissions the job rather than the person whose hands actually do the making.[35]

4. Use of the noun form ma'ăśeh. Of 236 occurrences of the noun, very few refer to things made, such as the work of a craftsman (usually idols, temple furniture, merchandise). When God's work is referred to (Job 14:15; 37:7; Ps 145:9–17 [4x]; Isa 29:16), it always refers to people, not to the cosmos. Note also Prov 16:11: "all the weights in the bag are of his [God's] making."[36] The term usually refers to activities that are done, achieved, or accomplished.

5. Use of the Participle. The participle occurs 20+ times as 'Creator'. Job 37:2–13 (NIV), in an extended context, provides a clear example of the works (*ma'ăśeh*) that the Lord does/makes (*'āśâ*).

---

33. *TLOT* 949; see Keel, *Symbolism*, 204–5.

34. The things made include garments, Noah's ark and merchant ships, buildings religious and otherwise, furniture religious and otherwise, cultic objects, meals and food, bricks, offerings, and reservoirs.

35. This observation was made by my student, Alyssa Walker, who also provided much help in gathering and sorting lexical information. See examples such as Gen 37:3; 1 Kgs 12:28; Jer 52:20; Eccl 2:5–6; 2 Chr 20:36; 32:29. Gen 12:5 is particularly intriguing as Abram is the subject of *'āśâ*, and the direct object is a person (*nephesh*). Obviously this means something other than material manufacture.

36. Note that this does not refer to God as manufacturing the weights but as determining them in some sense. These are not elements of cosmic geography.

Table 4.2. Use of the Participle 'Creator'

Reference	Object	Comments
Job 4:17	People	
Job 31:15	People in the womb	
Job 35:10	Oppressed people	The one who gives songs/strength in the night
Ps 95:6	Worshiping people	
Ps 115:15	Heaven and earth	
Ps 121:2	Heaven and earth	Source of help
Ps 124:8	Heaven and earth	Source of help
Ps 134:3	Heaven and earth	
Ps 136:4	Wonders	
Ps 136:5	Heavens	In his understanding
Ps 136:7	Great lights	Sun to govern day, moon and stars to govern night
Ps 146:6	Heaven and earth, sea and all in them	Source of help
Ps 149:2	Israel	// (divine) King
Prov 14:31	Poor	
Prov 17:5	Poor	
Prov 22:2	Rich and poor	
Isa 17:7	People	Will recognize their Maker
Isa 27:11	People	// *yrṣ*
Isa 29:16	Fashioned product	Here, Israel
Isa 44:2	People	Whom he formed in the womb
Isa 51:13	People	Who stretched out heavens and established earth
Isa 54:5	Israel	Your husband
Hos. 8:14	Israel	
Amos 4:13	Dawn to darkness	
Amos 5:8	Pleiades and Orion	

Listen! Listen to the roar of his voice,
to the rumbling that comes from his mouth.
He unleashes his lightning beneath the whole heaven
and sends it to the ends of the earth.
After that comes the sound of his roar;
he thunders with his majestic voice.
When his voice resounds,
he holds nothing back.
God's voice thunders in marvelous ways;
he does (*ʿāśâ*) great things beyond our understanding.
He says to the snow, "Fall on the earth,"

and to the rain shower, "Be a mighty downpour."
So that all men he has made may know his work (*maʿăśeh*),
he stops every man from his labor.
The animals take cover;
they remain in their dens.
The tempest comes out from its chamber,
the cold from the driving winds.
The breath of God produces ice,
and the broad waters become frozen.
He loads the clouds with moisture;
he scatters his lightning through them.
At his direction they swirl around
over the face of the whole earth
to do whatever he commands them.
He brings the clouds to punish men,
or to water his earth and show his love.

The above analysis suggests that the verb *ʿāśâ* and its cognate noun, *maʿăśeh*, when God is the subject, usually describe God as doing what is appropriate for him to do: run the cosmos; the text normally presumes that God made everything to be what it is and human beings to be who they are. One possibility is that, when deity is the subject of the verb (cf. Ps 103:6; Prov 14:31; 17:5; 22:2; Ezek 5:10), the semantics overlap with what in Mesopotamia is also divine activity: determining or decreeing (= making things be what they are). If so, again we find that the focus is on the functional aspect of reality, not the material. While this emphasis does not exclude concerns with the material, it reveals that the primary concern in the mind of the ancients was functional. At the very least, the data demonstrate that the mere presence of the verb *ʿāśâ* cannot be assumed as signaling a material process.

Heaven and Earth

Though Genesis recounts the division of the waters above from the waters below by the *rāqîʿa*, the text does not refer to heaven and earth as an original whole that had to be divided, unless this status is alluded to in v. 1. Above, I suggested that v. 1 should be understood as a literary introduction or heading to the chapter rather than as a report of creative activity. However, if Gen 1:1 is describing a creative act, it may in fact refer to an original separation of heaven and earth, and in this case, the etymological origin of *bārāʾ* (the notion of 'separation', discussed above) supports this reading. I believe that the case for taking v. 1 as a literary introduction is stronger, however. If the text were alluding to a separation of heaven and earth, we would expect the terminology for division that is used in the rest of the account, *byn . . . hbdyl*, to be used here as well.

Conclusion

In this extensive discussion of vocabulary and semantics, we have seen evidence of a functional orientation in Genesis 1, an orientation in which 'to create something' means to give it a function. This orientation is especially evident in the profile of the direct objects of the verb *bārā'*. If we do not arrive at the text of Genesis 1 with the preconception that the focus is on the bringing into existence of the material world, the context itself would not lead us to think in predominantly material terms. In the initial period, God brought the cosmos into existence (by setting up an ordered system and giving everything its role within that system). In this proposal, the text is making no comment on material origins. It is more interested in indicating how God set up the cosmos to function for human beings in his image. These functions define the idea of existence; the ancients had little interest in the material.[37]

Genesis 1:2 and the Precosmic Condition

When we investigated the precosmic condition as it was portrayed in texts from the ancient Near East that reflect the ancient cognitive environment, we noted that it was characterized not as a cosmos absent of matter but a world lacking function, order, diversity, and identity. The "before" picture comprised darkness, water, and the nondiscrete heaven and earth, on the positive side; and was absent of productivity, gods, and the operation of the cult, on the negative side.

Gen 1:2 is the biblical text that describes the precosmic condition as it was understood in Israelite thought. As in the rest of the ancient world, the cosmos is not absent of matter: primordial waters are already present. As in other texts from the ancient Near East, darkness characterizes this "before" picture. The other elements in the text that call for more detailed analysis are the hendiadys *tōhû* and *bōhû* and the role of the *rûaḥ* ('spirit' or 'wind').

---

37. Consider that, when the ancients looked up into the night sky and saw the moon, they did not think about a rock in space hovering an immense distance from earth, and reflecting the light of the sun. We might ask what alternative material description they had in mind, but it would be pointless to do so—they had no material description in mind, because the material aspects of the cosmos were largely insignificant to them.

Tōhû *and* Bōhû

Several scholars have recently made the case, and made it well, that neither of these words nor the hendiadys (two words that should be taken
together to refer to a larger whole) refers to 'chaos', either as a personified
being of some kind or as an active quality—an interpretation that has often
been put forward in the last one hundred years.[38] Most English translations
render *tōhû* as the absence of form or, alternatively (though exceptionally),
somewhat more negatively, as a wasteland (REB). All of these translations,
however, derive from a modern culture that is already thinking in terms of
a material ontology. Among much earlier translations, we have Augustine's
rendition: 'The earth was invisible and unorganized'.[39] The early Greek
translations offer a mixed assessment, with the LXX translators choosing
'unformed' (ἀκατασκεύαστος), but Aquila, Theodotion, and Symmachus
chose words that reflected nothingness, unworked material, and that which
is indistinguishable.[40] All of these still reveal some hint of a material focus.
The matter that needs to be determined is whether the synchronic lexical
data or the default ontology led interpreters to their material understanding.

Our main focus must be on the noun *tōhû*, because *bōhû* appears only
three times (in addition to Gen 1:2, only in Isa 34:11 and Jer 4:23) and only
appears in combination with *tōhû*, never alone. On the other hand, *tōhû*
appears 20 times (more than half in Isaiah [mostly in chaps. 40–49],[41] with
the others scattered between Job [3x][42] and single occurrences in Jer 4:23;
1 Sam 12:21; Deut 32:10; and Ps 107:40).

Deut 32:10, // "the wilderness," characterized by *yll* ('howling')
1 Sam 12:21, attributed to idols who can accomplish nothing

---

38. R. S. Watson, *Chaos Uncreated* (Berlin: de Gruyter, 2005), 16–17; D. Tsumura, *Creation and Destruction: A Reappraisal of the* Chaoskampf *Theory in the Old Testament* (Winona
Lake, IN: Eisenbrauns, 2005), 22–35.

39. Augustine, *Confessions* 12.22. This and the other examples here are gathered by Tsumura, *Creation and Destruction*, 9–10; and by A. Louth, *Genesis 1–11* (Ancient Christian Commentary on Scripture; Downers Grove, IL: InterVarsity Press, 2001), 4. Despite Augustine's
rendering in his commentary, he suggests that the words connote formlessness.

40. Aquila: κένωμα καὶ οὐθέν; Theodotion: θὲν καὶ οὐθέν; Symmachus: ἀργὸν καὶ
ἀδιάκριτον.

41. Isa 24:10; 29:21; 34:11; 40:17; 40:23; 41:29; 44:9; 45:18; 45:19; 49:4; 59:4. See listing in
A. Even-Shoshan, *A New Concordance of the Old Testament* (2nd ed; Grand Rapids, MI:
Baker, 1997), 1219.

42. Job 6:18; 12:24; 26:7.

Job 6:18, a wasteland away from wadis where caravans perish for lack of water

Job 12:24, a trackless waste in which one wanders

Job 26:7, what the north is stretched over

Psalm 107:40, a trackless waste in which one wanders

Jer 4:23, a specific description of *tōhû* and *bōhû*: light is absent; mountains are quaking; there are no people, no birds; the fruitful lands are waste; towns are in ruins.

The Isaiah texts include:

Isa 24:10, a *tōhû* settlement is described as desolate

Isa 29:21, with *tōhû* they turn aside righteousness (similar to Isa 59:4)

Isa 34:11, a measuring line of *tōhû* and a plumb stone of *bōhû*

Isa 40:17, worthlessness of the nations // *'yn* ('nothing') and *'ps* ('end?')

Isa 40:23, rulers of the world made (*'āśâ*) as *tōhû* // *'yn* ('nothing')

Isa 41:29, images are wind and *tōhû* // *'ps* ('end?') of their deeds

Isa 44:9, all who make images are *tōhû* // 'without profit'

Isa 45:18, God did not bring it into existence *tōhû* but formed it for habitation (intended function)

Isa 45:19, Israelites are not instructed to seek God in waste places // land of darkness

Isa 49:4, expending one's strength to no purpose (*tōhû*); // *ryq* and *hbl*

Isa 59:4, describes relying on empty arguments or worthless words (i.e., dissembling); // *šw'*

Not one of these references suggests anything about form or its absence. Whether the topic is geographical areas, nations, cities, people, or idols, the term refers to that which is nonproductive, nonfunctional, and of no purpose. This conclusion is fully supported by the contexts in which *tōhû* is used and by the terms that are used parallel to it.

Ugaritic usage is very similar to the Hebrew usage in passages with a trackless waste, but, significantly, the term appears in contexts where it is parallel to *ym* 'the sea'. All of these examples suggest that neither 'trackless' nor 'waste' carries the sense closest to the Hebrew word. On the other hand, the Egyptian concept *nonexistent* seems to be closer to the meaning of the Hebrew term. This connection may be particularly evident in Job 26:7:

nōṭeh ṣāpôn 'al-tōhû tōleh 'ereṣ 'al-bĕlî-mâ

NIV: 'He spreads out the northern skies over empty space; he suspends the earth over nothing'.

Here *tōhû* is parallel to the unique phrase *bĕlî-mâ*.[43] Ṣāpôn (NIV: 'northern skies'), as the place where heaven and earth meet and where the gods meet, is the center of the earth but also can be viewed as the dwelling place of the gods—therefore, heaven. This makes it difficult to determine whether *ṣāpôn* is used synonymously with *'ereṣ* or in antithetic parallelism, referring to the heavens. The use of the verb *nōṭeh* suggests that it is the heavens that are intended because they are usually the subject of this verb in cosmological contexts in the Hebrew Bible. If this is the case, then *tōhû* probably refers to the cosmic waters over which the heavens were stretched (cf. Ps 104:2–3).

Most commentators consider the word that is parallel to *tōhû*, *bĕlî-mâ*, to be a reference to the void; that is, that the earth is suspended over space that is empty of matter (an interpretation that could only result from the commentators' having a material ontology). But the biblical statement makes more sense if it is read in the context of the cosmology underlying the Egyptian sense of the nonexistent—something that is lacking function. In a functional ontology, the earth is seen as being suspended over the functionless cosmic waters below (cf. Ps 24:1; 136:6), parallel to the heavens that are stretched out over the upper cosmic waters. This perspective is supported in early versions of the Bible, at a time when a material ontology was not quite firmly established yet; thus, in the targum we have: "Over the *water* without anything supporting it."[44]

However, it is possible to be even more specific. The verb in the second clause, 'suspends' (*tlh*), most often refers to a form of execution ('hanged', Gen 40:19, 22; 41:13; Deut 21:22–23; Josh 8:29; 10:26; 2 Sam 4:12; 18:10; and often in Esther). In many of these references, *tlh* occurs in collocation with the preposition *'al* (as in Job 26), nearly always with the object *'ēṣ* ('tree', or, more likely, 'wooden pole/pike', since in ancient practice the corpse was impaled as a means of exposure and a denial of proper burial). These cases would be better translated 'suspended on' (not 'over'). Four other contexts use the combination *tlh 'al* (2 Sam 4:12, 'to hang next to'; Song 4:4, 'to affix shields to a wall'; Isa 22:24, 'to bear the family honor'; Ezek 15:3, 'to hang on a peg').

If *ṣāpôn* refers to the heavens, we ought to consider what the parallel term, *'ereṣ*, refers to. Though the word means 'earth' in hundreds of

---

43. Even-Shoshan's *Concordance* lists this as a single word without the *maqqep*. Also listed as a variant in *HALOT*. See E. Dhorme, *A Commentary on the Book of Job* (Nashville: Thomas Nelson, 1984), 371.

44. Cited in Dhorme, *Job*, 371.

passages, it is also used (both in the Hebrew Bible and in ancient Near Eastern cognate languages) to refer to the netherworld.[45] I favor the translation 'netherworld' here instead of 'earth', primarily because this poem does not begin discussing the earth until v. 10. Furthermore, the netherworld would be more appropriate as the opposite extreme of *ṣāpôn*.

This is not to say that *tōhû* and *bĕlî-mâ* are actually labels for the waters above and the waters below. Instead, they are words that describe the nonexistent, and the cosmic waters above and below belong to the category of the nonexistent. In addition to this apparent connection with the Egyptian concept of the nonexistent, there is an interesting parallel between the affirmation of God's work in Job 26:7 and the 32nd name of Marduk in *Enuma Elish*: Agilimma, "Creator of the earth above the waters, establisher of the heights."[46]

Thus, the adjective *tōhû* could refer to the precosmic condition, the functionless cosmic waters or, in the ordered creation, to the places on which order had not yet been imposed, the desert and the cosmic waters above and below, surrounding the ordered cosmos. This overlaps with but extends D. Tsumura's assessment that *tōhû* refers to that which is unproductive.[47] It also agrees with Westermann's conclusion that *tōhû* should be regarded as "the state that is opposed to and precedes creation."[48] "Opposed," however, may not be an appropriate description, because it hints at personification of the status and introduction of the notion of chaos. Perhaps "antithetical" would serve better, but "unordered" and "nonfunctional" are less prejudicial and preferable as simple labels for that which is not part of the ordered cosmos. This analysis implies that the Israelite conception of existence, the precosmic condition, and the continuing presence of the nonexistent in the cosmos are parallel to the perspective found in the ancient world. In none of the ancient Near Eastern literatures is the precosmic status personified.

Within a functional ontology, all of the uses of *tōhû* now come together. Just as the desert is described as nonexistent (nonfunctional) in Egyptian literature, *tōhû* is used to describe the desert in the Hebrew Bible. Just as Egyptian pharaohs used the concept of nonexistence to describe the end of

---

45. Exod 15:12; 1 Sam 28:13; Job 10:21–22; Eccl 3:21; Isa 26:19; Jonah 2:6. Akkadian: *erṣetu*; Ugaritic: *'arṣ*; J. Sasson, *Jonah* (AB 24B; New York: Doubleday, 1990), 188–89; N. Tromp finds many more examples, many of which are ambiguous at best: *Primitive Conceptions of Death and the Nether World in the Old Testament* (Rome: Pontifical Biblical Institute, 1963), 23–46.

46. *banu erseti eliš me mukin elati*, *Enuma Elish* VII line 83.

47. Tsumura, *Creation and Destruction*, 35.

48. Westermann, *Genesis 1–11*, 103.

those they destroyed, Biblical Hebrew uses *tōhû* to refer to the destruction of order and civilization. This use of *tōhû* is particularly evident in Jer 4:23, where the oracle refers to the cosmos's partial return to nonfunctionality.[49] Job 26:7 is the best example of *tōhû* referring to nonfunctional cosmic realms.

The cases where *tōhû* is applied to abstract nouns—referring to words, ideas, or actions without purpose or without result—fit nicely into this profile of nonfunctionality. And finally, prophetic rhetoric concerning divine images that labels them nonfunctional and, by virtue of being nonfunctional, effectively nonexistent is an essential component of the prophet's message in Isaiah.[50]

Tsumura at first appears to suggest that v. 2 describes a "bare" state, "without vegetation and animals as well as without man."[51] This is impossible, however, because Gen 1:2 does not describe an empty desert wasteland; the dry land has not yet emerged at this point in the narration. It is a watery condition that is described. By the end of Tsumura's treatment, he has modified his description, using the more vague terms 'unproductive and uninhabited',[52] but this phrase still falls short of precisely what is suggested by the semantic analysis above and our understanding of the ancient Near Eastern cognitive environment. All of the contexts that apply the term *tōhû* to a desert waste simply help to build the profile of the word as referring to any portion of the cosmos that is nonfunctional or, in Egyptian terms, nonexistent.

Furthermore, the common view that *tōhû* refers to Chaos cannot be sustained. As I noted above in the discussion of the ancient Near Eastern materials (see the discussion of Theomachy, p. 70), *chaos* is too strong a term for the precreation condition found in any of the ancient Near Eastern texts and is therefore a misleading idea that should not be introduced into discussions of Genesis 1.

---

49. Note that not every aspect of the cosmos becomes nonfunctioning in this text. Specifically, the functions that God assures will never again be disrupted in Gen 8:22 remain intact. The effect of the destruction is mostly on the functionaries rather than the functions. The light-bearers are not doing their job and there are no birds or people. The absence of people means that the towns are empty and that the land is unfruitful (perhaps this is more closely associated with Gen 2:5–6, which is also a description of nonfunctionality).

50. For a discussion of the existence of the gods in a functional ontology, see my *Ancient Near Eastern Thought and the Old Testament* (Grand Rapids, MI: Baker, 2006), 87–92.

51. Tsumura, *Creation and Destruction*, 33.

52. Tsumura, *Creation and Destruction*, 35.

Těhôm

The primeval waters *are* personified in both Akkadian and Egyptian literature (Tiamat in Akkadian literature, Nun in Egyptian), as are many of the elements of nature. The Israelites did not need to depersonify these terms; they simply did not share the ancient Near Eastern view that elements of the cosmos are represented by deities.

Not much can be added to Tsumura's thorough analysis of *těhôm*.[53] He demonstrates that, although *těhôm* has a cognate relationship with Akkadian *tamtum* and the related divine name Tiamat, there is no reason to think of the Hebrew term as a loanword, whether demythologized or not.[54] *Těhôm* is neither an enemy to be battled nor an adversary to be defeated. It is simply a term for the cosmic waters, applying either to the precreation context or to the waters at the boundaries of the ordered cosmos. That is, *těhôm* is one of the elements of cosmic geography that parallels what is found in the cognitive environment throughout the ancient Near East. In the precreation period, the *těhôm* covered everything. In the process of creation, it was pushed out to the edges of the cosmos, where it was restrained by the power of God. In its current location, it is identified as the cosmic waters that can be brought back at any moment by the deity, should its services be required. The term is applied very broadly, neither solely to salt water or sweet water nor only to subterranean waters or visible waters, such as seas. In Akkadian texts, the term is used of the Persian Gulf, Indian Ocean, and Mediterranean, as well as Lake Van and Lake Urmia.[55] It is probably best understood as a reference to cosmic waters in whatever form they are found.[56] In Egyptian thinking, these waters had both a negative significance, because they were functionless, and a positive significance, because they held all the potential of creation within them.[57] The Israelite portrayal does not present the precreation state as negative or personal/personified; instead, it is a neutral, functionless ambiguity.[58]

---

53. For a thorough treatment, see Tsumura, *Creation and Destruction*, 46–57; see also Horowitz, *Mesopotamian Cosmic Geography*, 301–6.

54. Tsumura, D., *Creation and Destruction*, 36–37.

55. Horowitz, *Mesopotamian Cosmic Geography*, 303.

56. Gilgamesh crosses the *tamtu* when he reaches the waters of death at the end of the world. In later texts, the Babylonian word *marratu* appears alongside *tamtu* as a synonym and represents the cosmic waters on the Babylonian world map. See Horowitz, *Mesopotamian Cosmic Geography*, 304–5, 332–33.

57. Tobin, "Myths: Creation Myths," *OEAE* 2:469.

58. C. Hyers, *The Meaning of Creation* (Atlanta: John Knox, 1984), 67.

Thus, the cognitive environment of the ancient Near East is reflected in Israel once again: the cosmic waters dominate the precreation state, and they have the same place in the cosmic geography. In contrast to the remainder of the ancient Near East, however, they are neither personified nor adversarial.

Spirit of God

Many interpreters have interpreted the prevalence of the winds in *Enuma Elish* as a basis for translating the Hebrew phrase *rûaḥ ʾĕlohîm* 'mighty wind' rather than 'spirit of God'. If this were true, the wind would be part of the precreation context. However, wind is *not* part of the precreation state in any of the other cosmology texts from the ancient Near East, and although *rûaḥ* can mean 'wind' in Hebrew,[59] it is never translated 'wind' elsewhere when it is modified by *ʾĕlohîm*. Consequently, it is unlikely that the phrase should be translated 'mighty wind' here. But regardless of how this controversy is resolved, and irrespective of the way that the phrase is translated, we must ask whether there are any parallels in the cognitive environment of the ancient Near East. Three differences between the *rûaḥ* of Genesis 1 and the wind in ancient Near Eastern texts may be noted: (1) wind is not part of the precreation state in ancient Near Eastern cosmological texts; (2) it is not deified/personified in the ancient Near East; and (3) in Genesis 1, the *rûaḥ* does not roil the waters aggressively.

Most of the elements of the cosmos are personified in the rest of the ancient Near East, but they are not personified in Genesis; in the case of the *rûaḥ*, however, the converse is true. Examples can be found in the Mesopotamian cosmology texts of the winds stirring up the sea.[60] The winds in those texts are not personified, though they are manipulated by one of the deities.[61] In contrast, in Genesis 1, the wind/spirit is personified and apparently deified by appending the modifier *ʾĕlohîm*. Given these characteristics, the only parallels for the 'wind' of Genesis 1 in the ancient Near Eastern cognitive environment are found in Egypt rather than in Mesopotamia.

---

59. The Ugaritic cognate is used only with the meaning 'wind', not 'spirit', and is never modified by *il* or *ilm* used as a superlative.

60. *Enuma Elish* I 105–10.

61. In *Enuma Elish* IV 42, the four winds are listed individually and are used by Marduk as weapons. But divine determinatives are not used in the list. In Adapa, the south wind whose wing is broken is vaguely personified (the other winds are identified as "your brothers") but not deified. For a discussion of the winds, see Horowitz, *Mesopotamian Cosmic Geography*, 196–204.

The Egyptian elements can be summarized from their appearance in a late (second-century A.D.) demotic cosmogony that draws heavily on a variety of earlier sources.[62] After the emergence of the Hermopolitan Ogdoad from Ptah, the eight gods coalesce into the single union called *Amun*. Fragment four of this papyrus, as interpreted by M. Smith, indicates that the four winds merge into a single wind, a manifestation of Amun, which then separates the sky from the earth. Smith suggests that the wind also forms or fertilizes the egg from which the solar deity emerges, who in turn becomes the Creator. In this account, the wind has a relationship to Amun that is similar to that of the spirit's relationship to *ĕlohîm* in Gen 1:2. The wind is also involved in initiating the most fundamental acts of creation, a notion that would not be foreign to the Genesis context but is not mentioned in it.

The very late date of this manuscript would usually disqualify it as a source to be considered for comparative studies. This situation can only be salvaged if evidence can be assembled to persuade us that it is simply a late copy of traditions that have their origins considerably earlier. Smith notes that "a number of Egyptian sources explicitly ascribe this separation [the primordial separation of the sky god, Nut, from the earth god, Geb] to the agency of the wind or a god associated with that element, most prominently Shu."[63] The Edfu Cosmogony (of Ptolemaic date, which of course is also relatively late) portrays the creative power of the wind as stirring a reed thicket.[64]

> A few sources make explicit reference to the wind's ability to create or fertilise eggs. Thus, in an inscription on the propylon of the temple of Montu at Karnak, the Theban nome is called *swhd.t pr m swhd*, "the egg which came forth from the wind."[65]

Earlier Coffin Texts recount the Heliopolitan tradition that the *ba* of Shu[66] speaks in the first person as one exhaled from the nose of Shu and is

---

62. M. Smith, *On the Primaeval Ocean* (Carlsberg Papyri 5; Carsten Niebuhr Institute 26; Copenhagen: Museum Tusculanum Press, University of Copenhagen, 2002), 194.

63. Smith, *Primaeval Ocean*, 59. He cites D. Kurth, *Den Himmel Stützen* (Brussels: Fondation Égyptologique Reine Élisabeth, 1973), 70–76, 78–80. Smith excerpts several of the texts, e.g., the inscription on the propylon of the Temple of Khonsu at Karnak that describes Khonsu-Shu as "the one who elevated the sky with a blast of air from his mouth."

64. Smith, *Primaeval Ocean*, 60.

65. Smith, *Primaeval Ocean*, 61. He refers also to S. Morenz's extensive treatment of this aspect of the wind in *Religion und Geschichte des alten Ägypten* (Weimar: Hermann Böhlaus Nachfolger, 1974), 469–76.

66. This is comparable to *rûaḥ*, since the *ba* is understood as the "sum of an entity less its material form" (*COS* 1.5, 8 n .1).

identified as being "exhale-like of form" and as saying, "My clothes are the wind of life." The *ba* claims to be the one who quiets the sky for Shu and silences the earth for him (these are preparatory acts for creation).[67] The preparatory role of the wind/air is also expressed in connection with its role in bringing the primeval hillock into being.

> At first calm and motionless, hovering over the sluggish primeval ocean, Nun, invisible as a nullity, it [the air] could at a given moment be set in motion, apparently of itself, could churn up Nun to its depths, so that the mud lying there could condense into solid land and emerge from the flood-waters, first as a "high-hillock" or as an "Isle of Flames" near Hermopolis.[68]

Smith summarizes the "wind" elements that are part of the cosmogony of the Carlsberg Papyrus 5 as follows:

> The four winds of the sky merged into a single high wind which brought the universe into existence by separating the sky from the earth and forming or fertilizing an egg from which the sun (= Pshai) emerged. The wind is personified by a being whose name is nowhere preserved.[69]

Smith identifies the personified deity as Amun, who as early as the New Kingdom is referred to as the wind and as the counterpart to the egg, as well as the one who separates earth and sky.[70]

This Egyptian context makes it very interesting that the same verb used to describe the activity of the *rûaḥ ʾĕlōhîm* in Genesis is a verb that refers elsewhere (Deut 32:11) to some activity of a bird over its nest. The NIV translation, 'hovering', is fairly common, not because it enjoys abundant supporting evidence, but because there is insufficient evidence to suggest other plausible alternatives. As a result, interpreters have frequently looked outside Hebrew to related (cognate) languages for lexical help. When we investigate the cognates of the root that Hebrew uses here, we discover that

---

67. CT 75 (*COS* 1.5).

68. Morenz, *Egyptian Religion*, 176, quoting Sethe, *Amun*.

69. Smith, *Primaeval Ocean*, 62.

70. Smith, *Primaeval Ocean*, 63. For another example of personification/deification of the wind(s), see the Egyptian Book of the Dead, spell 161, where each of the four winds is identified with a particular deity. These winds, however, are not involved in creation but enter into the nose of the deceased to restore him to life: "As for any noble dead for whom this ritual is performed over his coffin, there shall be opened for him four openings in the sky, one for the north wind—that is Osiris; another for the south wind—that is Re; another for the west wind—that is Isis; another for the east wind—that is Nephthys" (R. Faulkner, *The Egyptian Book of the Dead: The Going Forth by Day* [San Francisco: Chronicle, 1998], 125).

Syriac uses the same root for brooding protectively over a nest or incubating the eggs.[71] Ugaritic uses the same root to speak of vultures circling overhead, apparently waiting to devour the scraps of a feast.[72] As we consider a translation that can account for both Hebrew and Ugaritic usage and accommodate both biblical contexts, we might note that the verb in all contexts expresses a state of preparedness. Whether birds are brooding or hovering, they are preparing for what is to take place next. Significantly, in contrast, nothing in this verb could be associated with chaos.[73]

The reference to nest and eggs undoubtedly brings the Egyptian background to mind. The text of Genesis, however, is at best laconic: it fails to mention an egg, which in Egyptian thinking held the sun-god (or, alternatively, the Ogdoad), or the separation of heaven and earth by the *rûaḥ*. I propose, however, that Genesis is not simply being laconic, nor should the absence of the items that we see in the Egyptian context be considered accidental or polemical. Instead, what is clear is that the arena of discourse is shared by the Israelite and Egyptian environments, but the particulars have a shape unique to each tradition. It is commonplace to refer to the wind as having a role and to see the metaphor of bird-like brooding as preparation for creative activity. It is no surprise that this role for the wind in Israelite thinking inevitably takes on the identity of spirit and that it can be connected to none other than God.

More information from both the Old Testament and the ancient Near East confirm that the *rûaḥ* is related to the presence of the deity, preparing to participate in creation. In the Old Testament we find that, though the spirit is not mentioned in Genesis 1 after v. 2, other passages suggest that the spirit continues to act throughout the chapter. Mark Smith has recently elaborated on this point, though earlier scholars such as Wilf Hildebrandt had also presented the data.[74] Hildebrandt concludes his investigation, saying:

---

71. *HALOT* 3:1219–20.

72. *Tale of Aqhat*, see *ANET* 152 (iv 20–21). Ugaritic is more likely to be helpful than the Syriac, in that both the language and the literatures are closer to the time of the biblical narrative. Since the root is also used to describe bird behavior in Ugaritic, there is a good chance that Ugaritic usage and Hebrew usage had not developed in disparate ways. Nevertheless, even the Ugaritic uses are too few and unclear to allow for precise nuancing.

73. These two paragraphs are excerpted from my "Ancient Near Eastern Background of the Spirit of the Lord in the Old Testament," in *Power and Promise* (ed. D. Firth and P. Wegner; Leicester, UK: Inter-Varsity Press, 2011), 38–67.

74. M. S. Smith, *The Priestly Vision of Genesis 1* (Minneapolis: Fortress, 2010); Wilf Hildebrandt, *An Old Testament Theology of the Spirit of God* (Peabody, MA: Hendrickson, 1995).

It is evident that the *rûaḥ ʾĕlohîm* is not only superintending the work of creation but in fact brings creation about through the word. The passage is emphasizing the actual powerful presence of God, who brings the spoken work into reality by the Spirit. Thus, the Spirit and the word work together to present the fact that the one God is responsible for all that is seen in the physical universe.[75]

To summarize the evidence for the above conclusion:

Psalm 33:6. "By the word (*dabar*) of the Lord were the heavens made, their starry host by the breath (*rûaḥ*) of his mouth" (NIV). God's creative utterances (evident throughout Genesis 1) are here represented by the 'word' (*dabar*).[76] The parallel use of *rûaḥ* suggests that God speaks through the *rûaḥ*. We see the same connection in a bilingual hymn from the ancient Near East: "Your speech is a sweet breath, the life of the lands."[77]

Psalm 104:30. "When you send your Spirit (*rûaḥ*), they are created, and you renew the face of the earth" (NIV). Here the *rûaḥ* is the creative force.

Psalm 147:18. "He sends his word (*dabar*) and melts them; he stirs up his breezes (*rûaḥ*; note the singular in Hebrew), and the waters flow" (NIV). Though this verse refers to the control of nature rather than its initial creation, it still demonstrates that the *rûaḥ* carries out the divine utterances.[78]

Job 26:13. "By his breath (*rûaḥ*) the skies became fair; his hand pierced the gliding serpent." In this verse, the *rûaḥ* parallels God's power (*yād*) rather than his utterance but still in creative activities.

Isaiah 40:13. "Who has understood the mind (*rûaḥ*) of the Lord, or instructed him as his counselor?" (NIV). This verse immediately follows a description of God's creative activity—measuring the waters and marking off the heavens—with the *rûaḥ* as the active party. Hildebrandt points out that, in this creation context, the author asserts that none gave counsel to the *rûaḥ* in creation (the way that advisers in the divine council worked with Marduk).[79] These observations establish the *rûaḥ* as God's creative presence in creation.

Thus, as Smith indicates, we should equate the *rûaḥ* in Genesis 1 with the divine speech-acts of creation narrated throughout the chapter.[80] *Rûaḥ*

---

75. Hildebrandt, *An Old Testament Theology of the Spirit of God*, 35.

76. Smith, *Priestly Vision*, 54–55; cf. Hildebrandt, *An Old Testament Theology of the Spirit of God*, 41.

77. *CAD* Š/2 138b

78. Note the association in other noncreation passages such as Prov 1:23.

79. Hildebrandt, *An Old Testament Theology of the Spirit of God*, 40.

80. Smith, *Priestly Vision*, 54–55,

in Genesis 1 is the immanent manifestation of God the Creator. It is by the agency of the wind/spirit that he speaks creation into being. The verb *mĕraḥepet* reflects preparedness for action—waiting for the right moment.[81] Though typically associated with chaos in the ancient Near East, the winds of Genesis 1—along with other traditionally chaotic features, such as *tannin*—are presented as elements of the ordered cosmos.[82]

Consequently, in my view, *rûaḥ* should be translated 'spirit' of God but should be understood as having taken on some of the role of wind(s) known from ancient Near Eastern cosmologies. The activity of the *rûaḥ ʾĕlohîm* in this verse can also be considered in relation to the potentiality inherent in the precreation state. This potentiality is also seen in the Egyptian accounts in connection with the primeval waters.[83] The potentiality is realized through the *ka* ('vital force') of the creator-god, a force that is associated with regenerative concepts.[84] Meeks and Meeks summarize the belief that "The totality of creation . . . constituted the sum of the creator-god's vital force."[85]

Every element in Gen 1:2 has connections to the cognitive environment of the ancient Near East, yet there is neither direct mimicry nor complete dissociation from those roots in the Genesis text. As constituents of the same broad cultural environment, the Israelites thought about issues in the same context as peoples around them, even if the detailed shape of the perspective of each culture reveals distinctives.

The first two verses of Genesis 1 now appear to conform much more closely with Egyptian traditions than with Mesopotamian:

Israel	Egypt
In the Beginning	On the first occasion
Tōhû and *bōhû*	Nonexistent
The deep	Primeval waters
Rûaḥ ʾĕlohîm	Wind, *ba* of Shu, *ka* of creator, potentiality

---

81. This is true of the mother bird over the nest in Deut 32:11 and of the birds waiting to swoop down on the remains of the banquet in Ugaritic texts. In Genesis 1, the *rûaḥ* awaits the divine dispatch to bring life to creation.

82. Excerpted from my "Ancient Near Eastern Background of the Spirit of the Lord in the Old Testament."

83. Allen, *Genesis in Egypt*, 57. He points out that by the Ptolemaic period a dialectic between nonexistence and potentiality had developed.

84. See A. Bolshakov, "Ka," *OEAE* 2:215–17 for this element in the human *ka*; and D. Meeks and C. Favard-Meeks, *Daily Life of the Egyptian Gods* (Ithaca, NY: Cornell Univ. Press, 1996), 71 for the divine *ka*.

85. Meeks and Favard-Meeks, *Daily Life*, 71.

Consequently, it is no surprise that the Israelite account is similar to Egyptian literature in other respects, in that, for instance, it does not contain even a hint of theomachy. Just as the Egyptian cosmogonies are largely one-sided affairs, with the creator deities doing their work at will in unopposed serenity, so this is true of the biblical account: God does the work of Genesis 1 at his own pace, with no opposition. This picture is not a departure from the ancient Near Eastern cognitive environment; in fact, it is typical, because, as noted above, theomachy is more common in mythology concerned with divine rule than it is in cosmogonies, even in Mesopotamia.

Days 1–3 (Genesis 1:3–13)

In the ancient world, light, like darkness, was a phenomenon experienced by human beings, not an object with wave/particle characteristics, as in modern physics. For the ancients, darkness was created in the same way that light was created, because all phenomena were created as part of the ordering of the cosmos. A close reading of the account of Day 1, however, yields further information supporting the idea that Genesis 1 is focused on functions more than on materials. The salient ideas will be most easily drawn out by starting with the conclusion to the first day in v. 5: "God called the light 'day' and the darkness he called 'night.'"

The key observation here is simple, yet fundamental. The very names that are given by God imply that what has been created on Day 1 are not objects or even phenomena but periods, for it is lengths of time that are represented by the names "day" and "night." We thus should assume that the statement involves metonymy and understand the verse as saying, "God called the [period of] light 'day' and the [period of] darkness he called 'night.'" The same observation applies when we investigate v. 4. In v. 4, "God separated the light from the darkness." As in v. 5, the light and darkness are periods, not objects, for objects could not be separated in this fashion. No one today thinks of darkness as an object, and as objects, light and darkness could not be joined in a fashion that would permit them to be separated.[86] Like v. 5, this verse must also be understood as involving metonymy: "God separated the [period of] light from the [period of] darkness." Thus, v. 5 is the natural subsequence of v. 4: having separated the periods of light and darkness, God gives them each their appropriate names.

---

86. I am not attempting to force the text into purely modern terms by making these points; I *am* trying to demonstrate that people who converse in such terms are revealing their modernity.

Verse 4, in turn, is the result of v. 3. How did God separate the period of light from the period of darkness? When the account began, there was nothing but darkness (v. 2), so there was no *period* of darkness. But in v. 3, God created light—that is, not an object but a *period* of light that was to interrupt the darkness. But this did not mean that there was now to be perpetual light as there had previously been perpetual darkness. Instead, this was a period of light that was to alternate with periods of darkness; the two thus separated were named "day" and "night." Thus, day and night were created on Day 1—or, as we refer to the alternation of day and night, *time* was created. On Day 1, God created time, the first of the great functions that order our world and our existence.[87]

When we consider the ancient Near East, we discover that there are perspectives about time and its relationship to creation that are quite similar to the perspective outlined above as being present in Genesis 1. E. Hornung points out that in the Egyptian understanding of the precosmic condition there was neither time nor the alternation of day and night; both of these are part of the existent.[88] S. Morenz also identifies time as the thing created that divides the precosmic condition from the created order, citing the Hermopolis tradition that the elemental gods stepped onto the primeval hillock and created light as the first step of ordering the cosmos and thus are named the fathers and mothers of light.[89]

> The concept of time found in the myth is, first of all, characterized by its understanding of time as absolute. Time stems ultimately from the one primeval act of power before which there was not time and beyond which one cannot pass. This dividing line which separates the world of being from that of non-being marks off the beginning of time. . . . Although the origin of time is projected into the past to the primeval act of becoming, this is only a form in which an essentially timeless reality is clothed. Time

---

87. It has often been noticed that Gen 1:5 uses the cardinal number *'eḥād* ('day one') rather than the ordinal number, as is true of the other days. In light of the understanding of the account that I propose here, the text is *not* marking the first day but is explaining what constitutes a single day. A period of light had been inserted into the primeval darkness, so the first transition between time periods was an evening; then, when the next transition (i.e., morning) came, bringing the period of light, it constituted "one day"—one of each period (light and darkness) with their associated transitions.

88. Hornung, *Conception of God*, 175–76.

89. Morenz, *Egyptian Religion*, 176. He cites Theban temples 145b, 35c with texts and translation by K. Sethe, *Amun und die acht Urgötter von Hermopolis: Eine Untersuchung über Ursprung und Wesen des ägyptischen Götterkönigs* (Abhandlungen der Preussische Akademie der Wissenschaften 29; Berlin: Akademie der Wissenschaften, 1929), §96.

is always present and yet to come. It transcends the modern categories of empirical time.[90]

The god Shu, the god of the air, is the deity separating the heaven from the earth and holding up the sky. In the literature, he is related to both light and time:

> My clothing is the air of life,
> Which emerged for it around me, from the mouth of Atum
> And opens for it the winds on my path
> I am the one who made possible the sky's brilliance after Darkness.[91]
> I am Life, lord of years,
> Life of Eternal Recurrence, lord of eternal sameness.[92]

The gods are often associated with light in the Sumerian hymnic literature (mostly the sun-gods, moon-gods, and Inanna = Venus), but the creation of light is rarely mentioned, with only a few exceptions, such as in this example.

Song of the Hoe

Not only did the lord make the world appear in its correct form—the lord who never changes the destinies which he determines: Enlil, who will make the human seed of the Land come forth from the earth—and not only did he hasten to separate heaven from earth, and hasten to separate earth from heaven, but, in order to make it possible for humans to grow in 'Where Flesh Came Forth', he first suspended the axis of the world at Dur-an-ki. He did this with the help of the hoe—and so daylight broke forth.[93]

More frequent, but still relatively uncommon, are references to the creation of time or the cycles associated with time, as in the following example.

Great Astrological Treatise

> When An, Enlil, and Enki, the great gods,
>   in their infallible counsel,
>   among the great laws (me) of heaven and earth.
>   had established the crescent of the moon,
>   which brought forth day, established the months

---

90. B. S. Childs, *Myth and Reality in the Old Testament* (London: SCM, 1960), 72–73. Note also the observation of J. Stek ("What Says the Scripture?" 238): "The creation of light and the division of light and darkness into the alternation of day and night accords with the ancient perception of that alternation as the basic structure of cosmic time."

91. CT 80 (*COS* 1.8).

92. CT 80 (*COS* 1.8); cf. CT 78 (*COS* 1.7): "I am Eternal Recurrence."

93. http://etcsl.orinst.ox.ac.uk, 5.5.4, lines 1–8.

> and furnished the omens
> drawn from heaven and earth,
> This crescent shone in heaven,
> and one saw the stars shining in the highest heaven![94]

Akkadian literature likewise shows little interest in the creation of light and makes only sporadic reference to the creation of time. In a broken section of *Enuma Elish*, Marduk apparently creates time, because the text's references to the day and the year are followed by a reference to the watches of the night.[95]

We can conclude that in Genesis the subject of Day 1 is the creation of a function, time. We can also observe that time is considered a principal function that is noted, though infrequently, in the ancient Near Eastern creation accounts. In Akkadian literature, light is infrequently mentioned and is usually either represented in the function of the heavenly bodies or is part of the establishment of time.

Day 2: Cosmic Geography and the Rāqīʿa

The account of Genesis 1 addresses not only the ordering of time but also the ordering of space. The category "space" subsumes cosmic geography (Day 2), terrestrial geography (Day 3), and sacred space and integrates them, because cosmic geography gives definition to the sacred space of the cosmic temple.

The description of the acts of Day 2 does not address the universal scope of cosmic geography but focuses instead on a single aspect, the positioning of the *rāqīʿa* 'expanse, firmament' as something separating the cosmic waters above from those below. It is difficult to establish a precise meaning for this noun based on usage because it only occurs 17 times,[96] and the contexts in which it occurs provide very little help.[97] Ezekiel's vision of the moving throne of Yahweh provides the most helpful information (Ezek

---

94. Clifford, *Creation Accounts*, 67. In the Akkadian version, the three named gods charge the great astral gods to produce (*banu*) day and to assure the regular sequence of months for astrological observation.

95. *Enuma Elish* V 39–40, 46. See Foster, *Before the* Muses, 464; Horowitz, *Mesopotamian Cosmic Geography*, 117–18. It is also worth noting that, in one of the Babylonian god-lists, the first deity to exist is Duri ("Ever and Ever"), referring to time. See Lambert, "The Cosmology of Sumer and Babylon," 53.

96. Nine of the occurrences are in Genesis 1, 5 in Ezekiel 1 and 10, and once each in Ps 19:2, 150:1; and Dan 12:3.

97. Semitic cognates only begin to appear late in history. Semantic equivalents, such as Akkadian *burumu* (*CAD* B 344–45, only Standard Babylonian and Neo-Babylonian) are not widely used but clearly refer to the solid sky. The *burumu* is generally described as bright and

1:22, 23, 25, 26; and 10:1). In these visions, the throne is positioned above the *rāqīʿa*, which in turn is located above the creatures who serve as throne-bearers and may be thought of as filling the cosmic role of "sky-bearers." This specific cosmic imagery is known throughout the ancient Near East.[98] The *rāqīʿa* below the throne is parallel to the cosmic *rāqīʿa*.[99]

The verb *rqʿ*, from which the noun is derived, occurs 11 times in four different conjugations. The Qal (Isa 42:5, 44:24; Ps 136:6; Ezek 6:11; 25:6; 2 Sam 22:43) is used idiomatically of stamping one's feet or, specifically in cosmic contexts (Isaiah and Psalms), of spreading out the earth on the waters. Note that these references to the cosmos offer a different view from Genesis 1, where the dry land emerges, rather than God's spreading it out over the waters. The (Piel) occurrences (Exod 39:3; Num 17:4[16:39]; Isa 40:19; Jer 10:9) concern metalworking, particularly hammering out thin pieces of gold or silver for plating.[100] The single Hiphil occurrence (Job 37:18) draws the cosmic context together with a metalworking metaphor: "Can you join him in spreading out the skies, hard as a mirror of cast bronze?"(NIV) In all of its permutations, the verbal root expresses the action of flattening out. Nevertheless, it is important to notice that, in the single occurrence of the verb to describe cosmic activity in the heavens (Job 37:18), it is not the *rāqīʿa* that is spread out but the *šĕḥāqîm*.[101]

Since a noun may develop in a different semantic direction than the verbal root from which it is derived, especially when the noun becomes fixed in a technical usage, semantic similarity between verb and noun is not to be assumed. We must therefore reconsider the meaning of *rāqīʿa* especially in light of Job 37:18. In the first line, Elihu poses the question to Job about whether he thinks he could join God in "spreading out the skies." This use of *rqʿ* stands uniquely apart from the other occurrences in both its verbal form (the only Hiphil) and its direct object (connected with the "skies" instead of the earth). The word translated 'skies' (*šĕḥāqîm*, plural) is often

---

is named as a place where the gods dwell and stars are set. Marduk is said to hold up the ends of it.

98. Görg, "רקיע *rāqīʿa*," *TDOT* 13:649.

99. F. Hartenstein, "Wolkendunkel und Himmelsfeste: Zur Genese und Kosmologie der Vorstellung des himmlischen Heiligtums JHWHs," in *Das biblische Weltbild und seine altorientalischen Kontexte* (ed. B. Janowski and B. Ego; FAT 32; Tübingen: Mohr-Siebeck, 2001), 140 n. 60.

100. The connection with metal that is suggested by the use of the Hebrew verb is closely associated with the Egyptian use of *bỉ3* for the 'firmament'; see Görg, "*rāqīʿa*," 651.

101. Since Hebrew style does not hesitate to use a verb and direct object of the same root, this fact is significant.

rendered 'clouds' in its 21 occurrences.[102] Nevertheless, we should notice that, in this context, Job 37:21 (again, 'skies' in the NIV) cannot possibly refer to the clouds since it specifically refers to a cloudless sky. Furthermore, 2 Sam 22:12 speaks of the "clouds of the *šĕḥāqîm*," indicating that the clouds are part of the *šĕḥāqîm*, rather than the *šĕḥaqim* being clouds. We should also note that in another cosmological context it is obvious that establishing the *šĕḥāqîm* refers to an act of creation rather than to something God does now and then (Prov 8:28).

In light of these data, we must undertake a fresh examination of the *šĕḥāqîm*.[103] In terms of their role, we find that they are never identified as the source of rain (as clouds would be) but are identified as the source of other forms of moisture. The verbs used to express this (*nzl*, Job 36:28; Isa 45:8; and *rʿp*, Job 36:28; Prov 3:20) are connected with dew.

Structurally, the *šĕḥāqîm* are part of the heavens (*šāmayim*) and can appear parallel to the heavens (Deut 33:26; Job 35:5, as can *rāqîʿa*). They are said to contain the doors of heaven through which manna came (Ps 78:23). Their appearance is described as "hard as a mirror of cast bronze" (Job 37:18). From these structural observations, I propose that *šĕḥāqîm* pertains to the solid sky, a common component of ancient Near Eastern cosmology. It is commonly accepted that the Israelites also believed in a solid sky, but usually scholars identify this solid sky with the *rāqîʿa*.

Given this fresh analysis of *šĕḥāqîm*, I propose that *rāqîʿa* refers to the space created when the *šĕḥāqîm* were put in place. This would explain why the birds and sun and moon are seen to be *in* the *raqîʿa*. Both *šĕḥāqîm* and *rāqîʿa* can be used parallel to *šāmayim* and perhaps they could be viewed as constituting the plurality of *šāmayim*. Alternatively, and preferably, in some cosmological literature from Mesopotamia the solid sky is believed to be made up of three levels of stone, and the texts detail what stone each is made of and which gods are associated with each.[104] The regular use of *šĕḥāqîm* in the plural may plausibly suggest that the Israelites also thought in similar terms.

Any such proposal must also deal with the potential problems, and there are three passages that require explanation if this hypothesis is to stand up to scrutiny. The customary translation of Job 38:37 indicates that the

---

102. 3X singular (Isa 40:15; Ps 89:7, 38), the remainder in the plural.

103. This study is excerpted from my commentary on *Job* (NIVAC; Grand Rapids, MI: Zondervan, forthcoming).

104. Horowitz, *Mesopotamian Cosmic Geography*, 243–67.

šĕḥāqîm can be counted (Piel of *spr*). 'Count' is certainly one of the possible meanings of this verb (though typically with the Qal; however, this verse has a Piel), and if it is to be retained we might consider whether it refers to counting the levels of heaven. The Piel and Pual forms of *spr* regularly refer to giving an account through a report or proclamation. In these occurrences, the context almost always indicates someone to whom the report or account is being given. Fortunately, Job 28:27 offers us a similar type of syntax and context in which wisdom is the object of the verb (NIV: 'appraised').[105] I therefore conclude that Job 38:37 is not referring to "counting the clouds" but to "appraising the nature of the (solid) skies."

The next problem arises when we try to understand the significance of the two passages where the singular *šaḥaq* is used. Ps 89:6–7 describes *šaḥaq* as the place where God and the divine council are located. If we are right to think of the plural as referring to multiple levels of heaven as in Mesopotamia, we could suggest that, like the Babylonians, the Israelites associated a particular level with the location of God's heavenly residence. Thus the plural was used to refer to all the levels as a component of the cosmos, but one particular level was where God dwelt. Likewise, Ps 89:37 would be seen as a reference to one particular level where the faithful witness was established.

Finally, and by far the most difficult context is Isa 40:15. All translators have struggled with this because the context clearly demands something like 'dust' on the scales as it refers to the insignificance of the nations. This perception is strengthened by the parallel to a drop in a bucket in the previous line and to "fine dust" in the following line. Yet it is odd to take a word that otherwise refers to a macrocomponent of the cosmos and here translate it 'dust'.

The solution that I have to offer combines the needs of this context with the idea previously mentioned that the *šĕḥāqîm* were understood as the source of the dew. In ancient Near Eastern texts, the source of dew is the stars,[106] which are believed to be engraved on the underside of the lowest level of the solid sky.[107] This would demonstrate that connections between the dew, the stars, and the solid sky were made in the ancient Near East. Once the stars are in the picture, another Akkadian term takes on some significance for this discussion. One of the Akkadian terms for speaking of the heavens is *burumu*. It refers to the level of the skies that hold the night stars

---

105. Similar usage can be seen in Ps 26:7 and probably Ps 50:16
106. Horowitz, *Mesopotamian Cosmic Geography*, 243–44.
107. Horowitz, *Mesopotamian Cosmic Geography*, 13–15.

and specifically to the appearance of the stars as specks.[108] In the context of
Isa 40:15, the nations would then be likened to the appearance of the night
sky (the starry *šaḥaq*—not all the levels, just this one) on the scales. They
would thus be considered specks on the scale. The interpretation of the passage would not change, but, unlike previous readings, this one makes sense
of the metaphor. Isaiah refers to the great multitude of parts making up the
whole (same as drops in a bucket) and the corresponding insignificance of
each part. He uses the scale metaphor instead of just speaking of the stars
in the sky itself in order to bring in the assessment—the nations are being
weighed, measured, assessed, judged.

If *šĕḥāqîm* refers to the solid sky, then *rāqîʿa* must refer to something else.
Looking carefully at the contexts in which it is used, I agree with what has
been a common understanding—that it refers to the space between heaven
and earth (NIV "expanse"). In this connection, we should note that Genesis 1
identifies the *rāqîʿa* as a separator between the waters above and the waters
below, not between the waters above and the air (which would have been
a more accurate description of the solid barrier). If this is so, the *rāqîʿa* is
most comparable to the role of Shu (god of the air, who is positioned between earth and heaven, holding up the latter) in the Egyptian cosmology
rather than to Nut (sky-god representing the solid barrier and the starry
expanse). Shu actually has more prominence in the cosmological texts than
Nut does. He is described as having been given birth by Atum when he
parted Nut and Geb (sky and earth).[109] Since Sumerian and Akkadian texts
speak little of the space between heaven and earth, the Israelite ideas reflect,
again, more of the Egyptian perspective. Note J. Allen's description: "To
the Egyptians, the world of experience was a finite 'box' of light, space, and
order within an infinite expanse of dark, formless waters. The limits of this
space were defined by the earth below and the surface of the outer waters
above, held off the earth by the atmosphere."[110] Genesis 1 also reflects this
"box" perspective, and the *rāqîʿa* is that which creates the space—a bubble,
as it were—between the waters.

The fact that the *rāqîʿa*, operating in tandem with the *šĕḥāqîm*, separates
the upper waters from the lower waters identifies it as a feature of cosmic

---

108. Horowitz, *Mesopotamian Cosmic Geography*, 226. Horowitz points out that the noun
derives from the verb *baramu* 'to be speckled'.
109. Coffin Text spell 80, *COS* 1.8, p. 13 (from CT 2 39b–40b). For other examples of the
significance of Shu, see *COS* 1.6 and 1.7, Coffin Text spells 76 and 78.
110. Allen, *Genesis in Egypt*, 56.

geography known from the cosmogonies of the ancient world. A variety of images are used in the ancient world for the material of which the solid sky is made, and the Israelites may likewise have had a similar variety of pictures, but throughout the ancient Near East it was seen as solid because it held back the upper cosmic waters. The material itself is irrelevant: it does not matter whether it is a dome or a tent, made of metal or a stone pavement, or whether it is held up by mountains, poles, ropes, or the arms of a god.[111] Though the idea of something holding back the waters above is a commonplace in the ancient world, most cosmogonies do not recount the separation of the waters per se (this concept must be differentiated from the separation of heaven and earth). In fact, only Genesis 1 and *Enuma Elish* include this specific event, the separation of the waters above from the waters below, in the sequence of origins.[112]

If, as proposed in this analysis, the *rāqîʿa* is the space opened up by 'spreading out' (*rqʿ*, Job 37:18) the *šĕḥāqîm* to hold back the waters above, and by 'spreading' (*rqʿ*, e.g., Isa 42:5) the earth over the waters, it is not material by our scientific standards. The *rāqîʿa* and the *šĕḥāqîm* are pieces of ancient cosmic geography that have been rendered obsolete by modern cosmic geography because we have learned, through science, of the evaporation/condensation cycle. For the Israelites, as with everyone else in the ancient world, the solid sky is a material piece of the cosmos, though the Egyptian portrayal of it as a god (Nut) and the Babylonian portrayal of it as part of the divided body of Tiamat warn us against a view that is too material. Instead of objectifying this water barrier, we should focus on the important, twofold cosmic function that it played. The first role of the *rāqîʿa* was to create the space in which people could live; the second, and more relevant function for the context of Genesis 1, was to be a mechanism by which precipitation was controlled—the means by which rain and precipitation operated.[113] Order in the cosmos (for people especially) depended

---

111. A good summary of ancient views (not just from the Near East) can be found in P. Seely, "The Firmament and the Water Above," *WTJ* 53 (1991): 227–40. Seely includes in his survey early Jewish and rabbinic sources and the early church fathers; see p. 236. For a wide variety of iconographic representations of the solid sky being supported, see Keel, *Symbolism*, 24–47.

112. Tiamat's corpse is used as a cover (*ṣullulu*) for heaven (*šamami*) in *Enuma Elish* IV 138 and spread as a cover (*ṣullulu*) in V 62 (see entry in *CAD* Ṣ 239). This use of *ṣullulu* is semantically similar to the Hebrew use of the verb *rqʿ*.

113. Note that in *Enuma Elish* V 50–52 it is Tiamat's corpse (the solid sky) that is seen as the source of precipitation.

on the right amount of precipitation. Too little, and starvation resulted; too much, and damaging flooding occurred. The cosmic waters posed a continual threat, and the *rāqī'a* was created to establish cosmic order.

Genesis 1 does not provide a revised Cosmic Geography for Israel to adopt in contradistinction to the perception and belief systems of the rest of the ancient world. Instead, the known elements of cosmic geography are well represented in this text (and other biblical texts) and thoroughly integrated into it. Although slight variations occur in the biblical portrayal, the variations are not scientifically or theologically innovative. All of the elements of heaven and earth are located in the same places and have the same functions that they do throughout the ancient world. The differences are found in the role of deity and the relationship of deity to the cosmos. Furthermore, Day 2 concerns architectural design, not original composition. Thus, Genesis 1 uses cosmic geography to represent divine jurisdiction over the observable functions of the known material world—in this case, the function of weather, controlled in their understanding by the structure of the heavens.

Day 3: Creation of Fecundity

Day 3 begins with a gathering rather than a separating, but the gathering of the waters is undertaken so that the dry land might appear. Water and dry land do not need to be distinguished from one another because they are not viewed as unified. Likewise, in ancient Near Eastern materials, the dry land emerges rather than being separated from the waters.

Like Day 2, Day 3 is concerned with space, but in this case it is terrestrial space rather than cosmic space that is the focus. When commentators have studied the literary structure of Genesis 1, they have often observed that there appear to be two separate acts of creation on Day 3 (water/dry land, and vegetation), and it is usually suggested that there are likewise two separate creations on Day 6 (animals and people). Though this observation makes sense from a literary perspective, it must be recognized that these pairings only appear to be distinct units when they are considered from a material perspective. From a functional perspective, the soil, the water, and the principle of seed-bearing are all very much related: all are essential to the production of food. In Egypt, the dry land emerges in the form of the primeval hillock. This image reflects the yearly emergence of fertile soil from the waters of the Nile as the flooding subsides. This image makes it clear that the emergence of dry land has to do with the issue of fecundity.

It has also been noted that none of the verbs for 'to create' are used in the narrative of Day 3. This has led some commentators to raise the specific question What did God make on Day 3?[114] But asking this question only demonstrates how pervasive our material ontology is and illustrates the confusion caused when we impose it on the text. The text implies that God is indeed involved in creation on Day 3 just as much as on any other day, once the text is understood in its ancient context: creation is an ordering activity rather than a manufacturing enterprise. On Day 3, God created the basis for fecundity, fertility, vegetation, and agriculture—in short, he provided what was necessary to make the earth a source of food.

Functional versus Material Language

In earlier discussions of some of the key verbs used in Genesis 1 (*bārā'* and *'āśâ*), I have tried to demonstrate that they express activity related to the establishment of functions rather than to the manufacture of material. On Day 3, two additional verbs that have only functional aspects have appeared: 'separating' and 'naming'. In the ancient world, these verbs express the ways in which roles were assigned and functions were initiated. In a functional ontology, these are effectively verbs of creation.

Separating and Naming

Separating. It is interesting to note that the separating (1:4, 6–7, 14, 18; days 1, 2, and 4) and naming (1:5, 8, 10; days 1, 2, and 3) occur on the first three days. Although separating is mentioned on Day 4, the account simply differentiates further the periods that were already separated on Day 1: the periods of light and darkness. In this sense, no additional separation takes place on Day 4.

The prominence of separating and naming on the first three days distinguishes the first three days from the second three in Genesis 1 and demonstrates again the extent to which Genesis is at home in the cognitive environment of ancient Near Eastern cosmogony, for these activities permeate both Egyptian and Mesopotamian accounts.

In Mesopotamia, it is primarily the heaven and earth that are separated (see pp. 35–37). The fact, however, that texts report a state when "all lands were sea"[115] shows that additionally refined separations were necessary

---

114. Note Wenham's comment: "The work of the third involved no new creation, but more an organization of existing material" (*Genesis 1–15*, 20).

115. This statement appears in a Seleucid period text, *Cosmogony and the Foundation of Eridu*; cited by Clifford, *Creation Accounts*, 63.

in the process of creation. In Egypt, everything that exists was separated out at the appropriate stage from the original Monad that embodied everything in a singularity. "Creation is the process through which the One became the Many."[116] This is nothing like the separating that takes place in Genesis, but the Egyptian scenario demonstrates that the act of separating was considered to be a creative activity.

Naming. Egyptian literature identified the creator-god as the one who pronounced the name of everything.[117] It is this naming that called something into existence, for with the name comes an essence, a role, and a function.

> It was believed that the name of a living being or an object was not just a simple or practical designation to facilitate the exchange of ideas between persons but that it was the very essence of what was defined, and that the actual pronouncing of a name was to create what was spoken.[118]

Similarly, *Enuma Elish* begins with the heavens and the earth not yet named—when even the gods had not yet been given names. Then, Laḫmu and Laḫamu emerge, and their names are pronounced.

It is evident, then, that Genesis reflects the same way of thinking as in the rest of the ancient world when it considers separating and naming to be primary creative acts. But why are these activities restricted to the first three days of Genesis 1? The examination of the events of the first three days presented here has shown that on these days the establishment of the basis for time, weather, and food production occurred. These three principal functions are also grouped together in other ancient Near Eastern texts.

One observation that could be made is that days 1–3 in Genesis could be seen as paralleling the triad of chief gods in Mesopotamia: Anu is in charge of the calendar and the seasons; Enlil is a sky- and weather-god; Ea is the god of the *apsu*, the streams, and the fecundity that results from their watering the land. This is by no means a precise, one-to-one correspondence, however, because, for instance, Anu and Enlil both also have some responsibility for vegetation: Anu is referred to as the one who "makes the seeds sprout."[119] One could draw a similar correspondence to primeval deities in Egypt, where Time is represented by the sun-god, Weather by the

---

116. Allen, *Genesis in Egypt*, 57.

117. *Memphite Theology*, line 55

118. J. M. Plumley, "The Cosmology of Ancient Egypt," in *Ancient Cosmologies* (ed. C. Blacker and M. Loewe; London: Allen and Unwin, 1975), 38.

119. Jacobsen, *Treasures of Darkness*, 96.

air-god, Shu, and fecundity by Ptah.[120] But even were we to consider these correlations to be artificial, texts themselves evidence the same tripartite functions, as the following examples show.

The Sumerian Debate between Winter and Summer

> An lifted his head in pride and brought forth a good day. He laid plans for . . . and spread the population wide. Enlil set his foot upon the earth like a great bull. Enlil, the king of all lands, set his mind to increasing the good day of abundance, to making the . . . night resplendent in celebration, to making flax grow, to making barley proliferate, to guaranteeing the spring floods at the quay, to making . . . lengthen (?) their days in abundance, to making Summer close the sluices of heaven, and to making Winter guarantee plentiful water at the quay.[121]

This text focuses on the three functions—day and night, fertility, and the weather (Summer/Winter, sluices of heaven). A similar focus can be observed in *Enuma Elish*, in a fragmentary section of tablet V. Lines 39–40 refer to the day and the year, and line 46 refers to the watches of the night; in lines 47–52, Marduk creates precipitation, which is accompanied by clouds, winds, and fog; then, in lines 53–58, water sources on earth are established and dirt is piled up.[122] In this sequence, time, weather, and vegetation are addressed in order and in functional terms.[123] Compare the familiarity of this summary offered by a modern Assyriologist of Mesopotamian creation after the separation of heaven and earth:

> With Enlil, the modern universe is founded; he establishes just rule, and with the other Anunna decides the fates on the Holy Mound. Darkness turns into light, the moon and the sun, Nanna and Utu are born, Summer and Winter brought forth by Enlil and Hursag; undefined time turns into days, months, seasons and years.[124]

All of the elements are recognizable from our reading of Genesis 1. In Genesis, we discover that chap. 1 is not the only text in which this focus on the three primary functions is evident. It has long been recognized that the flood account is presented as a dismantling of the ordered cosmos, followed

---

120. Allen, *Genesis in Egypt*, 41.

121. http://etcsl.orinst.ox.ac.uk, 5.3.3.2.

122. Horowitz, *Mesopotamian Cosmic Geography*, 117–18.

123. W. G. Lambert ("Kosmogonie," *RlA*, 6:218–22) identifies three prime elements of the cosmos in ancient Mesopotamian literature: earth, water, and time. It would not take much imagination to see the relationship of these to the first three days of creation in reverse order.

124. Wiggermann, "Mythological Foundations," 286.

by a re-creation. As this re-creation, an echo of Genesis 1, is brought to a conclusion, God's promise concerning the stability of this re-creation is articulated in reverse order, reestablishing food, weather, and time (Gen 8:22):

As long as the earth endures,
Seedtime and harvest,
Cold and heat,
Summer and winter,
Day and night
Will never cease.

The first three days of Genesis 1 can therefore be seen as functional in orientation, treating the three functions most significant for human life, not only in the ancient world but in every culture of every time and place, even to the present day, regardless of technological accomplishments and scientific sophistication. Days 4–6, as we will see in the next chapter, though still operating within a functional ontology, focus on functionaries (and their functions) instead of on primary functions of the cosmos. The change in focus may also explain why separating and naming are linked primarily to days 1–3, since separating and naming are related to establishing functions. Days 4 through 6 are primarily interested in the installation of the functionaries into their appropriate realms.

It is useful to pause to assess how the analysis of Genesis 1 relates to the cognitive environment as it was laid out in the first half of this monograph. The functional ontology that was found to be prevalent throughout the ancient Near East has been confirmed to be present and operative in Genesis 1 through analysis of the verbs used to describe creative activity, through the analysis of the precreation state (especially with regard to *tōhû*), and through a close reading of days 1–3, which attempted to demonstrate that text's concerns are with functions rather than material things. The analysis has also shown that ancient world's cosmic geography is amply attested in Genesis as well. We will now consider the issue of the cosmic governing principles.

Cosmic Governing Principles

In an earlier chapter, I suggested that the cosmic governing principles comprised quintessential archetypes (ME/*parṣu*) and destinies (NAM/*šimtu*), each representing what was static or dynamic, respectively. These governing principles were part of the ordered cosmos and therefore not part of the

preexistent condition. The static MEs came into being with the cosmos and
the gods and were not created by the gods but were activated, administered,
and delegated by the gods. The dynamic destinies involved the assignment
of roles to functionaries; the tablet of destinies, representing the right to
decree destinies, was a symbol of rule.

How, then, were governing principles represented in Genesis 1? H. W. F.
Saggs notes that "there are no terms in Hebrew serving as near equivalents
of the Sumerian nam.tar and me."[125] Nevertheless, he proceeds to suggest
that there are instances in the Hebrew Bible in which Yahweh determines
destinies. For our purposes here, his inclusion of Gen 8:22 in the list of texts
of this sort, mentioned just above, is significant. In addition, Psalm 148, in
which the various inhabitants of creation are called upon to praise Yahweh,
is worth consideration in this connection (translation from NIV):

> Praise the LORD.
> Praise the LORD from the heavens,
>   praise him in the heights above.
> Praise him, all his angels,
>   praise him, all his heavenly hosts.
> Praise him, sun and moon,
>   praise him, all you shining stars.
> Praise him, you highest heavens
>   and you waters above the skies.
> **Let them praise the name of the LORD,**
>   **for he commanded and they were created.**
> **He set them in place for ever and ever;**
>   **he gave a decree that will never pass away.**
>
> Praise the LORD from the earth,
>   you great sea creatures and all ocean depths,
> lightning and hail, snow and clouds,
>   stormy winds that do his bidding,
> you mountains and all hills,
>   fruit trees and all cedars,
> wild animals and all cattle,
>   small creatures and flying birds,
> kings of the earth and all nations,
>   you princes and all rulers on earth,
> young men and maidens,
>   old men and children.

---

125. H. W. F. Saggs, *Encounter with the Divine in Mesopotamia and Israel* (London: Athlone, 1978), 73.

Let them praise the name of the LORD,
>for his name alone is exalted;
>his splendor is above the earth and the heavens.
He has raised up for his people a horn,
>the praise of all his saints,
>of Israel, the people close to his heart.
Praise the LORD.

Verse 5–6 are particularly significant because they portray Yahweh as the one who commanded the creation (*brʾ*) of these cosmic inhabitants and decreed (*ḥq ntn*) their destinies.[126]

These expressions suggest the possibility that Genesis 1 be understood in light of the concepts behind the ME/*šimtu* complex; if so, God's creative activities would be seen as establishing and maintaining order, just as do the ME. Perhaps days 1–3 should be associated with the ME of the cosmos but viewed, not just as activating something that was already part of the cosmos, but as initiating it into the cosmos. Days 4–6, then, could be seen as determining the destinies of the functionaries within the cosmos (again, therefore, not concerned with separating and naming). When the destinies of the gods were determined in the ancient Near East, powers and responsibilities were delegated to them. As a result, other gods became "working Enlils" when the MEs were given to them.[127] This process bears a resemblance to the biblical idea that human beings were created in the image of God and became beings who functioned as Elohim at some level.

In distinct contrast to Mesopotamian beliefs, however, Genesis 1, if it in fact is paralleling the idea of the MEs, positions them differently. Rather than positing deity as guardian of the cosmic MEs (which are not created by the gods, in Mesopotamian thought), Genesis portrays God as the one who initiates the cosmic MEs. This view coincides with the observations made on pp. 62–63 that in Genesis Yahweh is outside the cosmic system, although in the ancient Near East the gods are viewed as inside the system. Thus, the Mesopotamian gods are subject to the MEs, while Yahweh controls them. This is similar to the idea that in Israel Yahweh is considered the *source* of law, whereas in Mesopotamia Shamash is the *guardian* of law.

A similar distinction obtains with regard to the *šimati*: Yahweh does not need his *šimati* to be decreed by anyone, nor does he decree the *šimati* of other deities. Predictably, the Israelite God does not delegate powers to

---

126. Noticed also by Clifford, *Creation Accounts*, 68 n. 24.
127. Rosengarten, *Sumer et le Sacré*, 120, *Enliluti* ("l'Enlillité").

other gods but brings order to the cosmos by determining the destinies of its inhabitants. Similarly, in Genesis there is no Tablet of Destinies. Yahweh needs no emblem because he does not need to protect his power from usurpation by other deities such as Anzu or Kingu.

Before moving on, we should pause briefly to consider the proposal of F. Wiggermann that there was a development in Mesopotamian thought that shifted the emphasis from the ME to the destinies.[128]

> The meaning of this conflict [Enmešara's challenge of the main gods] for cosmogony lies in the tension between essences, me, and divine government, nam-tar, "decreeing the fates". The essences are by nature part of existence, they came into being with what was created, but they are not created themselves. Enlil, An and Enkig represent active rulership, they distribute the essences over the gods and assign each his task, nam-tar. The essences are made subservient to the purposes of just rule. The brainless old cosmos of essences had to go, but it did not give way without a struggle, it rebelled: Enmešara, "Lord all Essences", tried to know namtar and rule like Enlil, but he was defeated. What there is was subordinated to divine government for good.[129]

One might claim that Genesis 1 undertakes a similar task, in that it offers a cosmogony that is entirely and thoroughly hegemonic.[130] Nonetheless, the rulership of Yahweh is portrayed not as the result of a shift in emphasis but by a theological positioning that places him outside the cosmos and makes him the creator and ruler of all governing principles, controlling functions, and functionaries.

Two final issues that appear prominently in Genesis can now be considered anew in light of the relationship suggested between Genesis 1 and the ME/*šimtu* complex. These two are a regular part of the formulas that characterize Genesis 1: creation by speech, and the assessment that "it was good."

Creation by Speech

It has often been noted that creation by speech is a commonplace in Egyptian literature.

> Old Testament scholars are familiar with the *Memphite Theology* as a creation by fiat that predates Genesis. However, this concept is found elsewhere in Egyptian literature, too. In CT II, 23 life is created "according to

---

128. Wiggermann, "Mythological Foundations," 279–306.
129. Wiggermann, "Mythological Foundations," 288.
130. In the rest of the Pentateuch, use of magic is also excluded from acceptable behavior as part of an unacceptable aspect of the surrounding cognitive environment.

the word (*ḥft mdw*) of Nun in Nu, in Hehu, in *tnmw*, in Keku." The command (*wd*) of Atum is responsible for the creation of animal life in CT II, 42–43. Similar to the logos creation of Ptah in the Memphite theology is that attributed to Ptah on the little known stela of Ptah and Sekhmet. This late 18th or early 19th Dynasty text says of Ptah: *dd.tw m ib.f mʒ ḥpr.sn* "One says in his mind (lit., heart), 'Look, may they come into being'."[131]

In contrast to Egyptian literature, it is typically claimed that Mesopotamian cosmologies do not evidence creation by the spoken word. This assessment, however, is colored by what is understood as "creation." If creation was viewed in terms of functional ontology, it would not entail deity calling material objects into existence by the spoken word but would refer to establishing and assigning functions by fiat. And if we grant this definition, Mesopotamian literature is replete with creation by the spoken word, in that the decreeing of the destinies is always accomplished in this way. Consider this Hymn to Enki for Išme-Dagan:

> Lord who among the gods makes the clever decisions, most prominent among them from the south to the uplands; who holding a staff in his hand determines their destinies as the Anuna gods come to him; who possessing all the divine powers is alone surpassing; a great lord, who ... the living things; who alone is proclaimed as their god—you are their .... You, whose utterances make justice flourish, strengthen the divine powers of heaven and earth. You, who examine the ordinances and carry them out correctly, are proclaimed as their great prince.[132]

In similar fashion, Genesis 1 portrays God as issuing decrees, by the spoken word, that establish functions in the cosmos and install the functionaries (decreeing their destinies) in their appropriate spheres. If this comparison is followed to its logical conclusion, it becomes apparent that the role of the spoken word in Genesis 1 takes on a new level of comparison, since the MES were also established by the spoken word.[133]

It Was Good

In addition, the MES were considered "good"—the best possible expression of world order.[134] The recurring formula in Genesis 1—"it was good"—offers this same assessment of the creative acts that brought order to the cosmos: the cosmos now functioned well. The evidence that this is the

---

131. Hoffmeier, "Thoughts on Genesis 1 and 2," 45.
132. http://etcsl.orinst.ox.ac.uk (Išme-Dagan X) 2.5.4.24, lines 1–6.
133. Rosengarten, *Sumer et le Sacré*, 219–20.
134. Rosengarten, *Sumer et le Sacré*, 12, 74.

nuance of the Hebrew word *ṭob* (which admittedly has a wide semantic range) comes from the context. Contextually, it is useful to consider the nuance that the word has by asking what it would look like for something *not* to be good. Fortunately, the context does indicate something that is not good: "It is not good for the man to be alone" (Gen 2:18). The word *ṭob* in this context concerns proper functioning; it is not a negative assessment of craftsmanship or moral purity. We can therefore infer that the recurring assessment that things were good in Genesis 1 does not refer to the absence of corruption or flaw. It instead is an affirmation that the functions were set to operate according to their design.[135] This is the same sort of statement that is also made in the hymnic literature when the gods of Mesopotamia are praised for their perfect designs and efficacious utterances.

But there is one more important contribution made by Gen 2:18. This text makes it clear that the focus of the designed functions is not on God but on humanity. The biblical text is not interested in the scientifically investigatable functions of the various parts of the cosmos. That is to say, the function of time established by the alternating periods of light and darkness has no meaning or significance apart from people. This function serves neither the divine realm nor the "natural" realm. Not only is the sun not a manifestation of deity in Genesis, but it neither functions for deity's sake nor is it simply a burning ball of gas.[136] As v. 14 reports, the function of the lights is to mark signs, festivals,[137] days, and years—precisely the uses that humans have for these functionaries.

Conclusion: Threefold Functions

Although Gen 1:1–2 contains elements that support the functional understanding of Genesis 1, days 1–3 provide the bulk of the evidence that this is indeed the perspective underlying the text. The three functions—time, weather, and food production—are called into existence by the utterance of God and are given their functions through acts of separating and naming, with both the functions themselves and the actions that make them operational having precedents in the cognitive environment of the ancient

---

135. This interpretation is also found in Coote and Ord, *In the Beginning*, 56.

136. Note the conversation in C. S. Lewis's *Voyage of the Dawn Treader* between one of the children and a "retired" star: "'In our world,' said Eustace, 'a star is a huge ball of flaming gas.' 'Even in your world, my son,' replied the old man, 'that is not what a star is, but only what it is made of.'"

137. For the evidence that *môʿădîm* here refers to 'festivals' rather than 'seasons', see W. Vogels, "The Cultic and Civil Calendars of the Fourth Day of Creation (Gen 1,14b)," *SJOT* 11 (1997): 178–79; D. J. Rudolph, "Festivals in Genesis 1:14," *TynBul* 54/2 (2003): 23–40.

Near East. They are evaluated and found to be perfectly functional ("good") for the human world. These functions are comparable to the quintessential archetypes (MES) that are featured prominently in Mesopotamian literature, except that, in Genesis, God is positioned differently in relationship to them. The creative activity therefore involves bringing these functions into action in a system ordered around human beings. This concept is also recognized by Vanstiphout in his observations about *Enki and the World Order*:

> The interest lies not so much in the material goods themselves—they were there anyway—but in the possibility of realizing their potential. The things themselves were already in existence: the need was for a system by which they could be used efficiently.[138]

The scene is set to continue on to days 4–6, when the functionaries are installed and, in Mesopotamian terms, their destinies are decreed.

Days 4–6 (Genesis 1:14–31)

As indicated in the previous chapter, though the account in days 4–6 remains function oriented, it now has to do with installing functionaries into their appropriate areas of responsibility and giving them roles within their respective realms. This action is similar to the decreeing of destinies in Mesopotamian literature and, like the acts of days 1–3, constitutes an act of rule by God.

Day 4

The cosmic geography of the ancient world is reflected in Genesis 1 by the fact that the celestial bodies are all located in the *rāqîʿa*. If the meaning of creation in Genesis 1 is governed by a functional rather than material focus, the age-old question about how light could exist during Day 1 when the sun was not created until Day 4 has been answered. The account is not describing material origins. Functions (such as time) appropriately are given pride of place; they are introduced before the mere functionaries (such as celestial bodies) that inhabit time and perform their tasks for humanity are commissioned.

The choice of the term "lights" need not be polemical; the label is, instead, the clearest functional term. It is possible, however, that the biblical author wanted to be clear that he intended no decreeing of destinies for

---

138. Vanstiphout, "Why Did Enki Organize the World?" 122.

lesser gods in this context, which was often the case in the Mesopotamian accounts. This is especially important because the function that is attributed to the lights is ruling.[139]

The functions listed for the lights are separating,[140] designating calendrical periods or moments,[141] lighting, and governing—all notions that obtain their meaning from an anthropocentric perspective and are related to time, which had been established on Day 1. A similar list of functions for the celestial bodies is found in the *Great Astrological Treatise*:

> When An, Enlil, and Enki, the great gods,
>   in their infallible counsel,
>   among the great laws (ME) of heaven and earth,
>   had established the crescent of the moon,
>   which brought forth day, established the months
>   and furnished the omens
>   drawn from heaven and earth,
> This crescent shone in heaven,
>   and one saw the stars shining in the highest heaven![142]

Day 5

The spoken word is also prominent on Day 5, as living creatures are installed in the areas established in Day 2. The birds fly across the face of the *rāqîʿa*, and the fish swim in the waters below. The waters above have no inhabitants.

It is significant that the text makes special note of the *tannînim* in Gen 1:21. The narrative returns to using the verb *bārāʾ*, thus marking these sea creatures as part of the ordered world of the existent, not representatives of disorder or threats to order from within the "existent," the latter being a role that Apophis had, as we noted above (p. 72).[143] Furthermore, the *tannîn*

---

139. Note the absence of the the sun(-god)'s usual role in maintaining justice. The governing referred to in Genesis has nothing to do with a ruler providing justice for humanity but only with providing light.

140. Note that God's separating is not an act of creation but his using of the celestial bodies to maintain the separation that was put in place at the first, on Day 1.

141. Note that the word *ʾōtōt* 'signs' is used without hesitation or polemic, despite how close it comes to validating the ideas behind celestial divination. The establishment of the festivals in ancient times is also portrayed in *KAR* 4, line 63 (as cited by Clifford, *Creation Accounts*, 51, line 46).

142. Clifford, *Creation Accounts*, 67. In the Akkadian version, the three named gods charge the great astral gods to produce (*banu*) day and to ensure the regular sequence of months for astrological observation.

143. For a helpful introduction to all of these beasts, see J. Westenholz, *Dragons, Monsters and Fabulous Beasts* (Jerusalem: Bible Lands Museum, 2004).

are not to be compared to the 11 composite creatures that aid Tiamat in *Enuma Elish*.[144] As is true throughout Genesis 1, the absence of theomachy is notable.

The Hebrew Bible refers to a variety of cosmic sea creatures (see Isa 27:1 and Ps 74:13–15). *Tannîn* occurs 14 times in the Hebrew Bible[145] and is usually considered to be related to the Ugaritic noun, *tunnanu*, which in the literature from Ras Shamra is a great sea monster defeated by Anat and Baal.[146] Wakeman contends that *tannîn* is "unlike Rahab and Leviathan in being more properly a generic term for the mythical monster than a personal name."[147] Of the 14 occurrences in the Hebrew Bible, 8 refer to zoological creatures, presumably a crocodile, at least in some contexts.[148] The remaining 5 occurrences, as in Genesis 1, refer to cosmic creatures. In Job 7:12, *tannîn* occurs parallel to *yam* (which is either the sea, generically, or, because of the parallel, the creature representing the sea, Yamm, as in Ugaritic Literature).[149] In Ps 74:13–14, the *tannîn* is portrayed as having multiple heads and occurs in poetic parallelism to Leviathan, an opponent overcome by Yahweh. The background of battle is also present in Isa 51:9, where the cosmic creatures *tannîn* and *Rahab* are defeated. In Isa 27:1, *tannîn* is among the cosmic creatures historicized as enemies to be defeated. Finally, in Ps 148:7, the text that presents the *tannin* most like the image in Gen 1:21, the *tannin* is simply another creature called upon to praise Yahweh.[150] In this text, it is probably a cosmic creature but not an adversary.

---

144. *Ee* I 133–43. See the discussion in W. G. Lambert, "Ninurta Mythology in the Babylonian Epic of Creation," *Keilschriftliche Literaturen: Ausgewälte Vorträge der XXXII. Rencontre assyriologique internationale* (ed. K. Hecker and W. Sommerfeld; Berliner Beiträge zum Vorderen Orient 6; Berlin: Reimer, 1986), 56–58.

145. See the discussion in M. Wakeman, *God's Battle with the Monster* (Leiden: Brill, 1973), 68–82.

146. There are eight occurrences in Ugaritic literature: twice in personal names, three times as a monster defeated by Anat, and three times in fragmentary contexts that do not permit complete analysis; *DDD²*, 835; see S. B. Parker, *Ugaritic Narrative Poetry* (SBLWAW 9; Atlanta: Society of Biblical Literature, 1997), 111, line 40.

147. Wakeman, *God's Battle*, 79.

148. In Exod 7:9–12 and Ps 91:13, the *tannîn* is probably a crocodile, as well as in Ezek 29:3 and 32:2, in both of which it is used as a metaphor representing Pharaoh. In Deut 32:33, the *tannîn* appears to be a zoological creature, but in this case it cannot be a crocodile because it has venom.

149. The understanding of *tannîn* and *Yamm* as chaos creatures has been persuasively disputed by Watson, *Chaos Uncreated*, 282–89.

150. Watson concludes that in Ps 148:7 the term is "all-embracing," referring to all marine creatures (*Chaos Uncreated*, 210).

The blessing given in Gen 1:22 is part of the decreeing of destinies and further describes the function of these creatures: they are to multiply on the earth.

Day 6

Land animals are the inhabitants of the dry land that emerged on Day 3. There are relatively few texts in the ancient world that recount the creation of animals, and in many cases, they are only referred to in passing; a few are cited here.

A Babylonian text entitled *Two Insects* describes the gods' meeting in assembly after they had created heaven and earth: "They brought into being the animals . . . large wild animals, wild animals, small wild animals . . . they allotted their respective domains to the cattle and the small domestic animals."[151] In this text, creation included putting animals in their appropriate habitat.[152]

Enki and the World Order

He made this good place perfect with greenery in abundance. He multiplied the animals of the high plain to an appropriate degree, he multiplied the ibex and wild goats of the pastures, and made them copulate.[153]

Exploits of Ninurta

Let its meadows produce herbs for you. Let its slopes produce honey and wine for you. Let its hillsides grow cedars, cypress, juniper and box for you. Let it make abundant for you ripe fruits, as a garden. Let the mountain supply you richly with divine perfumes. . . . Let the mountains make wild animals teem for you. Let the mountain increase the fecundity of quadrupeds for you.[154]

In both of these texts, the centrality of animal fecundity parallels the blessing provided in Genesis. The animals are also placed in the context of greenery, a connection that is represented in Genesis by the relationship between Day 3 and Day 6. Finally, in the *Exploits of Ninurta*, it is the mountains that make the animals teem, paralleling the function that the dry land has in Genesis.

---

151. Clifford, *Creation Accounts*, 65.

152. See also the so-called *Eridu Genesis*, COS 1.158, line 14. Jacobsen's translation implies that the animals are coming forth from the ground, as in Genesis, but the translation on the Oxford Sumerian literature site differs: http://etcsl.orinst.ox.ac.uk, 1.7.4, 14.

153. http://etcsl.orinst.ox.ac.uk, 1.1.3.

154. http://etcsl.orinst.ox.ac.uk, 1.6.2

Humanity

As we have noted repeatedly in the comparative analysis undertaken in this study, the shared ancient Near Eastern cognitive environment is evident in the Genesis account, even though there is often a marked departure in the specifics. As in the ancient Near Eastern literature, the text of Genesis 1 is role oriented: it focuses on the station of people in the cosmos and the functions that they have been assigned to carry out. But Genesis offers a different assessment of the station and function of humanity; it answers the questions underlying the ancient Near Eastern texts in ways that differ from them.

First, it is important to observe that, even though Genesis 2 turns its attention to a specific human couple, Genesis 1 is concerned only with the role and functions of humanity in general—a concern that parallels accounts from the rest of the ancient Near East. If the text of Genesis 1 were fully to represent the Mesopotamian perspective, the destiny of all of humankind would be decreed in this account. And the focus of Genesis, corresponding to the ancient cognitive environment, remains archetypal in its narrative. Both in the discussion of humanity as a whole in Genesis 1 and also in the treatment of Adam and Eve as individuals in Genesis 2, the description consistently identifies characteristics of humanity as a whole.[155] Thus, even when physical materials are mentioned, it is only for archetypal purposes and not as description of chemical composition or physical anatomy. But because there are no *divine* ingredients—no rhetorical "biological" connection to deity—we can agree with W. Brown that "humanity's correspondence with God through the *imago Dei* is one of function and form, not substance. Language of this sort, at the very least, transfers the tasks and trappings of royalty and cult, the offices of divine representation and habitation to humanity."[156]

As was noted on pp. 74–86, the image of God is rarely applied to humanity as a whole in the rest of the ancient world (the major exception

---

155. Thus, all people are made from the dust of the ground, because "dust you are and to dust you shall return." Woman is archetypally drawn from the side of man because it is universally observable that "for this cause a man shall leave his father and mother and cleave to his wife." These are archetypal portraits.

156. W. Brown, *The Ethos of the Cosmos* (Grand Rapids, MI: Eerdmans, 1999), 44; see P. Bird, "'Male and Female He Created Them': Gen. 1:27b in the Context of the Priestly Account of Creation," *HTR* 74 (1981): 138–40; J. Barr, "The Image of God in the Book of Genesis: A Study in Terminology," *BJRL* 51 (1968): 11–26; S. D. McBride, "Divine Protocol: Genesis 1:1–2:3 as Prologue to the Pentateuch," in *God Who Creates: Essays in Honor of W. Sibley Towner* (Grand Rapids, MI: Eerdmans, 2000), 3–41.

being in *The Instruction of Merikare*). When the image of deity was attached to specific individuals—invariably kings—in either Assyria or Egypt, it endowed the king with divine sonship and enabled the king to function on behalf of the deity. That is, the "image of god" operated within the political/ bureaucratic model in which the ruling function of deity was carried out on earth by the king. In Genesis, the functions assigned to humanity also have to do with ruling but at a different level.

> The description of the ancient Near Eastern kings as the image of a god, when understood as an integral component of Egyptian and/or Mesopotamian royal ideology, provides the most plausible set of parallels for interpreting the *imago Dei* in Genesis 1. If such texts—or the ideology behind them—influenced the biblical *imago Dei*, this suggests that humanity is dignified with a status and role vis-à-vis the nonhuman creation that is analogous to the status and role of kings in the ancient Near East vis-à-vis their subjects. [157]

Instead of ruling over people and kingdoms, as in Assyria and Egypt, all humanity in the Genesis account rules over its segment of the cosmos, subduing and ruling the world that people inhabit. In this respect, human beings are functioning on behalf of deity, in whose image they were created. Thus, the royal aspect of the image of God is maintained but located in a different arena.

Differences that are even more remarkable can be observed in the centrality of humankind, both in the Genesis account and in the cosmos as portrayed in Genesis. This centrality is apparent in that, in the seven-day structure of Genesis 1, all of the functions are established in relation to people—not to provide an environment for a god or the gods. This is in stark contrast to Mesopotamia, where the cosmos functions as a world that exists for the sake of the gods, and the role of people vis-à-vis the world is secondary: they are to serve the gods in their world. The only other ancient text where the former concept is evident is *The Instruction of Merikare*, in which all of creation (i.e., sky and earth, sun, and daylight) is made to function for people, and people are provided for by deity. *The Instruction of Merikare* is much closer to Genesis than much of the rest of ancient Near Eastern literature, but Genesis elevates the portrayal of people, treating them not as cattle but as rulers. Thus, Genesis merges ideas from different ends of the cognitive environment: all humanity is in the image of God and

---

157. Middleton, *Liberating Image*, 121.

collectively functions in a ruling capacity. People are central in the account of Genesis 1 (all functions are directed toward them) and central in the cosmos, functioning as rulers in the image of deity.

The station of humanity in the cosmos as portrayed in Genesis 1 is, therefore, almost precisely opposite of the picture in Mesopotamian literature, where people are slaves of the gods and thus involved in helping the gods do their work. In Genesis, humanity is a partner in the work of ruling. Furthermore, people are given a role as partners because the functional nature of humanity is identified with its maleness and femaleness, both in the image of God. This is a radical departure, to view women as partners with men, but is essential to the first aspect of the blessing: being fruitful and multiplying.

The blessing itself ("be fruitful and multiply") is a departure from the occasional notion in ancient literature that overpopulation is a problem that must be controlled by the gods. This problem is particularly evident in the *Atrahasis Epic*, in which a variety of strategies to reduce the population are attempted before the flood is settled upon as the solution.[158] In Genesis, population growth is encouraged as a means by which the other aspects of the blessing (subduing and ruling) can be carried out.

The foregoing observations make it clear that Genesis 1 completely restructures the the position and role of the participants on the cosmic stage. For instance, in Genesis, humanity is granted a role that is reminiscent of the role of some gods in Mesopotamian literature. In *Enki and the World Order*, Inanna complains that she has not received any control attributes to administer. In *Inanna and Enki*, she is given some. Compare this to the Genesis account, in which God transfers some control attributes to Adam and Eve by means of the image of God and the blessing, allowing them to decree destinies within the purview of these control attributes—thus, for instance, naming the animals (= decreeing the destinies?). Humanity is given a subordinate ruling responsibility, similar to the position delegated to the lower gods by the higher gods in Mesopotamia, a role that is eventually also delegated to kings. Thus, Genesis 1 bequeaths to humanity a dignity that is not attested in the rest of the ancient Near East. In Genesis, God is outside the cosmos, not inside or a part of it, and he has no origin. He is responsible for the origin of all the governing principles. Human beings are

---

158. A. D. Kilmer, "The Mesopotamian Concept of Overpopulation," *Or* 41 (1972): 160–77.

positioned as rulers in the cosmos, with all of the functions of the cosmos organized on their behalf.

Conclusion

Days 4 through 6 concern the installation of functionaries and the decreeing of the destiny of these functionaries as they operate in the anthropocentric cosmos. The structure presented by the text reflects a degree of political/bureaucratic concerns without introducing mid-level deities, as is common in the ancient Near East. Though the shape of the cosmos is seen in terms quite similar to the literature of the ancient Near East, the elements of the cosmos have no corresponding deities, and the structure of the cosmos is radically different. By the way in which Genesis 1 uses the shared ancient Near Eastern cognitive environment, it asks the same questions that lie behind all of the other ancient cosmologies and operates from the same metaphysical platform but gives quite different answers that reflect the uniqueness of the Israelite world view and theology.

Day 7 (Genesis 2:1–3):
Temple and Rest in Genesis

Pages 101–119 described the close interrelationship between temple and cosmos in the ancient world and also addressed the role of divine rest in relationship to both. In that chapter, we noted that the building of temples was described in cosmic terms, that the temples were described as having cosmic functions, that temples were understood as models in miniature of the cosmos and were replete with cosmic symbolism, that cosmic origins were sometimes associated with temple building, that temples were sometimes thought to represent the world, and that deities rested in temples that had been constructed for precisely this purpose. To use Levenson's terms, the temple and the cosmos were congeneric and homologically connected. The temple was the hub of the cosmos and the rest of the deity in the temple was essential to his rule of the cosmos.

When we consider the import of these ideas for our reading of Genesis, to evaluate the extent to which they are reflected in the cognitive environment of Israel, it is appropriate to ask, "Is there any reason to think that a temple metaphor is present in any way in the Genesis cosmology?" If it is true that there is a close association between temple and cosmos in the cognitive environment, and if there is occasionally a connection between cosmology and temple building, it would hardly be surprising to find this kind of association in Genesis 1. Furthermore, in a variety of places elsewhere in the Hebrew Bible, the connection between temple and cosmos is evident, so the idea is hardly foreign to Israelite thinking. Particularly notable in this regard is Isa 66:1, which refers to a cosmos-sized temple, a connection between temple and rest, and a connection between creation and temple.

Isaiah 66:1–2

This is what the LORD says:
"Heaven is my throne,
and the earth is my footstool.
Where is the house you will build for me?
Where will my resting place be?
Has not my hand made all these things,
and so they came into being?"
declares the LORD.

Though there is no explicit mention of a temple per se in the Genesis account, two items that are specifically mentioned help to connect the idea of temple in the ancient Near Eastern and biblical contexts: rest on the seventh day and the Garden of Eden.

Rest on the Seventh Day

The relationship between temple and rest in Israelite thinking, as exemplified in Isa 66:1, was noted above. Additional extensive comment is given by the Psalmist in Psalm 132.

Psalm 132:7–8, 13–14

Let us go to his dwelling place;
let us worship at his footstool—
"Arise, O LORD, and come to your resting place,
you and the ark of your might."

For the LORD has chosen Zion,
he has desired it for his dwelling:
"This is my resting place for ever and ever;
here I will sit enthroned, for I have desired it."

What is the nature of divine rest in the Hebrew Bible? In the ancient Near Eastern literature, we have noted a range of activities (and inactivity) that were involved in rest: from peaceful sleep, to leisure time for entertainment and banquets, to sovereign rule. Some have interpreted the rest in Genesis 1 as representing disengagement and the enjoyment of relaxation.

Thus, Levenson comments that the text "leaves us with an impression of the deity in a state of mellow euphoria, benignly fading out of the world that he has finished and pronounced to be 'very good.'" [159] It should be noted, however, that the "disengagement" form of rest in the ancient Near East is consistently based either in polytheism (e.g., social activities among and entertainment with other gods) or in the belief that the gods had humanlike needs and desires (e.g., sleep or sexual activity).

In contrast, N. Andreasen recognized the "engagement" aspect of divine rest in Genesis. The relationship between God's rest and the world's stability suggests that stability is assured by activity rather than inactivity.

> It is curious, however, that precisely the Old Testament should make Yahweh rest and even refresh himself after his creative work, for Yahweh is not a God who would tire or retire in the face of new and extraordinarily heavy activities, or before other aggressive powers, nor is the world's stability assured by his inactivity, but on the contrary by his activity within creation. [160]

In fact, however, although the idea of divine rest in the ancient Near Eastern includes retirement as one possibility, other texts examined above showed rest as the freedom to rule (pp. 113–115). In the Hebrew Bible, Psalm 132 provides a key passage, in which not only is the temple identified as the resting place of Yahweh but we also find rest identified with rule, for in the temple he sits enthroned. In this sense, divine rest is not primarily an act of disengagement but an act of engagement. No other divine rest occurs in the Hebrew Bible than the rest that is associated with his presence in his temple. [161] This, combined with the data that were presented concerning divine rest in temples in the ancient Near East, confirms that the idea of deity resting, as on the seventh day in Genesis 1, is a clear indication to the reader that a temple metaphor underlies the understanding of the deity's status. [162]

---

159. J. Levenson, *Creation and the Persistence of Evil* (Princeton: Princeton University Press, 1988), 109.

160. N.-E. Andreasen, *The Old Testament Sabbath: A Tradition-Historical Investigation* (SBLDS 7; Missoula, MT: Scholars Press, 1972), 183.

161. For an extensive study of the Hebrew terminology, see J. Laansma, *"I Will Give You Rest"* (Tübingen: Mohr Siebeck, 1997), 17–76.

162. For the inevitable conclusion that rest after creation is to be equated with rest in the temple, see Laansma, *"I Will Give You Rest,"* 72. The verbs for 'rest' and the nouns for 'resting place' appear very infrequently with Yahweh as subject. Instead, he is usually giving rest to (or withholding rest from) his people. In the early verses of Genesis 2, *šbt* in the Qal only appears with God as the subject. *Nwḥ* in the Qal only occurs with God as the subject in Exod 20:11 (an indication that Exod 20:11 and Genesis 2 should be interpreted in light of one another). The

This connection is further substantiated by the fact that the rest takes place on the seventh day. Several examples of temple inaugurations from ancient Near Eastern literature, cited above, show that these rites took place in the course of seven days and that the deity entered the temple to take up his rest on the seventh day.[163] Mark Smith, in his discussion of the motif of seven days in Genesis 1, concludes, with Hurowitz, that "creation in Genesis 1 uses the language of temple-building."[164] Regardless of whether Genesis 1 is understood as reflecting a temple-building account (like the building of Baal's Temple in seven days) or a temple-inauguration account (like the temple inauguration in Gudea Cylinder B), the connection between Genesis 1 and temple imagery is confirmed.

---

only other allusions to divine rest in the Hebrew Bible are the occurrences of the noun *mnḥwt* when it refers to the Jerusalem temple (Ps 95:11; 132:8, 14; Isa 66:1).

163. Scholars have long expressed curiosity about the possibility of a relationship between Genesis 1 and the Akitu celebration, because the Akitu includes the recitation of *Enuma Elish*, the great Babylonian literary work about the establishment of order in the cosmos under Marduk's rule. Nonetheless, no clear relationship has been established. Both the Akitu festival and Genesis 1 present an ordering of the cosmos that climaxes with the deity entering rest. Parallels beyond this, if they exist at all, are very sketchy. If we consider van der Toorn's observation that the Akitu ritual really begins on Day 4 ("The Babylonian New Year Festival: New Insights from the Cuneiform Texts and Their Bearing on Old Testament Study," *Congress Volume: Leuven, 1989* (VTSup 43; Leiden: Brill, 1991]) 332 n. 7.), the 12-day festival has the potential of more closely paralleling the seven days of Genesis. In this scheme, Akitu Day 11 would be the equivalent of Genesis Day 7 as the day of divine egress. Akitu Day 4 would be preliminary, setting the stage for the next seven days, with the covering of Anu and Enlil representing the shrouding of heaven and earth, when nothing but the cosmic waters existed. Day 4 is when *Enuma Elish* was recited. Akitu Day 5 would presumably then be equivalent to Genesis Day 1, when the darkness was dispelled and the "golden heaven" appeared, representing light, and the prayer to Marduk was offered: "O (Divine) Bull, brilliant light which burns the darkness, O burning of Anu." Beyond these somewhat vague and debatable similarities, the Akitu and Genesis 1 both involve the decreeing of destinies. Any of the possible similarities between the Akitu and Genesis 1 cited here are much too general or simply too circumstantial to claim some kind of direct relationship between the two texts. Nonetheless, note that the Akitu recalls the cosmic establishment of Marduk's kingship and temple building associated with rituals intended to maintain and reenact enthronement. Genesis 1, in my proposal, envisions a cosmic-temple establishment, inauguration, and divine enthronement as a representation of a cosmogony, using the known (temple) to describe the unknown (cosmogony) in conceptually comprehensible (analogical) and theologically expressive ways.

164. M. S. Smith, *The Ugaritic Baal Cycle*, vol. 1: *Introduction with Text, Translation and Commentary of KTU 1.1–1.2* (Leiden: Brill, 1994), 78; referring to Hurowitz, *I Have Built*, 242. Furthermore, note J. Klein's outline of the structure of Sumerian Temple Hymns: Commissioning of the restoration; carrying out the divine command; beautification of the various parts of the building (decoration and embellishment); dedication of the restored temple; blessings given. Many of these can also be identified at least in part in Genesis 1. J. Klein, "Building and Dedication Hymns in Sumerian Literature," *Acta Sumerologica* 11 (1989): 27–67; see p. 36.

Seven-day temple inaugurations are the norm in biblical temple-building accounts. In the account of the construction of Solomon's temple, a seven-day dedication, to which was added a seven-day feast/banquet (2 Chr 7:9; 1 Kgs 8:65), followed the completion of construction. Levenson observes the repeated use of the number seven in the account and concludes that the account is modeled on the seven days of creation.

> 1 Kings 6:38b tells us that it took Solomon seven years to build his Temple. According to 1 Kings 8, he dedicated it during the Feast of Booths (*Sukkot*), which occurs in the seventh month (verse 2) and which, in the Deuteronomic tradition, is a festival of seven days' duration (Deut 16:13–15). . . . Can the significance of the number seven in this Temple dedication be coincidence? In light of the argument on other grounds that Temple building and creation were thought to be congeneric, this is improbable. It is more likely that the construction of the Temple is presented here as a parallel to the construction of the world in seven days.[165]

However, because the number seven occurs frequently in texts reflecting the ancient Near Eastern cognitive environment, it might be more likely that the association is the reverse—namely, that the Genesis 1 account is modeled after a temple-inauguration account. Indeed, McBride states forthrightly this same conclusion: "This day of silent divine rest is a consummation of all that has gone before because it inaugurates God's residence within the cosmic temple."[166]

Once this possibility is raised, other connections to temple-inauguration accounts can be suggested. For example, in the case of Gudea's temple inauguration, most of the ceremony was taken up with proclaiming the functions that the temple would have and installing the functionaries so that the deity could enter the temple (on the seventh day) to take up his rest, at which point it became functional. If we agree that Genesis 1 has to do with the assigning of functions (= ME) to the cosmic temple, days 4–6 bear some similarity to the temple inaugurations in which the functionaries are installed in the temple and their *šimati* ('decrees') declared prior to the de-

---

165. J. Levenson, "The Temple and the World," *JR* 64 (1984): 275–98; see esp. pp. 288–89; see Hurowitz, *I Have Built*, 275–76. R. E. Averbeck ("Sumer, the Bible, and Comparative Method: Historiography and Temple Building," in *Mesopotamia and the Bible* [ed. M. W. Chavalas and K. L. Younger Jr.; Grand Rapids, MI: Baker, 2002], 119–20) offers a 15-point comparison between the Gudea texts and biblical temple texts, including the seven-day temple dedication.

166. S. D. McBride, "Divine Protocol: Genesis 1:1–2:3 as Prologue to the Pentateuch," in *God Who Creates: Essays in Honor of W. Sibley Towner* (Grand Rapids, MI: Eerdmans, 2000), 3–41; see p. 14. In his n. 25, he suggests comparison with the Egyptian ceremony of "Ceding the Temple to Its Lord."

ity's taking up his rest.[167] In the context of a functional ontology, the deity's entering the temple was the point at which the temple came into existence. The temple-inauguration accounts make the presence of deity in the temple central but also emphasize that the deity's presence functioned for the benefit of the people.

All of these details resonate with the Genesis account. The ways in which the cosmic temple of Genesis 1 will function for humanity are proclaimed (and thus come into existence), and the functionaries who carry out the activities that follow are installed. Then the deity comes to rest in the temple and the temple becomes a functional structure. Like the temple-inauguration in the Gudea texts, the "furniture" and staff are installed, the fish fill the rivers, and the animals fill the land. Then the prince enters, and finally the deity takes up his rest in the throne room.

As is the case in temple construction, the mere completion of the material construction phase does not produce a functioning temple. Only when the functions are identified, the functionaries installed, and the deity has entered the temple does it begin to function. *This is creation* as it was understood in the ancient Near East. Even in the biblical picture of creation in Genesis 1, the manner in which the material stuff of the cosmos came into being and the time involved in this process had little significance. The amount of time is unspecified, and the manner in which the material stuff came to exist is also unspecified. Creation takes place when the cosmos/temple is made functional for its human inhabitant by means of the presence of God.

To claim that both the Bible and the ancient Near Eastern texts draw on a similar cognitive environment and describe the processes of "origins" in similar ways in no way suggests that Genesis "borrowed" from Gudea or any other piece of ancient Near Eastern literature. To insist that these similarities could only be the result of borrowing is a gross misunderstanding of appropriate methodology, something that I have attempted to make clear from the beginning of this book. Instead, the Israelites shared with the rest of the cultures of the ancient world certain basic concepts about temples, rest, and cosmos that are naturally reflected in an account such as Genesis 1. The claim is not that Genesis 1 borrows the literary form of temple-inauguration accounts but that it is informed by the same cognitive environment that can be observed in contemporary (in the broad sense of that term) temple-

---

167. Gudea B vi–xii.

inauguration accounts. The fact that so much in common can be observed is evidence of the broad range of the cognitive environment.

The Garden of Eden

A second element in the Genesis account that communicates a connection with ancient Near Eastern temple ideology is the Garden of Eden (in Genesis 2, of course; not in Genesis 1). The place of the Garden of Eden in ancient creation and temple ideology has received extensive attention in recent decades.[168] Many have noted that the Jerusalem temple reflects many elements of the Garden of Eden. Thus, E. Bloch-Smith refers to the temple as a "virtual garden of Eden"[169] V. Hurowitz similarly concludes, "The decorations in the Temple and their distribution were significant and logical. It seems as if the Temple was not merely Yhwh's residence, but a divine garden on earth."[170] The converse relationship, that the Garden of Eden reflects temple symbolism, has been explored by G. Wenham.

> The garden of Eden is not viewed by the author of Genesis simply as a piece of Mesopotamia farmland but as an archetypal sanctuary—that is, a place where God dwells and where man should worship him. Many of the features of the garden may also be found in later sanctuaries particularly the tabernacle or Jerusalem temple. These parallels suggest that the garden itself is understood as a sort of sanctuary.[171]

---

168. C. L. Meyers, *The Tabernacle Menorah* (ASOR Dissertation 2; Missoula, MT: Scholars Press, 1976); D. Jericke ("Königsgarten und Gottes Garten: Aspekte der Königsideologie in Genesis 2 und 3," in *Exegese vor Ort* [ed. C. Maier, R. Liwak, and K.-P. Jörns; Leipzig: Evangelische Verlag, 2001], 161–76) draws out the similarities between the Garden of Eden and the royal gardens of the ancient Near East; he considers them to be cosmic gardens (pp. 172–74); L. Stager ("Jerusalem as Eden," *BAR* 26/3 [2000]: 41) lists biblical references to waters flowing from the temple. Other discussions: M. Dietrich, "Das biblische Paradies und der babylonische Tempelgarten," in *Das biblische Weltbild und seine altorientalischen Kontexte* (ed. B. Janowski and B. Ego; Tübingen: Mohr Siebeck, 2001), 281–323 (esp. pp. 290–93); E. Bloch-Smith, "Solomon's Temple: The Politics of Ritual Space," in *Sacred Time, Sacred Place: Archaeology and the Religion of Israel* (ed. B. Gittlen; Winona Lake, IN: Eisenbrauns, 2002), 83–94; V. Hurowitz, "Yhwh's Exalted House: Aspects of the Design and Symbolism of Solomon's Temple," in *Temple and Worship in Biblical Israel* (ed. J. Day; London: Continuum/T. & T. Clark, 2005), 63–110; G. J. Wenham, "Sanctuary Symbolism in the Garden of Eden Story," in *"I Studied Inscriptions from before the Flood"* (ed. R. S. Hess and D. T. Tsumura; Sources for Biblical and Theological Study 4; Winona Lake, IN: Eisenbrauns, 1994) 399–404; M. Weinfeld, "Gen. 7:11, 8:1–2 against the Background of Ancient Near Eastern Tradition," *WO* 9 (1978): 242–48.

169. Bloch-Smith, "Solomon's Temple: The Politics of Ritual Space," 88.

170. Hurowitz, "Yhwh's Exalted House," 87.

171. Wenham, "Sanctuary Symbolism," 399.

Among the parallels, Wenham includes: God walking to and fro (as he does in a temple); cherubim guarding the gates (as temples have guardian figures); the entrance is on the east; various trees, including a tree of life, the idea of fullness of life in the temple, and the presence of trees at worship locations; Adam's job is very like priestly duties; Adam and Eve are clothed specially, and the priests also wear special garments; the presence of water, gold, and precious stones (all characteristic of temples); the similarity of the tree of knowledge to the description of the Torah, which was kept in the holy of holies of the tabernacle/temple; and the warning against touching or eating certain restricted items, such the fruit of the tree of the knowledge of good and evil (in the garden) or touching the ark of the covenant (tabernacle and temple), with violation of the warning leading to death.[172] Thus, the text of Genesis describes a garden, a park landscaped with exotic trees and stocked with wildlife,[173] and these features were common accoutrements of temples and palaces in the ancient world.

Temple complexes often featured gardens that symbolized the fertility provided by the deity.[174] The produce of these temple gardens was used in offerings to the deity, just as the temple flocks and herds were used for sacrificial purposes. The gardens were watered by the fertile waters that flowed from temples.[175] The idea of four streams flowing from the temple or palace to water the four corners of the earth is common in ancient Near Eastern iconography. In the eighteenth-century B.C. palace of Zimri-Lim at Mari, a fresco painted on the walls shows an investiture scene. In one of the panels, two goddesses hold jars, and out of each flow four streams of water in different directions. The artifactual and archaeological evidence offers more information about palace gardens than about temple gardens.[176]

---

172. Wenham, "Sanctuary Symbolism," 401–3. Meyers (*Tabernacle Menorah*, 35) has a similar list in which she names elements of the sacred center, including a "cosmic mountain," garden, waters flowing from a cosmic source, sacred trees at the center, and a guardian. She also identifies the menorah as symbolizing the cosmic tree, which represented God's presence (p. 180).

173. For an illustration, see the marble panel from Ashurbanipal's palace that portrays a garden with flowing water channels, adjoining a temple, with the god pictured inside; a photo of this panel can be viewed on the British Museum Web site, http://www.thebritishmuseum.ac.uk/compass.

174. K. Gleason, "Gardens," *OEANE* 2:383. All of these elements are also discussed in *NIDOTTE* 1:875–78.

175. Lundquist, "What Is a Temple?" 208–9; see S. Tuell, "The Rivers of Paradise: Ezekiel 47.1–12 and Genesis 2.10–14," in *God Who Creates* (ed. W. P. Brown and S. D. McBride; Grand Rapids, MI: Eerdmans, 2000), 171–89.

176. See Gleason, "Gardens," 383; Keel, *Symbolism*, 135. It should be noted that temples and palaces often shared adjoining space (Bloch-Smith, "Who Is the King of Glory?" 26).

Nonetheless, evidence for temple gardens is not lacking. Archaeologists have discovered a temple near Assur with many rows of tree pits—that is, holes in which trees presumably were planted—in the courtyard.[177] In Egypt, holy groves at times were associated with a temples. Artificial pools, exotic trees and plants, fish and waterfowl, and produce grown for the provision of the gods were all components of these temple gardens. The fertility and ordered arrangement of these gardens symbolized order in the cosmos.[178] Temple ideology often associates the temple with waters bringing life and fertility that flow forth from a spring, within the building itself—or, rather, the temple is viewed as incorporating within itself a water source or as having been built on a spring. Springs are associated with temples because they were perceived as the primeval waters of creation—Nun in Egypt, Abzu in Mesopotamia—and as a result, the temple was founded on and remains in contact with the primeval waters.[179] In the Hebrew Bible, this idea is present in Ezekiel's vision of a temple, which features waters flowing out from the threshold of the sanctuary to provide perpetual fertility (Ezek 47:1–12).[180]

As in any ancient Near Eastern temple, the Presence of God was essential to the garden, and this would be true for the ancient understanding of the Garden of Eden as it was for a temple garden in, say, Mesopotamia. God's presence in Eden is understood to be the source of all life-giving waters. "It is not only the dwelling place of God. It is also the source of all the creative forces that flow forth from the Divine Presence, that energize and give life to the creation in a constant, unceasing outflow of vivifying power."[181] In conclusion then, the Garden of Eden is understood to function as the antechamber of the holy of holies in the cosmic temple complex.[182]

---

177. Stager, "Jerusalem as Eden," 43.

178. R. Germer, "Gardens," *OEAE* 2:5.

179. Lundquist, "What Is a Temple?" 205–20; cf. p. 208.

180. Other, briefer references appear in Zech 14:8 and Ps 46:4. Perhaps the most familiar picture, however, comes from Rev 22:1–2 in the New Testament, where the river of the water of life flows from the throne of God.

181. D. Neiman, "Gihon and Pishon: Mythological Antecedents of the Two Enigmatic Rivers of Eden," in *Proceedings of the Sixth World Congress of Jewish Studies* (Jerusalem: Magnes, 1973), 321–28; see p. 324

182. Genesis 2 does not attempt to develop the idea that Eden is the place of God's presence or the holy of holies of the cosmic temple. This idea is assumed by both author and audience. The text is most interested in the garden as the means by which God provided food for humanity (v. 9). The trees of the garden provided food, not for the deity (as in the parks that sometimes adjoined temples), but for the people who served the deity. By providing food, the garden actualized the benefits that had been granted in the blessing given in Gen 1:29–30.

Because the creation narrative of Genesis refers to God's resting at the conclusion and because the account is immediately followed with a description of the Garden of Eden, we can conclude that the cosmology of Genesis 1 is built on the platform of temple theology: both of these ideas—rest and the garden—are integral to the temple theology of the ancient world.

> We should not be surprised to find that the texts describing the creation of the world and those describing the construction of a shrine are parallel. The Temple and the world stand in an intimate and intrinsic connection. The two projects cannot ultimately be distinguished or disengaged. Each recounts how God brought about an environment in which he can find 'rest.'[183]

Cosmos as Temple in Genesis 1

If we can now grant that the temple homology[184] underlies the account of Genesis 1, it is appropriate to explore the nature of the homology and the extent to which it coincides with what is found in the ancient Near East. The evidence that has been presented thus far confirms that the temple in Israel was seen as a microcosmos, particularly through its identification with the symbolism of the Garden of Eden.[185] The next question to address is whether the cosmos itself is viewed as a temple, or the temple is merely seen as the hub of the cosmos which, part for the whole, represents the cosmos. The latter perspective was common in the ancient Near East, but the former is hinted at in Isa 66:1–2. Which picture, if either, is reflected in Genesis 1?

Levenson has suggested that the Isaiah 66 text does reflect the idea of cosmos as temple.[186] He also notes Ps 78:69: "He built his sanctuary like the heights, like the earth that he established forever." Here, it is clearly stated that God modeled the temple after the cosmos. But Levenson also provides evidence that the temple was considered the center of the world,[187] pointing

---

183. Levenson, "Temple and World," 288. Smith (*The Ugaritic Baal Cycle*, 77) summarizes Levenson: "Creation can be rendered in terms of temple-building and vice-versa." Note the connection between sabbath and sanctuary in Lev 19:30, 26:2—the two are related through the concept of rest.

184. For the distinction that the correlation is homological, not metaphorical, see p. 109 n. 327.

185. But not solely through identification with the Garden of Eden. For example, Levenson ("Temple and World," 287) shows that the creation and completion of the tabernacle are described in similar language (Gen 2:1–2 = Exod 39:32, 40:33–34; Gen 2:31 [*sic*; he means 1:31] = Exod 39:43; Gen 2:3 = Exod 39:43; Gen 2:3 = Exod 40:9).

186. Levenson, "Temple and World," 296.

187. Levenson, "Temple and World," 284–85.

to biblical texts such as Ezek 5:5 and 38:12, as well as citations from Josephus and rabbinic literature.

Midrash Tanḥuma: Kedoshim 10

Just as the navel is positioned in the center of a man, thus is the Land of Israel positioned in the center of the world, as the Bible says, "dwelling at the very navel of the earth" (Ezek 38:12), and from it the foundation of the world proceeds. . . . And the Temple is in the center of Jerusalem, and the Great Hall is in the center of the Temple, and the Ark is in the center of the Great Hall, and the Foundation Stone is in front of the Ark, and beginning with it the world was put on its foundation.

Philo (De Specialibus Legibus 1.66)[188]

The highest, and in the truest sense the holy, temple of God, is, as we must believe, the whole universe, having for its sanctuary the most sacred part of all existence, even heaven, . . .

Josephus (Jewish War 5.213–14)[189]

Nor was this mixture of materials [of the entrance veil] without its mystic meaning: it typified the universe. For the scarlet seemed emblematical of fire, the fine linen of the earth, the blue of the air, and the purple of the sea. . . . On this tapestry was portrayed a panorama of the heavens, the signs of the Zodiac excepted.

Levenson discusses additional points of symbolism identified by Josephus and then concludes by observing the role of the temple as implied by the historian's symbolism.

Josephus' point in all this Hellenistic allegory is that the Temple is an *eikon*, an image, an epitome of the world. It is not one of many items in the world. It is the world *in nuce*, and the world is the Temple *in extenso*.[190]

Should we conclude that Genesis 1 considers the cosmos to be a temple, or that it uses temple symbolism and temple-inauguration imagery to describe the creation of the cosmos? Is the temple an image of the cosmos, or is temple-building a useful way of describing cosmogony because cos-

---

188. Philo, *De Specialibus Legibus* (LCL; Cambridge: Harvard University Press, 1937), 137.

189. Josephus, *Jewish War* (LCL; Cambridge: Harvard University Press, 1928), 265. For additional discussion of Josephus and Philo, see G. K. Beale, *The Temple and the Church's Mission: A Biblical Theology of the Dwelling Place of God* (Downers Grove, IL: InterVarsity Press, 2004), 45–47.

190. Levenson, "Temple and World," 285.

mos and temple are homologous? Because there is no explicit reference to a temple as distinct from the cosmos in Genesis 1, and because the functions and functionaries described in the narrative are cosmic, the view that the cosmos itself is being portrayed as a temple seems to be the more likely conclusion. And Levenson draws just this conclusion from Isa 66:1 as well.

> Yhwh has already built his Temple, which is the world, "heaven" and "earth." The endurance of the created order renders its earthly replica, or antitype, superfluous. This is anything but the desacralization of sacred space. It is, instead, the infinite extension of sacred space, the elimination of the "profane," that which stands *pro fano*, "in front of the Temple." The world in its fullness is the Temple.[191]

The biblical cosmic temple allows people to live and serve in the presence of deity; the functions of the cosmic temple are for their sake.[192] This is a significant differentiation from the ancient Near Eastern cognitive environment, in which, as Clifford notes, "The world is not created for human beings but for 'cult,' the housing and feeding of the gods."[193] In Genesis, the focus of the cosmology is the support of the life of the people, not the life of the gods.

In Genesis, the entire cosmos can be portrayed as a temple because the cosmos and temple serve the same functions, as shown in table 4.3.

Table 4.3. Functions of Temples and Cosmos

	Cosmos	*Temple*
Theocentric	OT, ANE	OT, ANE
Anthropological Orientation	OT, ANE (mes for people)	OT
Gods, Needs/benefits	ANE	ANE
People, Needs/benefits	OT	OT

The temple is sometimes viewed in biblical texts, as in the ancient Near East, as the center of the cosmos. This is probably the case with the scenario

---

191. See Levenson, "Temple and the World," 296.

192. Just as humans are blessed as part of their destiny in connection with the dedication of the cosmic temple in Genesis 1, the idea of blessing following the dedication of a temple is familiar in the ancient Near Eastern world. So, for example, after the dedication of the restored Ekur, Urnammu is blessed by Enlil, giving him superiority over other kings; this is equivalent to decreeing his destiny. In the epilogue of the dedication text, this blessing is the basis for Urnammu's subduing the world (in this case, his foreign enemies, but compare this to the instruction in Genesis 1: "subdue and rule"); cf. Klein, "Building and Dedication Hymns in Sumerian Literature," particularly pp. 34–35.

193. Clifford, *Creation Accounts*, 65.

in Genesis 2, where the source of the waters and the garden defines sacred space within the cosmos but nonsacred space exists, outside the garden, where the offending couple is driven after their sin. But there is another sense in which the cosmos in its entirety is a temple. In Israel, the temple was intended to be a place where the world of God's existence and the world of people's existence became intertwined (in the concept of sacred space, the people are in effect placed in the garden). If this concept is extended back to Genesis, the world of the deity and the world of the people could be viewed as coextensive at the creation and ideally so in later time.

Conclusion

In the traditional interpretation of Genesis 1, it often appears to readers that they are left with only vague theological notions when they finally arrive at Day 7. The main work has been done in the preceding six days, the climax has been reached and passed (creation of people), and all that remains is a theological etiology for the Sabbath or for the length of the week. In a purely material ontology, the seventh day is not part of "creation" because nothing is made on that day. It is only an esoteric postscript.

However, if the text is read in light of a functional ontology that relies on a temple identity, we discover that Day 7 is far from a postscript. The climax of a temple inauguration is when the deity enters his prepared residence and rests there, as he assumes the rule of the cosmos from his temple-throne. The former acts are mere preliminaries to this grand finale.

The analysis presented in this chapter leads to the conclusion that the seven-day structure of Genesis 1 reflects the intention of the author to present creation of the cosmos in terms of the inauguration of a cosmic temple. As in a temple inauguration, which in its core elements is the initiating of sacred space and its commensurate ritual functions, the creation account at its core is a narrative of the initiation of the functioning of the cosmos by recounting the primary purposes for which the elements of the cosmos have been put in place and by officially installing the appropriate functionaries in their place. The entire cosmos is viewed as a temple designed to function on behalf of humanity; and when God takes up his rest in this cosmic temple, it "comes into (functional) existence" (real existence in ancient thinking) by virtue of his presence. The rest that God thereby achieves and enjoys facilitates his rule of the cosmos by providing the means by which he engages in the control of the cosmos that he has set in order (which is what is meant, in modern terms, by "he created"). Many of these points were already made by M. Weinfeld three decades ago,[194] so they are not new at all, though they have only gradually been making their way into the mainstream of biblical scholarship. Weinfeld's seven points are as follows:[195]

1. God's dwelling in his sanctuary is considered as "rest", parallel to the concept of the sanctuary in the ancient Near East, and to the seventh day's rest in Genesis.
2. The completion of the Tabernacle is parallel to the completion of the universe in Genesis.
3. The seventh day as the day of completion appears both in the Tabernacle accounts and in the Creation stories.
4. Creation and Temple building in the ancient Near East are associated with and tied to the notion of enthronement.
5. Creation and the Enthronement of God are interrelated in the Old Testament.
6. The Sabbath and the enthronement of God are related together in Jewish liturgy.
7. The *Sitz im Leben* of Gen. 1:1–2:3 is to be sought in Temple liturgy.

When we review the elements bearing on this topic from the cognitive environment of the ancient Near East, we find that the Hebrew Bible as a whole is in general agreement with them. But since Genesis does not explicitly mention the temple, we cannot find there specific affirmation of what we know about temples and temple building from ancient Near Eastern literature and what is sometimes reflected in the remainder of the Hebrew Bible. The basic cognitive environment may be summarized as follows:

- building of temples was described in cosmic terms (Ps 78:69)[196]
- temples were described with cosmic functions (the closest example is Ezek 47:1–12, where the rivers flowing from the temple provide a source of fertility for the land)
- temples were understood as models of the cosmos and were replete with cosmic symbolism (a fact that is evident in the furnishings)[197]

---

194. Weinfeld, "Sabbath, Temple and the Enthronement of the Lord," 501–12.

195. Weinfeld, "Sabbath, Temple and the Enthronement of the Lord," 512.

196. These data were compiled by G. K. Beale, *The Temple and the Church's Mission: A Biblical Theology of the Dwelling Place of God* (Downers Grove, IL: InterVarsity Press, 2004), 31–38.

197. Beale, *Temple*, 32–50; Hurowitz, "Yhwh's Exalted House," 63–110; Levenson, "Temple and the World," 285–86.

- cosmic origins were sometimes associated with temple building (not attested in the Hebrew Bible unless this association is present in Genesis 1, as I have proposed) [198]
- temples could be understood as representing the world (Isa 66:1) [199]
- deities rested in temples that had been constructed for precisely this purpose (cf. 1 Chr 28:2; 2 Chr 6:41; Ps 132)

In reality, it could be claimed that, by reading Genesis 1 in the context of ancient Near Eastern temple building, the canonical flow of the Hebrew Bible or even the entire Christian Bible comes into clearer focus. [200] Levenson, for instance, notes the inclusio that is present in the Hebrew Bible:

> Perhaps it is not coincidence that the Hebrew Bible begins with an account of the creation of heaven and earth by the command of God (Gen 1:1) and ends with the command of the God of heaven "to build him a Temple in Jerusalem" (2 Chron. 35.23 [sic 36.23]). It goes from creation (Temple) to Temple (creation) in twenty-four books. [201]

The Genesis account is distinguished from the temple theologies of its ancient Near Eastern context by virtue of the application of the temple identity to the entire cosmos; in the Hebrew Bible, the temple is much more than just the hub of the cosmos that sometimes represents the whole; it is the entire cosmos. Levenson's observation is a fitting conclusion:

> The world which the Temple incarnates in a tangible way is not the world of history but the world of creation, the world not as it is but as it was meant to be and as it was on the first Sabbath. [202]

---

198. However, see Levenson's attempt to demonstrate "the connection between world building and temple building" (Levenson, "Temple and the World," 288–91).

199. See Levenson, "Temple and the World," 295.

200. See Beale, *Temple*.

201. Levenson, "Temple and the World," 295. For the Christian canon, one could point to a similar inclusio with the end point being the new heavens and new earth in Revelation 21–22.

202. See Levenson, "Temple and the World," 297.

Chapter 5

Conclusions

The six short sections of this chapter summarize the conclusions drawn in this book regarding the extent and nature of the intersection between Genesis 1 and ancient cosmology. The six sections are:

1. Ways in which the Hebrew Bible shared in the broad ancient Near Eastern cognitive environment, accompanied by recognition of distinctive Israelite application of the information
2. Ways in which Israel shared only with Egypt, accompanied by recognition of distinctive Israelite application of the information
3. Ways in which Israel shared only with Mesopotamia, accompanied by recognition of distinctive Israelite application of the information
4. Aspects of thought about creation and cosmology that were distinctive to Israel but based on an ancient Near Eastern platform
5. Evidence that Israel possessed novel ideas that show no antecedents or connections whatsoever with ancient Near Eastern thought
6. Ideologies that were prominent in the ancient Near East but of which Israel shows no knowledge or (apparently) chose to ignore

1. Shared Broad Cognitive Environment

Most importantly and fundamentally, Israel shared a belief in the functional ontology of the ancient Near East. The belief that existence was defined by having a function in an ordered cosmos is evident in all ancient cosmological texts and is reflected both at the lexical/semantic level and at the conceptual level. Similarly, the precosmic environment is portrayed throughout the ancient world as involving primordial waters and darkness; it is a world without function, not a world without matter. Creation accounts in the ancient Near East are teleological: they feature divine cause and purpose, even if the final goal is not identified plainly. Naming and separating as creative activities are evident in the cosmologies of every culture, although they are not as prominent in some as in others. Once we have concluded that naming and separating are creation activities, the idea of creation by speech can be seen as common ground across the ancient world.

The most prominent functions in the cosmos pertain to time (understood in relation to alternating periods of day and night and the calendar), weather (as regulated by the sky), and fecundity (a result of fertile land, rivers and other water sources, and seeding and harvesting).

In the ancient world, the cosmos is filled with functional entities, not merely with material objects. This is evident in the common formulation of cosmic geography throughout the ancient world, a formulation that Israel largely shares. The functions of the cosmos are understood as serving the inhabitants of the cosmos—gods and people in the ancient Near East, and people alone in Israel. This focus on beings rather than on objects results in understanding the cosmos as being similar to a company or kingdom rather than a machine. The most important question answered by every ancient cosmology is: Who is in charge? Divine rule in the cosmos is the primary answer. Divine rule is exercised from the temple and occurs in a context of divine rest, which consistently takes place in a temple. This results in a close association between temple and cosmos throughout the ancient Near East. This association is always evident in temple ideologies, though it is less consistently built into cosmologies.

When cosmologies include the creation of humanity as a component, archetypal interests dominate. Archetypal issues are framed by discussion of the materials used for making people and by indications of humanity's station and role. The function of human beings most frequently concerns their relationship to deity.

Even though Israel shares in these broad ideological commonalities, there are distinctive ways in which Genesis 1 interacts with and develops them. These distinctives have mostly to do with the divine and human characters. For instance, in the realm of divine rule, the monotheism of Genesis inevitably results in a different description of the station of deity. The primordial waters are neither deified nor personified; nor are any other elements of the cosmos. Similarly, the Israelite view of deity results in a different understanding of functions in the cosmos. The God portrayed in Genesis 1 does not set up the cosmos to function for himself but for humanity alone, though his presence in the ordered cosmos is important for maintaining this order. Finally, the role and station of humanity in the cosmos is different. The archetypal presentation in Genesis relates people to God only through his image, thereby delegating to them a ruling role in the cosmos (not just over other people); furthermore, it views them as serving deity not by meeting his needs but by caring for sacred space. Thus, Israel shares with the rest of the ancient Near East the idea that cosmology deals with questions regarding human archetypes, but the archetype that is developed has a different shape entirely. Another distinctive is that Genesis develops the archetype in part through a monogenesis perspective (at least in Genesis 2) rather than the familiar polygenesis approach observable in ancient Near Eastern texts.[1]

2. Shared with Egypt Only

The elements in Israelite cosmology that elsewhere are only evident in Egypt appear mostly in the first two verses of Genesis in the description of the precosmic status. These elements include the identification of a "first occasion" ("in the beginning") as an initial period during which the cosmos was ordered. Prior to this ordering, there was only the 'nonexistent' (Hebrew *tōhû wabōhû*), a functionless condition, which was acted upon by a wind/spirit.

Israelite distinctives appear in the nature of the *rûaḥ*, which is personified and at least quasi-deified, with its role only vaguely demarcated—leaving out the sense of 'wind' almost entirely and ignoring the egg-fertilizing concept found in Egyptian literature, even as it uses a verb usually related to the activity of avians. The text of Genesis leaves both the identity and role of the spirit/wind unclarified.

3. Shared with Mesopotamia Only

Given the prominence that has historically been given to *Enuma Elish* in the study of comparative cosmologies, it is striking how little of Israelite cosmology is traceable to Mesopotamian sources or ideas alone. Naming activity in relation to creation may be more prominent in Mesopotamia, but it is not absent from Egypt, and the same observation can be made about temple rest. The relationship of temple building to cosmology is perhaps the most important Mesopotamian feature we have discussed, though it must be admitted that this element is not explicit in the text of Genesis, despite the

---

1. *Monogenesis* refers to the idea that all of humanity emerged from a single human pair—ostensibly the general viewpoint in the Hebrew bible (cf. 1 Chronicles 1–9); *polygenesis*, reflected in the rest of the ancient Near East, is the view that humans were created en mass—a logical procedure, since the gods desired slave labor.

evidence that it is clearly implied. Temple building is accompanied by the idea that the seven-day temple inauguration makes the temple functional.

The idea that the functionality of the cosmos and everything in the cosmos is regulated by quintessential archetypes (MES) and the decreeing of destinies is prevalent in Mesopotamian literature and has been proposed here as a model for what is described in Genesis. What seems to be different in the Israelite view is its more narrow perspective on divine rest (since several of the Mesopotamian concepts concerning divine rest were founded in the community of the gods, who had needs; in Israel, divine rest has nothing to do with divine needs) and on God's relationship to the control attributes.

4. Israelite Distinctives Based on the Ancient Near Eastern Platform

The Image of God

The idea that at least some people are in the image of God was a familiar idea in the ancient world, but Israel has its own perspective on this. First, this ideology is applied universally to all humans (unlike in Mesopotamia). In Egypt, when it is applied universally, it does not pertain to a ruling function. In Genesis, the image of God has to do with rule and relationship to deity, but the rule is terrestrial rather than political, and the relationship presents humanity much like lower-echelon deities in the other cultures (though it could be perhaps argued that the image of God that was applied to royals in the ancient Near East accomplished the same purpose).

Cosmos as Temple

Despite the intrinsic relationship that existed between cosmos and temple in the ancient world, the concept never seems to have been extended so far as to consider the entire cosmos a temple. It is also uncertain that Genesis contains this picture, though the evidence points in the direction that it did.

Human Roles

The basic ancient cosmological environment claims that humanity exists to serve deity. This is what I have referred to as the "Great Symbiosis," in which people are expected to serve the needs of the gods (housing, clothing, food), and in return the gods protect and provide for the people.

But service can conceivably take many forms. The Mesopotamian picture was service as slave labor designed to meet the needs of the gods. Egyptian cosmological literature does not deal with this issue, but the more general Egyptian picture indicates the importance of the priesthood and of the rituals for meeting the needs of the gods. In Genesis, humanity is created to serve God, but human service stems from a relationship in which God first meets individuals' needs. In this view, God has no needs. Eventually in Israelite thinking, the Great Symbiosis is replaced with a Covenant Symbiosis, in which God meets the Israelites' needs as the people are faithful to the covenant. A final element of the distinctive picture is the fact that a blessing is pronounced on humanity instead of a burden of service being imposed on them. This blessing, however, deals with familiar topics in the ancient world.

5. Israelite Distinctives That Have No Known Antecedents

Not a single element of Israelite cosmology can be identified as having no antecedents whatsoever in the ancient world, though, as we have noted, the configuration of Israelite cosmology is not without distinctions. There are, however, no new ideas about cosmology in ancient Israelite thinking, though there are divergent concepts regarding the nature of God and the roles of human beings. No new cosmological models are offered; no new questions are asked, though some innovative answers are presented.

6. Ancient Near Eastern Distinctives That Have No Israelite Reflections

When we turn to distinctive elements in ancient Near Eastern cosmology, the list is more substantial. On the level of cosmology, the main difference is the absence of the separation of heaven and earth in Israelite cosmology. The detail of Israelite cosmology that comes closest to this idea is the related separation of the waters above from the waters below.

With regard to humanity itself, the main distinctive is the prevalence in the ancient Near East, especially Mesopotamia, of the inclusion of aspects of civilization and society in creation accounts. W. Brown observes that the connection between creation and civilization was the hallmark of ancient Near Eastern cosmologies.

Unlike their modern counterparts, ancient Near Eastern cosmologies presumed a seamless connection between cosmos and society. Without categorical distinction, nature and civilization, cosmos and community were the inseparable products of divinely instituted creation.[2]

Genesis 4, much later, addresses some aspects of society in its presentation of the genealogical development of the second generation, thus making it clear that the development of society is not part of Israelite cosmology.

The greatest differences in both degree and number pertain to the divine world. Israelite thinking has no element of theogony, for the Creator-God of Israel has no beginning, and there are no other gods whose existence needs to be explained. Furthermore, divine functions are not related to cosmic functions in Israel as they are in the rest of the ancient world, so the origins of cosmic functions (i.e., their existence) is not related to the existence of deity.

The entire idea of a divine bureaucracy does not exist in Israel,[3] so there is neither struggle for rule (theomachy) nor a restructuring of the divine world or a decreeing of destinies for deities, as there is elsewhere in the ancient Near East.

Conclusion

It is interesting to note that the precosmic picture in Genesis is more like the portrayal of this status in Egypt literature, while the seven-day establishment of order has greater similarity to Mesopotamian ideas. The role of humanity as presented in Genesis 1 has some points of contact with both Egypt and Mesopotamia but is the topic on which Israelite theology is most distinct. If we may borrow a clichéd metaphor, the wheel was not reinvented in Genesis, but it was put on a different axle (temple dedication?), on a different vehicle (monotheism). In the process of doing so, a few of the spokes were replaced.

The most important result of this study for the interpretation of Genesis is the realization that the Genesis account pertains to functional origins

_____

2. W. Brown, *The Ethos of the Cosmos* (Grand Rapids, MI: Eerdmans, 1999), 1–2. Brown reads Genesis 1 as also reflecting the intrinsic connection between cosmos and societal order, and while we might agree that the text points us in this direction, the extent to which other ancient cosmologies include this connection is not present in Genesis 1.

3. Israelite thinking *does* include a divine council, but it is construed somewhat differently. For further discussion, see my *Ancient Near Eastern Thought*, 92–97; idem, "Interpreting the Bible as an Ancient Near Eastern Document," in *Israel: Ancient Kingdom or Late Invention?* (ed. D. Block; Nashville: Broadman Holman, 2008), 298–327; see esp. pp. 305–9.

rather than material origins and that temple ideology underlies the Genesis cosmology. These conclusions have significant ramifications for the public discussions and controversies of our time, including those concerning the age of the earth, the relationship between Genesis and science, the interpretation of the biblical text in relation to evolution and Intelligent Design, and the shape of public science education. In the world of biblical studies, this analysis serves as an illustration of the role that studying and knowing the cognitive environment can have in hermeneutics and how comparative studies can advance our understanding in very productive ways. Furthermore, I hope that some of the findings presented here will help in the establishment of a more vital biblical theology of creation and, within certain confessional circles, aid in the clear definition of the nature of biblical authority and revelation.

Bibliography

Abusch, T. "Ghost and God: Some Observations on a Babylonian Understanding of Human Nature." Pp. 363–83 in *Self, Soul and Body in Religious Experience*, ed. A. Baumgarten, J. Assmann, and G. Stroumsa. Leiden: Brill, 1998.

Allen, J. *Genesis in Egypt*. New Haven, CT: Yale University Press, 1988.

Anderson, B. W. *Creation versus Chaos*. New York: Association Press, 1967.

Andreasen, N.-E. *The Old Testament Sabbath: A Tradition-Historical Investigation*. SBLDS. Missoula, MT: Society of Biblical Literature, 1972.

Assmann, J. *The Mind of Egypt*. New York: Metropolitan Museum of Art, 1996.

_____ . *The Search for God in Ancient Egypt*. Ithaca, NY: Cornell University Press, 2001.

Averbeck, R. E. "Myth, Ritual and Order in 'Enki and the World Order.'" *JAOS* 123 (2003): 757–71.

Bahrani, Z. *The Graven Image: Representation in Babylonia and Assyria*. Philadelphia: University of Pennsylvania Press, 2003.

Barr, J. "The Image of God in the Book of Genesis: A Study in Terminology." *BJRL* 51 (1968): 11–26.

Batto, B. "Paradise Reexamined." Pp. 33–66 in *The Biblical Canon in Comparative Perspective: Scripture in Context IV*, ed. K. L. Younger, W. W. Hallo and B. F. Batto. Lewiston, NY: Edwin Mellen, 1991.

_____ . *Slaying the Dragon*. Louisville: Westminster John Knox, 1992.

_____ . "The Sleeping God: An Ancient Near Eastern Motif of Divine Sovereignty." *Bib* 68 (1987): 153–77.

Beale, G. K. *The Temple and the Church's Mission*. Leicester: Apollos / Downers Grove, IL: InterVarsity Press, 2004.

Bird, P. "'Male and Female He Created Them': Gen. 1:27b in the Context of the Priestly Account of Creation." *HTR* 74 (1981): 138–40.

Blacker, C., and M. Loewe. *Ancient Cosmologies*. London: Allen and Unwin, 1975.

Bloch-Smith, E. "Solomon's Temple: The Politics of Ritual Space." Pp. 83–94 in *Sacred Time, Sacred Place: Archaeology and the Religion of Israel*, ed. B. Gittlen. Winona Lake, IN: Eisenbrauns, 2002.

_____ . "'Who Is the King of Glory?' Solomon's Temple and Its Symbolism." Pp. 18–31 in *Scripture and Other Artifacts*, ed. M. Coogan, J. C. Exum, and L. E. Stager. Louisville: Westminster John Knox, 1994.

Brown, W. *The Ethos of the Cosmos*. Grand Rapids, MI: Eerdmans, 1999.

_____ , and S. D. McBride Jr. *God Who Creates*. Grand Rapids, MI: Eerdmans, 2000.

Clifford, R. *The Cosmic Mountain in Canaan and the Old Testament*. HSM 4; Cambridge: Harvard University Press, 1972.

_____ . "Cosmogonies in the Ugaritic Texts and in the Bible." *Or* 53 (1984): 183–201.

_____ . *Creation Accounts in the Ancient Near East and the Bible*. CBQMS 26; Washington, DC: Catholic Biblical Association, 1994.

_____ , and J. J. Collins. *Creation in Biblical Traditions*. Washington DC: Catholic Biblical Association, 1992.

Coote, R. B., and D. R. Ord. *In the Beginning*. Minneapolis: Fortress, 1991.

Cornelius, I. "The Visual Representation of the World in the Ancient Near East and the Hebrew Bible." *JNSL* 20 (1994): 193–218.

Curtis, E. "Man as the Image of God in Genesis in Light of Ancient Near East Parallels." Ph.D. diss., University of Pennsylvania, 1984.

Dalley, S. *Myths from Mesopotamia*. Oxford: Oxford University Press, 1991.

Day, John. *God's Conflict with the Dragon and the Sea*. Cambridge: Cambridge University Press, 1985.

Deist, F. E. "Genesis 1:1–2:4A: World Picture and World View." *Scriptura* 22 (1987): 1–17.

Farber-Flugge, G. *Der Mythos "Inanna und Enki" unter besonderer Berücksichtigung der Liste der me*. Studia Pohl, Dissertationes scientificae de rebus orientis antiqui 10. Rome: Pontifical Biblical Institute Press, 1973.

Fields, W. W. *Unformed and Unfilled*. Green Forest, AR: Master Books, 2005.

Fisher, L. R. "Creation at Ugarit and in the Old Testament." *VT* 15 (1965): 313–24.

Foster, B. *Before the Muses*. 3rd ed. Bethesda: CDL, 2005.

George, A. R. "Sennacherib and the Tablet of Destinies." *Iraq* 48 (1986): 133–46.

Gleason, K. "Gardens in Preclassical Times." P. 383 in vol. 2 of *Oxford Encyclopedia of Archaeology in the Near East*, ed. E. Meyers. New York: Oxford, 1997.

Groenback, Jakob H. "Baal's Battle with Yam: A Canaanite Creation Fight." *JSOT* 33 (1985): 27–44.

Handy, L. *Among the Host of Heaven: The Syro-Palestinian Pantheon as Bureaucracy*. Winona Lake, IN: Eisenbrauns, 1994.

Harrelson, W. "The Significance of Cosmology in the Ancient Near East." Pp. 237–52 in *Translating and Understanding the Old Testament*, ed. H. Frank and W. Reed. Nashville: Abingdon, 1970.

Hasel, G. F. "The Significance of the Cosmology in Genesis 1 in Relation to Ancient Near Eastern Parallels." *Andrews University Seminary Studies* 10 (1972): 1–20.

Heidel, A. *The Babylonian Genesis*. Chicago: University of Chicago Press, 1951.

Hess, R. S. "Genesis 1–2 and Recent Studies of Ancient Texts." *Science and Christian Belief* 7 (1995): 141–49.

_____ . "Eden—A Well-Watered Place." *BR* 7/6 (1991): 28–33.

Hoffmeier, J. K. "Some Thoughts on Genesis 1 and 2 and Egyptian Cosmology," *JANES* 15 (1983): 39–49.

Hornung, E. *Conceptions of God in Ancient Egypt*. Ithaca, NY: Cornell University Press, 1982.

Horowitz, W. *Mesopotamian Cosmic Geography*. Mesopotamian Civilizations 8. Winona Lake, IN: Eisenbrauns, 1998.

Hurowitz, V. A. *I Have Built You an Exalted House*. JSOTSup 115; Sheffield: JSOT Press, 1992.

_____ . "Yhwh's Exalted House: Aspects of the Design and Symbolism of Solomon's Temple." Pp. 63–110 in *Temple and Worship in Biblical Israel*, ed. J. Day. LHBOT 422. New York: Continuum / London: T. & T. Clark, 2005.

Hyers, C. *The Meaning of Creation*. Atlanta: John Knox, 1984.

Jacobsen, T. "The Eridu Genesis." *JBL* 100 (1981): 513–29.

_____ . *The Harps That Once . . . : Sumerian Poetry in Translation*. New Haven, CT: Yale University Press, 1987.

Janowski, B., and B. Ego. *Das biblische Weltbild und seine altorientalischen Kontexte*. FAT 32; Tübingen: Mohr Siebeck, 2001.

Jericke, D. "Königsgarten und Gottes Garten." Pp. 161–76 in *Exegese vor Ort*, ed. C. Maier, R. Liwak, and K-P. Jörns. Leipzig: Evangelische Verlag, 2001.

Kapelrud, A. S. "Temple Building, a Task for Gods and Kings." *Or* 32 (1963): 56–62.

_____ . "The Mythological Features in Genesis Chapter 1 and the Author's Intentions." *VT* 24 (1974): 178–86.

Keel, O. *The Symbolism of the Biblical World: Ancient Near Eastern Iconography and the Book of Psalms,* trans. Timothy J. Hallett. New York: Seabury, 1978. Reprinted Winona Lake, IN: Eisenbrauns, 1997.

Kingsbury, Edwin C. "The Seven Day Ritual in the Old Babylonian Cult at Larsa." *HUCA* 34 (1963): 1–34.

Klein, J. "Building and Dedication Hymns in Sumerian Literature." *Acta Sumerologica* 11 (1989): 27–67.

Kloos, C. *Yhwh's Combat with the Sea: A Canaanite Tradition in the Religion of Ancient Israel*. Leiden: Brill, 1986.

Kragerud, A. "The Concept of Creation in Enuma Elish." Pp. 39–49 in *Ex Orbe Religionum*. 2 vols. Studies in the History of Religions 21–22. Leiden: Brill, 1972.

Kramer, S. N., and J. Maier. *Myths of Enki, the Crafty God*. New York: Oxford University Press, 1989.

Laansma, J. *I Will Give You Rest*. Tübingen: Mohr Siebeck, 1997.

Lambert, W. G. "The Cosmology of Sumer and Babylon." Pp. 42–65 in *Ancient Cosmologies,* ed. C. Blacker and M. Loewe. London: Allen and Unwin, 1975.

_____ . "Destiny and Divine Intervention in Babylon and Israel." Pp. 65–72 in *The Witness of Tradition: Papers Read at the Joint British-Dutch Old Testament Conference Held at Woudschoten, 1970*. OtSt 17. Leiden: Brill, 1972.

_____ . "A New Look at the Babylonian Background of Genesis." *JTS* 16 (1965): 287–300.

_____ . "Ninurta Mythology in the Babylonian Epic of Creation." Pp. 56–58 in *Keilschriftliche Literaturen: Ausgewälte Vorträge der XXXII. Rencontre assyriologique internationale*, ed. K. Hecker and W. Sommerfeld. Berliner Beiträge zum Vorderen Orient 6. Berlin: Reimer, 1986,.

_____ , and A. R. Millard. *Atra-Hasis: The Babylonian Story of the Flood*. Oxford: Oxford University Press, 1969. Reprinted Winona Lake, IN: Eisenbrauns, 2009.

Lawson, J. *The Concept of Fate in Ancient Mesopotamia of the First Millennium*. Wiesbaden: Harrassowitz, 1994.

Lesko, L. "Ancient Egyptian Cosmogonies and Cosmology." Pp. 88–122 in *Religion in Ancient Egypt*, ed. B. Shafer. Ithaca, NY: Cornell University Press, 1991.

Levenson, J. D. *Creation and the Persistence of Evil*. Princeton: Princeton University Press, 1988.

_____ . "The Temple and the World." *JR* 64 (1984): 275–98.

_____ . *Theology of the Program of Restoration of Ezekiel 40–48*. HSM 10. Missoula, MT: Scholars Press, 1976.

Loewenstamm, S. "Biblical Studies in the Light of Akkadian Texts." Pp. 256–64 in *From Babylon to Canaan*. Jerusalem: Magnes, 1992.

Lundquist, J. "What Is a Temple? A Preliminary Typology." Pp. 205–19 in *The Quest for the Kingdom of God: Studies in Honor of George E. Mendenhall*, ed. H. B. Huffmon, F. A. Spina, and A. R. W. Green. Winona Lake, IN: Eisenbrauns, 1983.

Luyster, R. "Wind and Water: Cosmic Symbolism in the Old Testament." *ZAW* 93 (1981): 1–10.

Machinist, P. "The Question of Distinctiveness in Ancient Israel." Pp. 420–42 in *Essential Papers on Israel and the Ancient Near East*, ed. F. E. Greenspahn. New York: New York University Press, 1991.

_____ . "Rest and Violence in the Poem of Erra." *JAOS* 103 (1983): 221–26.

McBride, S. D. "Divine Protocol: Genesis 1:1–2:3 as Prologue to the Pentateuch." Pp. 3–41 in *God Who Creates: Essays in Honor of W. Sibley Towner*, ed. W. Brown and D. McBride. Grand Rapids, MI: Eerdmans, 2000.

Meyers, C. L. *The Tabernacle Menorah*. ASOR Dissertation 2. Missoula, MT: Scholars Press, 1976.

Middleton, J. R. *The Liberating Image*. Grand Rapids, MI: Brazos, 2005.

Millard, A. R. "A New Babylonian 'Genesis' Story." *TynBul* 18 (1967): 3–18.

Miller, P. D. "Eridu, Dunnu, and Babel: A Study in Comparative Mythology." *HAR* 9 (1985): 227–51.

Morenz, S. *Egyptian Religion*. Ithaca, NY: Cornell University Press, 1973.

Niditch, S. *Chaos to Cosmos: Studies in Biblical Patterns of Creation*. Scholars Press Studies in the Humanities 6. Chico, CA: Scholars Press, 1985.

Nigosian, S. A. "Roots of Biblical Cosmogonic Concepts." *Theological Review* 19 (1998): 91–106.

Oden, R. A. "Divine Aspirations in Atrahasis and in Genesis 1–11." *ZAW* 93 (1981): 197–216.

_____. "Transformations in Near Eastern Myths: Genesis 1–11 and the Old Babylonian Epic of Atrahasis." *Religion* 11 (1981): 21–37.

Ornan, T. *The Triumph of the Symbol*. OBO 213. Fribourg: Academic Press / Göttingen: Vandenhoeck & Ruprecht, 2005.

Ortlund, Eric Nels. *Theophany and Chaoskampf: The Interpretation of Theophanic Imagery in the Baal Epic, Isaiah, and the Twelve*. Piscataway, NJ: Gorgias, 2010.

Parpola, S. "The Assyrian Tree of Life." *JNES* 52 (1993): 161–208.

Pettinato, G. *Das altorientalische Menschenbild und die sumerischen und akkadischen Schöpfungsmythen*. Heidelberg: Carl Winter, 1971.

Renckens, H. *Israel's Concept of the Beginning*. New York: Herder & Herder, 1964.

Rosengarten, Y. *Sumer et le Sacré*. Paris: Boccard, 1977.

Rudolph, D. J. "Festivals in Genesis 1:14." *TynBul* 54/2 (2003): 23–40.

Seely, P. "The Firmament and the Water Above." *WTJ* 54 (1992): 31–46.

_____. "The Geographical Meaning of 'Earth' and 'Seas' in Genesis 1:10." *WTJ* 59 (1997): 231–55.

Simkins, R. A. *Creator and Creation*. Peabody, MA: Hendrickson, 1994.

Smith, M. *On the Primaeval Ocean*. Carlsberg Papyri 5. Carsten Niebuhr Institute 26. Copenhagen: Museum Tusculanum Press, University of Copenhagen, 2002.

Smith, M. S. "Like Deities, Like Temples (Like People)." Pp. 3–27 in *Temple and Worship in Biblical Israel*, ed. John Day. LHBOT 422. New York: Continuum / London: T. & T. Clark, 2005.

_____. *The Priestly Vision of Genesis 1*. Minneapolis: Fortress, 2010.

Sommer, B. D. "The Babylonian Akitu Festival: Rectifying the King or Renewing the Cosmos?" *JANES* 27 (2000): 81–95.

Stadelmann, L. *The Hebrew Conception of the World*. AnBib 39; Rome: Pontifical Biblical Institute, 1970.

Stager, L. "Jerusalem as Eden." *BAR* 26/3 (2003): 36–47.

Stek, J. "What Says the Scripture?" Pp. 203–65 in *Portraits of Creation: Biblical and Scientific Perspectives on the World's Formation*, ed. H. J. Van Till. Grand Rapids, MI: Eerdmans, 1990.

Toorn, K. van der. "The Babylonian New Year Festival: New Insights from the Cuneiform Texts and their Bearing on Old Testament Study." Pp. 331–44 in *Congress Volume: Leuven, 1989*. VTSup 43. Leiden: Brill, 1991.

Tsumura, D. T. *Creation and Destruction: A Reappraisal of the* Chaoskampf *Theory in the Old Testament*. Winona Lake, IN: Eisenbrauns, 2005.

_____. "Genesis and Ancient Near Eastern Stories of Creation and Flood: An Introduction." Pp. 27–57 in *"I Studied Inscriptions from before the Flood": Ancient Near Eastern, Literary, and Linguistic Approaches to Genesis 1–11*, ed.

R. S. Hess and D. T. Tsumura. Sources for Biblical and Theological Study 4. Winona Lake, IN: Eisenbrauns, 1994.

Tuell, S. "The Rivers of Paradise: Ezekiel 47.1–12 and Genesis 2.10–14." Pp. 171–89 in *God Who Creates*, ed. W. P. Brown and S. D. McBride, Jr. Grand Rapids, MI: Eerdmans, 2000

Vanstiphout, H. *Epics of Sumerian Kings*. SBLWAW 20. Atlanta: Society of Biblical Literature, 2003.

_____. "Why Did Enki Organize the World?" Pp. 117–34 in *Sumerian Gods and Their Representations*, ed. I. L. Finkel and M. J. Geller. Groningen: Styx, 1997.

Vogels, W. "The Cultic and Civil Calendars of the Fourth Day of Creation (Gen 1,14b)." *SJOT* 11 (1997): 163–80.

Wakeman, M. *God's Battle with the Monster*. Leiden: Brill, 1973.

Walton, J. *Ancient Near Eastern Thought and the Old Testament: Introducing the Conceptual World of the Hebrew Bible*. Grand Rapids, MI: Baker, 2007.

_____. "Genesis." Pp. 2–159 in vol. 1 of *The Zondervan Illustrated Bible Backgrounds Commentary*, ed. J. Walton. Grand Rapids, MI: Zondervan, 2009.

_____. *Genesis: From Biblical Text . . . to Contemporary Life*. New International Version Application Commentary. Grand Rapids, MI: Zondervan, 2001.

Wasilewska, E. *Creation Stories of the Middle East*. London: Kingsley, 2000.

Watson, R. S. *Chaos Uncreated: The Reassessment of the Theme of "Chaos" in the Hebrew Bible*. Berlin: de Gruyter, 2005.

Weinfeld, M. "Gen. 7:11, 8:1–2 against the Background of Ancient Near Eastern Tradition." *WO* 9 (1978): 242–48.

_____. "Sabbath, Temple, and the Enthronement of the Lord: The Problem of the Sitz im Leben of Genesis 1.1–2.3." Pp. 501–12 in *Mélanges bibliques et orientaux en l'honneur de M. Henri Cazelles*, ed. A. Caquot and M. Delcor. AOAT 212. Kevelaer : Butzon & Bercker / Neukirchen-Vluyn: Neukirchener Verlag, 1981.

Wenham, G. *Genesis 1–15*. WBC. Waco, TX: Word, 1987.

_____. "Sanctuary Symbolism in the Garden of Eden Story." Pp. in 399–404 *"I Studied Inscriptions from before the Flood": Ancient Near Eastern, Literary, and Linguistic Approaches to Genesis 1–11*, ed. R. S. Hess and D. T. Tsumura. Sources for Biblical and Theological Study 4. Winona Lake, IN: Eisenbrauns, 1994. Reprinted from pp. 19–25 in *Proceedings of the Ninth World Congress of Jewish Studies*, Division A: *The Period of the Bible*. Jerusalem: World Union of Jewish Studies, 1986.

Westermann, C. *Genesis 1–11: A Commentary*, trans. John J. Scullion. Minneapolis: Augsburg, 1984.

Wiggermann, F. "Mythological Foundations of Nature." Pp. 279–306 in *Natural Phenomena: Their Meaning, Depiction and Description in the Ancient Near East*, ed. D. J. W. Meijer. Amsterdam: Royal Netherlands Academy of Arts and Sciences, 1992.

Wolde, Ellen van. *Reframing Biblical Studies: When Language and Text Meet Culture, Cognition, and Context*. Winona Lake, IN: Eisenbrauns, 2009.

Woods, C. "The Sun-God Tablet of Nabu-apla-iddina Revisited." *JCS* 56 (2004): 23–103.

Wright, J. E. "Biblical versus Israelite Images of the Heavenly Realm." *JSOT* 93 (2001): 59–75.

Wyatt, N. "The Darkness of Genesis 1:2." *VT* 43 (1993): 543–54.

_____ . "Killing and Cosmogony in Canaanite and Biblical Thought." *Ugarit-Forschungen* 17 (1986): 376–81.

Index of Authors

Index of Scripture

Old Testament

New Testament

Index of Ancient Sources

Egyptian

Ugaritic

Hittite

Classical Sources